CUCINA DEL

Mare

ALSO BY EVAN KLEIMAN

CUCINA FRESCA
(with Viana La Place)

PASTA FRESCA
(with Viana La Place)

CUCINA RUSTICA
(with Viana La Place)

CUCINA DEL
Mare
FISH AND SEAFOOD ITALIAN STYLE

EVAN KLEIMAN

DESIGNED AND ILLUSTRATED BY SARAJO FRIEDEN

WILLIAM MORROW AND COMPANY, INC. NEW YORK

It is the policy of William Morrow and Company, Inc., and its imprints and affiliates, recognizing the importance of preserving what has been written, to print the books we publish on acid-free paper, and we exert our best efforts to that end.

Library of Congress Cataloging-in-Publication Data

Kleiman, Evan.
    Cucina del Mare : fish and seafood Italian style / Evan Kleiman.
        p.   cm.
    Includes index.
    ISBN 0-688-09916-5
    1. Cookery (Fish).   2. Cookery (Seafood).   3. Cookery, Italian.
    I. Title.
    TX747.K56   1993
    641.6′92—dc20   92-31205
                                                     CIP

Printed in the United States of America

First Edition

1 2 3 4 5 6 7 8 9 10

BOOK DESIGN BY SARAJO FRIEDEN

To my mother, Eadie Kleiman

Her cooking
of simple, honest flavors
and her earthy embrace
of life and food
prepared me to fully appreciate
the ingenious simplicity
of the Italian kitchen

ACKNOWLEDGMENTS

I have many people to thank. My partner in life, Michele Saee, for his support of my eternal juggling act of chef/restaurateuse and author. All of my Angeli staff in the restaurants and the general offices, in particular Frank Ternay and Ivana Athey for their forbearance and understanding while finishing this project.

To the angels who helped with the recipe testing—thank you, Kathy St. Hilaire, Kathy Ternay, Tom King, Marianne Deery, Laura Guagliano, and Meg Grosswendt.

To my editor, Ann Bramson, and my agents, Maureen and Eric Lasher—your understanding and patience will endear you to me forever.

But most of all to Ilana Sharlin Stone, my collaborator on this project as well as my major domo in the restaurant kitchens—I give you my endless gratitude. You have made my life easier and richer during the last two years. You have become like a sister to me. Thank you.

CONTENTS

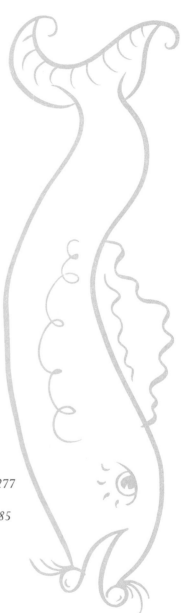

INTRODUCTION

For those of you who know me only from my previous collaborations with Viana La Place—*Cucina Fresca, Pasta Fresca,* and *Cucina Rustica*—I thought I should mention a bit about my restaurants in Los Angeles.

My cookbook career and my professional cooking career began simultaneously nearly twelve years ago when I began cooking in restaurants in my hometown, Los Angeles. My obsession with Italian food stems in great part from years spent studying the language, literature, and culture on my way to a B.A. in Italian literature. Eventually this obsession led me to open a small caffe-pizzeria called Angeli. Over the years this small caffe has been joined by three other restaurants, Trattoria Angeli, which focuses on regional Italian cooking; Angeli Mare, which offers fish and seafood; and Angeli in the Rodeo Collection, which embraces the Mediterranean cooking of southern France and Greece.

I like to describe the food I cook as being regional versus international, poor versus rich, artisanal versus industrial. The best compliment I can think of is when a customer exclaims, ''This reminds me of my mother's (or grandmother's) cooking!'' I think learning traditional tastes is an indispensable step in developing a palate that allows one to take off in new directions. Many of my customers say they love my food because it is simple, natural, and undemanding, yet filled with flavor. I hope to impart through this book a bit of the same spirit.

Many of us who have fallen under the magic spell of Italian culture, countryside, and food have a personal benchmark memory, one that recognizes an insatiable desire for the places, tastes, and visuals of Italy. For some it's the rich cultural stimulations of museums, incomparable ruins and palazzi. Others salivate at the mere mention of a Tuscan idyll among the vineyards. For me it was a blazingly hot August afternoon in the early seventies. My friends and I, after spending hours on a rocky Ligurian beach, charring our bodies to the appropriate shade to which all youth aspires, staggered about twenty feet to a small palm-covered shack on the beach. There in a haze of cool drinks and salt-drenched bodies we were treated to the essential Italian seafood meal: simple, unpretentious, and perfect. The antipasto started with a huge platter of shiny black mussels steamed in garlic, parsley, wine, and brilliantly green Ligurian oil, the cooking juices sopped up with crusty bread. It was followed by a pyramid of crunchy shrimp, fried in the shell in olive oil. We dived in with our hands, slipping the tender pink crescents out of the shells, then chewing on the potato chip–like heads. Then came a tangle of spaghetti tossed with a garlicky sauce of tiny clams still in the shell and moistened with the clam juices, barely tinted with tomato. After stuffing ourselves, we discovered that the meal was just beginning. The main course was a simply grilled whole fish, its natural juices enhanced by a squeeze of lemon and fresh herbs. We finished with a salad of tender lettuce and fresh basil leaves dressed only with coarse salt and that fragrant Ligurian oil. A truly great meal that will always exemplify to me a consonance of place, style, and taste. I realized that the Italians' approach to food is instinctively simple yet brilliant. The fish is treated as simply as possible to reveal its natural attributes. Along the way classic Italian ingredients such as lemons and oranges, herbs, capers, and olives are showcased.

Until that meal, fish had always seemed a bit of a mystery to me. And, I must admit, at home in Los Angeles at that time, fish was inevitably a white square in a small plastic-wrapped packet, lacking in color, character, or any sensory appeal.

Why do so many of us shrink from cooking fish at home, when it is what we order most often when we dine out? It is almost as if we are afraid of it when we find ourselves head to head with it, so to speak, in the market.

Looking for fish in fresh fish markets can be an adventure. The other-worldliness of fish is immediately apparent. The luminescent, shimmering blues, reds, and yellows of whole fishes with those staring gelatinous eyes following you about, the scraggly blue-pinky-reds of the shrimp, the flat white of squid with its menacing maroon-brown tentacles—in all, a vision of creatures from another world, the world of water. And the legacy of a life in water is tenderness. Nearly all the fish and most of the seafood in markets devoted to selling truly fresh fish are meltingly tender in their natural state.

This legacy of tenderness means that on the whole, fish needs little cooking. Its subtle flavor marries well with nearly all cooking techniques and tastes. Once heat is applied to fish, no matter what the cooking method, it usually cooks in a few short minutes. For this reason many of my recipes call for adding flavor to fish before cooking with marinades, herb mixtures, and pastes made of piquant condiments. Braising in aromatic liquids, and serving fish accompanied by simple yet highly flavored sauces are additional techniques to deepen and vary flavors. I am convinced that fish cookery often yields the most impressive results for the smallest investment in time and, often, money.

While traditional regional Italian fish dishes can range from the minimalist to the baroque, fish and seafood are prepared substantially the same as any other food on the Italian table. The main difference is the quick preparation of most fish dishes, making them a good fit for our desire for ease of preparation. And as a bonus fish provides low-fat meals that can be prepared quickly.

Not all regions of Italy are equal in yielding a large variety of indigenous fish and seafood recipes. Obviously geography plays a role. Liguria, the region along the Mediterranean called the Italian Riviera, pairs its fish and seafood with many fragrant herbs, mushrooms, nuts, and great olive oil. Sicilia, surrounded by seas full of sardines, tuna, and swordfish, contributes the flavors of citrus, saffron, and fennel. Venezia pairs the delicacy of crabs, scallops, and many varieties of clams with the richness of butter and cream and, of course, risotto and polenta. Naples and its environs, including the island of Capri, give us gutsy simplicity with the addition of tomatoes, oregano, hot pepper, capers, and anchovies. Apulia is special for the economical yet inventive use of its everyday ingredients, especially potatoes, rice, sun-dried tomatoes, and greens, in conjunction with the day's catch.

I leave it to other cookbook authors to write encylopedic volumes on fish types and appropriate nomenclature. My primary interest is to get you from the cookbook to the stove to the table with as little fuss or trepidation as possible.

Cooks tend to take two different approaches in preparing for a meal. There are those who are recipe driven and those who are ingredient driven. Some people are both. Sometimes you'll want to search all over town for the ingredients to make a specific dish. But often inspiration is in the ingredients themselves. Strolling through a Chinese fish market, for example, you'll come across some compact-looking little silvery guy that cries out to you, and you'll be seduced into buying it. When you get such impulse ingredients home, let your intuition guide you. Many of these recipes are simple enough to encourage you to explore.

I offer a variety of straightforward recipes, all of which have their roots firmly planted in the Italian seas. This book contains a combination of authentic and traditional regional recipes and new, lighter dishes, inspired by the traditional ones, that have proved easy to make and have found a contented audience in my home, restaurants, and cooking classes. Enjoy!

Fish Essentials

We have all had that perfectly sautéed piece of tender sole in a restaurant and lamented to ourselves, Why is it impossible to get a crisp yet yielding surface like this at home? Or the server presents us with a long fish fillet or steak with grill marks that seem practically painted on, the scent from the slightly charred edges still lingering, and we marvel, Why don't the chefs here lose half the fish through the grates like I do? Home cooks become discouraged when they attempt to sauté or grill because they often end up with a flaking, peeling mess. If there is a secret for grilling or sautéing fish well, it is *heat*—high, intense heat in the first few seconds—very hot fat, and well-seasoned or nonstick skillets or grills.

When first trying to get that perfect crust on a piece of sautéed fish, *use a nonstick pan.* Don't subvert your admirable desire to expand your repertoire by setting up obstacles through equipment and technique.

Certain fish with a dense structure more like that of red meat, such as tuna, shark, mahimahi, and swordfish, can take a bit more abuse, so it makes sense to concentrate on learning how to cook these well before graduating to the more tender and flaky whitefish, snapper, salmon, or sole. Remember that you can also get a taste similar to grilling by oven broiling close to the heat source.

If you're not a technician and have no desire to be, start first with the braised, broiled, and baked dishes; the pasta and risotto recipes are simple. When you do approach the grill and the sauté pan, pick a time when you aren't under pressure. A few calm, comfortable sessions and you'll have it down. Relax, practice—and your confidence in your ability will grow. What is the restaurant cook's biggest secret? Practice and repetition.

FISH TYPES

The lists that follow are a guide to help you choose the fish that is most suitable for the recipe you wish to cook. Although there are exceptions, as a rule, fragile, delicate fillets lend themselves to sautéing; thicker, oilier fish and steaks are good on the grill, in the broiler, and in the oven. Tougher, lean fish, such as rockfish, are great for soups and braises although tender, fattier fishes often do as well. I don't pretend to include every fish available but I think you will get the point. At the top of each recipe, I give additional suggestions for fish that can be used, recognizing that there are regional variations in availability. There is some obvious overlap in the lists as many fish of course are suitable for more than one cooking technique.

For Quick Sautés

cod	sand dabs	turbot
John Dory	sole (Dover, English, gray, petrale, rex)	whitefish
perch		winter flounder
plaice	tilapia	yellowtail flounder

For Grilling and Broiling

bluefish	mullet	shad
bonito	perch	shark
grouper	pompano	snapper
halibut	salmon	sturgeon
lingcod	sea bass (black,	swordfish
mackerel	Chilean, Mexican,	trout
mahimahi	or *baquetta*)	tuna

For Baking

bluefish	haddock	perch
cod	halibut	salmon
grouper	mackerel	tilefish

For Soups and Stews

angler
baccalà
bonito
carp
catfish
cod
corvina
croaker
fluke

grouper
haddock
halibut
mahimahi
monkfish
perch
pike
pollock

rockfish
scup
sheepshead
snapper
sturgeon
swordfish
tilefish
tuna

Small Whole Fish for Baking, Grilling, and Sautéing

anchovies
bream
Coho salmon
moon fish
pompano

porgy
sardines
shiner
smelts
striped bass

tilapia
trout
whitebait
whiting

How to Purchase, Clean, and Prepare Fish and Shellfish

For the adventurous who are willing to spend a bit more time, I've included descriptions of how to purchase, clean, and prepare the most commonly available fish and shellfish. It is not cheating, however, to have a good fishmonger do the dirty work. If buying fish already cleaned and prepped is what you need to do to incorporate it into your cooking routine, do it!

But I beg you to search out fresh fish markets, either in a good farmer's market, at a waterfront market, or in ethnic specialty fish markets such as those found in Thai, Vietnamese, Chinese, and other communities that thrive on a varied selection of fish. In large urban areas, purveyors who provide high-quality product to restaurants often have small retail outlets for the home cook.

Whole Fish

Purchase whole fish that have a glossy look and tight, smooth scales, and are firm and resilient to the touch. The eyes should be clear. The further away the fish is from this ideal, the older and more deteriorated it is.

When serving a whole fish, I always present it with the head and tail on. Some of the most tender meat is found in the head. In addition, cooking with the head and tail on adds additional flavor and moisture to the fillet meat by protecting it. If you feel you must remove the head, do so with a clean, sharp chop after the fish has been cooked. If you plan to remove both tail and head, forget whole fish; buy boneless fillets and adapt the recipe to them.

The basic method of preparation is the same for most recipes that call for whole fish, even though fish come in different shapes and sizes. If you plan to hold the fish in the refrigerator for more than a few hours before cooking, it's still a good idea to clean the fish as soon as possible, as the bacteria in the viscera multiply quickly and speed up spoilage. Once the fish is cleaned, it can be wrapped in plastic, stored in a pan filled with ice, and refrigerated for forty-eight hours or even longer if it is very fresh. Of course, the sooner it is cooked, the better the flavor.

How to Clean Whole Fish Most fishmongers will scale and clean the fish for you, but it's easy to do this yourself. First remove the scales: Hold the fish by the tail under cold running water and scrape away from you with a fish scaler or a dull knife. (Put a layer of newspaper in the sink to catch the scales.) Then rinse the fish well. To eviscerate the fish, use a very sharp knife to cut a shallow slit along the length of the belly, from the tail to the vent opening. If the head has not been removed, cut all the way to the cheeks, lift the gill covering, and remove the gills. Be careful not to cut into the entrails. Remove all the entrails from the belly cavity and rinse the fish inside and out under cold running water. Remove the fins if you like; when I am grilling a whole fish, I usually leave them on to help maintain the shape of the fish during cooking. Before serving, simply remove them with a firm tug.

How to Eat a Fish with Bones Some fish, naturally, are bonier than others. But whatever variety you are eating, confront the task of boning methodically. When presented with an individual-sized whole fish, use your fork to steady the fish and, with your knife, make an incision along the back of the fish. Then gently insert the knife between the top fillet and the skeletal structure. Guide the knife along this structure until the fillet is freed from it.

The top fillet is now ready to eat, without having to lift it off the bones. When you finish eating the top fillet, the bone structure of the fish will be clearly visible. Again, take your knife and guide it between the bones and the bottom fillet until the fillet is freed. Then cut the small connection to the fillet at the tail end. Lift up the tail and, voilà, the bones, tail, and head easily come off. Discard these on a plate placed on the table for this purpose, and eat the bottom fillet. Why go to all this trouble? Because whole fish are delicious, rustically simple, and completely Italian.

FILLETS VERSUS STEAKS

A fish fillet is cut away from the backbone along the length of a fish. It may have some remaining smaller bones that should be removed with sturdy tweezers or needle-nosed pliers. Sometimes the bones are not readily visible, but can be found by running your hand lengthwise along the fillet. The fillet can then be cut down to portion size, depending on the size of the fish: One salmon fillet, for example, can serve as many as seven or eight people, whereas a tilapia fillet will only serve one. A fish steak is a flat piece cut crosswise through a large fish.

Because fish steaks are flat, they are ideal for grilling. Fillets are also wonderful grilled, but require a little more care, since they are usually thinner and not flat. Their versatility makes them ideally suited for other methods of cooking, such as sautéing or frying, baking, and braising.

When purchasing fish fillets, look for translucent flesh. Fish steaks should be moist and meaty.

BACCALÀ (SALT COD)

No discussion of the Italian way with fish would be complete without the mention of baccalà and stoccafisso. Baccalà is cod that has undergone a salt cure; stoccafisso is salted mackerel. Of the two, baccalà is more commonly found in the United States. Most baccalà I've seen here is fairly moist, and soaking isn't an endless chore. Stoccafisso is so dry and stiff that my Uncle Alfonso once informed me that it was his mother's instrument of choice for disciplining the kids.

I've been asked many times why anyone would bother with this salted fish when fresh varieties are so readily available. My answer is always that the Italian seafood kitchen would be impoverished by the lack of baccalà. Anyone who is a first-generation Italian or who has spent any considerable time in Italy has baccalà inextricably entwined in his or her memory bank. The entire preparation, from soaking and deboning through cooking, is a ritual filled with such distinct smells and flavors that one easily becomes addicted.

If you purchase a whole side of baccalà, first cut it into pieces that will fit into a large pan for soaking. Cover the baccalà with abundant water and soak for a minimum of twenty-four hours, in a cool place like a basement, or, if necessary, the refrigerator. Change the water three or four times. After twenty-four hours, taste a bit of the fish for saltiness. If it is still very salty, change the water and soak for twenty-four hours longer, again changing the water three or four times.

Normally, baccalà is ready to use when it has nearly doubled in bulk. Just trim off the skin and cut it into portions for your recipe.

To cook baccalà, put it in enough simmering water (or half water and half milk) to cover. Cut a lemon in half, squeeze the juice into the water, and throw in the squeezed halves. Add a bay leaf and a few black peppercorns if you wish. Cook for a few minutes, or until fish is opaque and flakes easily. The baccalà is now ready to be incorporated into casseroles.

CLAMS

In general, I like to cook with soft-shell clams, such as Manila, rather than the hard-shelled Eastern clams. I prefer soft-shell clams because their sweet, tender meat resembles the clams of the Mediterranean, while the Eastern clams have a tougher, chewier texture. Choose clams with tightly closed shells or shells that close when they are tapped lightly. Place the clams in abundant salted water to soak. (When cleaning a large quantity of clams, use the kitchen sink instead of a bowl.) The water should be as salty as the sea to convince the clams to relax, open up a little, and give up their last traces of sand. Soak clams for half an hour. Lift them out of the water a few at a time, rinse under cold running water, and place in another bowl. Clean the sink or soaking bowl thoroughly of all sand and fill again with cold water and salt. Gently add the clams to the water and let soak for another half hour. Lift the clams out of the water, rinse under cold water, and place them in a bowl. Discard any that are open and do not close at your touch, any with cracked shells, and any that feel heavy (they are probably filled with mud). Cover the bowl with a damp towel and refrigerate until ready to use. Do not be alarmed if the slithery ''tongue'' of the clam makes an appearance outside its shell—remember that clams are living things and should be treated gently.

To prepare clams to serve on the half-shell, open them while holding them over a bowl to catch any juices. If you lack practice in opening clams, place the clam on a counter atop a thick pad of kitchen towels for added stability. Hold the clam so that the hinge faces your palm. Use a clam knife, and work the blade between the shell halves; as the knife slides into the mollusk, cut the muscle at the hinge. Pry open the shell, and cut the clam's connection to the top shell.

CRABS, SOFT-SHELL

Available fresh only in the spring and summer months, soft-shell crabs are blue crabs that have shed their old shells and are waiting for new larger shells to grow in. Purchase only live crabs. Once again, it requires a bit of chutzpah to prepare these delicious crustaceans. Just before cooking them, cut their faces off, behind the eyes, with a pair of scissors or a sharp knife. Gently lift each side of the top shell and remove the underlying gills. Lay the crab on its back and pull off the flap, or apron, that covers the belly. Soft-shell crabs should be used the day they are purchased.

LOBSTER

We've all experienced the comical frenzy associated with submerging live lobsters into boiling water. As familiar as this method is, it is not the best. For the most flavorful lobster, muster up your courage and cut the live lobster in half lengthwise down the back with a very sharp knife; start by plunging the tip of the knife into the back part of the head, which will kill it instantly. Remove the stomach sac behind the head and the dark intestinal vein that runs to the end of the tail. If you do want to boil a whole lobster, start it in cold water. As the water temperature rises, the lobster will be lulled into unconsciousness. Lobsters should be cooked within twenty-four hours of purchase.

MUSSELS

I prefer black mussels for nearly all the recipes in this book. However, the larger green-lipped New Zealand mussels are impressive when stuffed for antipasti. Choose mussels with tightly closed shells or shells that close when they are tapped lightly. Unlike clams, mussels do not need to be soaked clean. Just scrub them gently (the shells are delicate) but well under cold running water, until the shells are completely free of sand and grit. Hold them hinge side up under the running water so the mollusk does not fill with water, a sure death knell. Discard any mussels that are broken or not firmly clamped shut. To remove the beard (the bit of fiber that protrudes from the shell), pull firmly until it releases. To hold mussels for cooking, store in a bowl covered with a damp towel in the refrigerator.

OYSTERS

Oyster cultivation has virtually exploded in the past ten years, and today there are hundreds of varieties of oysters farmed in the waters of the Pacific and the Atlantic. Oyster connoisseurs will tell you that the flavors of each variety are as distinctive as those of different wines from the same varietal, ranging from briny to melony. Purchase oysters with tightly closed shells. Rinse them free of debris under cold running water before opening. I have found that the best way to open oysters to be served raw on the half-shell is to use an old-fashioned can opener (church key). Position the pointed end between the two shells of the oyster at the hinge. Gently but firmly push down until the muscle releases. Carefully run a paring knife along the inside of the top (flat) shell to disconnect the muscle that holds the oyster to the shell. Of course, if you like, you can use an oyster knife. For the sake of convenience, oysters can be purchased already shucked, for frying, stewing, and baking.

SCALLOPS

Scallops are almost always sold to the fish market shelled and packed in their own liquid. Rather than rinsing away their natural liquid, I simply drain them if necessary before cooking. Before cooking sea scallops, simply peel off the tough muscle that clings to the side of the scallop. Bay scallops are so tiny that you can forego this step. Check to be sure there are no remaining bits of shell.

SHRIMP

The terms *shrimp* and *prawn* are used loosely and almost interchangeably in the United States. Scampi are lobsterlike crustaceans from the Atlantic and Mediterranean that are also referred to as *langoustine.* Fresh shrimp are very perishable; for this reason, most shrimp available in the market are ''fresh-frozen,'' that is, frozen as soon as they are caught and thawed later for market. Truly fresh shrimp, which are flown into many metropolitan markets, are usually sold with the heads still on. Simply twist them off and reserve for stock. To prepare any shrimp, peel off the shell, cut a shallow incision along the back curve of the shrimp, and pull out the dark vein. Rinse under cold running water. For a more rustic look, leave the part of the shell covering the tail on.

SQUID

Squid or calamari come in many sizes, from giants over a foot long to tiny ones that measure barely two inches. Most of those sold in fish markets are about four to six inches long. Cleaned squid is widely available. Sometimes it is fresh; often it is frozen. But for many cooks, cleaned squid, even if frozen, is the product of choice because of its ease of preparation. Some fish markets also carry squid steaks, which are usually tenderized pieces cut from very large squid. They can be treated with any of the marinades or herb pastes in this book and quickly grilled.

To clean squid, gently pull off the head and tentacles from the body sac. Cut the tentacles above the eyes. Pop out the little ball, or beak, in the center of the tentacles. Discard it and the greenish innards. Reach into the body sac and pull out and discard the quill-shaped plasticlike bone. Peel off the purplish skin and the ''ears'' that protrude from the body sac. Peel these side fins; they are edible. Use a sharp knife to cut the body sacs crosswise into rings.

FISH PANTRY

If you keep the following indispensable staples on hand, you'll find it much easier to incorporate fish and shellfish into your everyday cooking.

PESCE AZZURO

Despite the fact that peninsular Italy juts into the Mediterranean and Adriatic seas and has as political appendages several islands, fish has historically been a precious and often expensive commodity. Italians who lived near the seas learned to preserve nearly everything that came from their nets. Almost every type of fish was salted, smoked, or packed in oil or vinegar. And so, while in our culture canned tuna, sardines, and anchovies have a reputation for ordinariness or as mere convenience foods, they have long been a valued part of every Italian pantry.

Italians classify anchovies, sardines, and tuna as *pesce azzuro*, "blue fish." The *blue* refers to the richness and high fat content of their meat rather than the color of their skin. The high concentration of polyunsaturated fatty acids (beneficial in controlling cholesterol) and the ease with which these fish are digested make canned anchovies, sardines, and tuna an attractive and sensible choice when both economic and health concerns are at issue.

ANCHOVIES

Anchovies are available filleted and packed in oil (flat, or rolled and stuffed with capers) and whole, or filleted and packed in salt. Anchovies packed in salt are closest in taste to fresh anchovies, and they still retain their meaty texture. Salt-packed anchovies should be rinsed well and the bones removed before using. If you really like anchovies, there is no substitute for salt-packed. When using anchovies packed in oil, it is customary but not necessary to rinse them before cooking. Anchovy paste, the lazy person's alternative, has added spices and vinegar that add unwanted flavors; avoid it. Anchovies are used in fish cookery to reinforce and deepen flavor much like reductions and demiglace in meat cookery. I often liken their flavor to earthy salt.

SARDINES

Canned sardines are most often imported from Spain or Portugal, packed in oil. A connoisseurship has developed around canned sardines similar to that surrounding red wine. Aging canned sardines mellows their flavor, as the olive oil and fish intermingle. It is thought that canned sardines of high quality are at their best after five or six years. Because fresh sardines are rarely found in American fish markets, I have not included the recipes that make up the Italian sardine repertoire.

TUNA

Although the most delicious canned tuna is Italian-style dark tuna packed in olive oil, most people invariably buy albacore packed in spring water for health reasons. Since most of my recipes that call for canned tuna also include olive oil and many herbs, you needn't worry about missing the rich flavor of the oil-packed variety.

BREAD CRUMBS

Fresh Bread Crumbs Fresh bread crumbs are easy to make in a food processor. Using the steel blade, process cubes of fresh high-quality bread into coarse crumbs. The crumbs are used to bread delicate fillets for sautéing or can be spread out on a cookie sheet and baked for homemade dried bread crumbs.

Garlicky Bread Crumbs My dear friend and colleague Kathy Tenay taught me this enrichment of a Sicilian tradition. Garlicky Bread Crumbs are my addiction; I seem to have topped nearly everything at one time or another with these flavorful coarse crumbs. To make Garlicky Bread Crumbs, toss fresh bread crumbs in a bowl with minced garlic to taste, salt, and black pepper. Add enough olive oil to slightly moisten the crumbs. Spread the seasoned bread crumbs on a baking sheet and bake in a preheated 350° oven until golden brown. Watch carefully, as crumbs can burn in a matter of seconds.

CAPERS

Capers are the piquant bud of a hardy Mediterranean plant that thrives on rocky sun-baked soil. They are either pickled in brine or salted to preserve them. If you are lucky, you can find large capers packed in salt from Pantelleria, a tiny island off the coast of Italy. They have the reputation for being the finest, most perfumatic capers in the world. Capers are generally available in two sizes: Nonpareil are the smaller, and ''Spanish'' capers are very large. I prefer to use the nonpareil for cooking and the Spanish capers for salads. Few condiments add as much punch per square inch as these, and they are uniquely suited to fish cookery. Pair with tomato sauces, olives, or bread crumbs—let your imagination run wild!

CARAMELIZED GARLIC

This all-purpose condiment is indispensable in the Angeli kitchens. We use it for everything from topping goat cheese to tossing into salads. The garlic-infused oil can be drizzled onto grilled fish, puréed into herb pastes, or added to salad or cooked vegetables of any kind.

Peeled garlic cloves
Olive oil to cover

Place the garlic cloves in a small deep saucepan, and cover with olive oil. Cook over low to medium heat until the garlic is golden, watching constantly, as it cooks very quickly. Remove from the heat and allow to cool. Store the garlic submerged in the cooking oil in the refrigerator.

CHEESE

Don't use it. Seriously, in Italy, Parmesan cheese is almost never offered with fish pastas or risotti. In those few cases where cheese is appropriate, choose a high-quality imported Italian grana padana or Reggiano cheese.

CLARIFIED BUTTER

When you clarify butter, you remove the solids and water, which are what cause the butter to burn at high heat. Once the water has evaporated and the solids are discarded, the butter takes on the characteristics of a cooking oil and can stand much higher temperatures without burning.

To clarify butter, place unsalted butter in a deep heavy saucepan; two pounds is a reasonable amount to start with. Set over low heat until the butter is completely melted. Then turn the heat up so that butter barely simmers, and allow to simmer until the water in the butter has evaporated and the foamy solids have condensed and sunk to the bottom of the pan, leaving a liquid butter the color of a golden oil. Let the clarified butter cool slightly, and pour it through a sieve into a glass or metal container, being careful not to disturb the deposits on the bottom of the pan. Covered and refrigerated, clarified butter will last for months. To use for sautéing simply spoon some out of the container and heat until liquified.

LEMONS

An essential complement, either as an intrinsic ingredient or as a garnish, to most fish dishes. Look for thin-skinned juicy lemons.

OLIVE OIL

Use extra-virgin olive oil for all cooking except deep-frying.

OLIVES

When buying green olives, look for small unpitted olives. Two types of black olives I like and are fairly easy to find are Kalamata and Moroccan. Kalamatas are flavorful Greek olives packed in brine. I use them primarily for cooking, in sauces, pastas, and stews. Moroccan olives are oil-cured, with a glossy look and deep, meaty flavor that adds to salads and makes them great for nibbling. French Niçoise or Italian Gaetas are small, mild, brine-cured black olives that are wonderful with fish.

Olio Santo

It is typical of the Italian sense of humor to call an oil that has as its main characteristic the spicy bite of the devil *holy oil*. Easy to make, this oil is indispensable in simple fish cookery, adding a lift with each drizzle. (If you eat a lot of spicy food, you may wish to use a full liter bottle of oil, in which case, simply double the other ingredients.)

> 1 ½-liter bottle extra-virgin olive oil
> 2 tablespoons red chile pepper flakes or 10 whole dried cayenne peppers, broken in half
> 2 or 3 bay leaves
> 1 large sprig fresh rosemary

Remove and set aside the cork or screwtop and stopper from the bottle of olive oil. Pour out about 2 tablespoons oil to make room for the herbs. Using a funnel, add the pepper flakes to the oil; if using dried cayenne peppers, drop the pieces into the oil. Thread the bay leaves and rosemary onto a short bamboo skewer and insert the skewer into the bottle. To prevent the possibility of mold, make sure the herbs are completely submerged in the oil. Replace the cork or stopper and screwtop. Set the bottle in a cool dark spot for a minimum of one month before using.

Pasta

I almost always use dried durum wheat pasta to make fish dishes. Its bland flavor and sturdy texture go well with fish and shellfish. Use only imported Italian dried pasta. Some brand names to look for are Rustichella, Martelli, De Cecco, and Barilla. The latter two are the most widely distributed; the first two are basically handmade small-production products.

Vinegar

Use aged red or white wine vinegars, and use balsamic vinegar that is at least eight years old.

Antipasti

hose of you familiar with my previous books or my restaurants know that this is how I like to eat. I would rather make a meal of a few small bites of many dishes than have an enormous plate of only one. The frugal nature of the Italian kitchen lends an enormous creativity and ingenuity in creating masterful antipasti from a few simple ingredients. The recipes in this chapter range from relatively austere cocktail-sized crostini topped with a garlicky anchovy paste to a wide-ranging repertoire of *ripieni,* stuffed mussel and clam recipes. Use this chapter to create casual and abundant buffets that can tease the palate or easily make an entire meal.

CROSTINI

Italian cookbooks and restaurant menus are likely to use the word *crostini* to describe everything from the most delicate appetizer canapés to substantial portions of grilled country bread with toppings. I use the word *crostini* to describe small slices of toasted bread used as a base for Italian canapés, and the word *bruschetta* for the larger toasts. Toasting good-quality bread brushed with olive oil and garlic results in crunchy, garlickly croutons that act as a foil for a variety of savory toppings, and are a must in Caesar salads.

Watch crostini carefully when they are baking because it takes only a matter of a minute or two for the toasts to go from golden brown to burnt. Stored in an airtight tin or plastic container, crostini will keep for several days.

½ cup extra-virgin olive oil

4 garlic cloves, peeled and minced

**1 good-quality baguette or other small-diameter loaf
    cut into ¼-inch slices (approximately 40 slices)**

Preheat the oven to 400°. Mix the oil and minced garlic together in a small bowl. Place the bread slices on a cookie sheet. Using a pastry brush, brush some oil and bits of garlic onto each slice of bread. Turn the slices over and brush again with the garlickly oil. Place the cookie sheet in the preheated oven and bake until the toasts are golden. Remove from the cookie sheet and let cool. Store in airtight tins or plastic containers.

Fresh Tuna Toasts

CROSTINI AL TONNO

Serves 4 to 6

Although I offer canned tuna as an alternative here, the rich taste and texture of a fresh tuna purée is unusually satisfying. Before you automatically reach for the canned variety, try using fresh for this recipe at least once.

> 6 ounces cooked fresh tuna or 1 6½-ounce can Italian-style tuna packed in oil, drained
>
> ½ cup chopped fresh Italian parsley
>
> 1 tablespoon capers
>
> 2 tablespoons olive oil
>
> Salt and freshly ground black pepper to taste
>
> Juice of ¼ lemon
>
> 1 recipe Crostini (page 19)
>
> Capers

Place all the ingredients except the crostini and capers in a blender or a food processor with a steel blade. Process for approximately 30 seconds; for a finer texture, use a rubber spatula to scrape the fish purée off the sides of the blender container or processor bowl and process for an additional 30 seconds to 1 minute. Transfer the purée to a bowl, cover, and refrigerate until ready to use. This purée is best eaten within a few hours, but it can be made as much as 2 days ahead.

Spread the tuna purée on the crostini. Garnish with capers, and serve.

GARLICKY ANCHOVY TOASTS
CROSTINI FORTE

Makes ½ cup purée

The anchovy purée that tops these crostini is a good example of the versatility of Italian food. Served on delicate crostini with cocktails at dusk, this bitingly briny pate is a perfect formal cocktail accompaniment. The topping is full of super-strong flavors—the perfect foil for a sharp drink. Yet when spread on a thick slice of country bread with a slather of sweet butter, the purée mellows and becomes inspired picnic food.

4 green onions, root ends and green tops trimmed
1 2-ounce can anchovy fillets packed in olive oil, drained
1 garlic clove, peeled
Salt and freshly ground black pepper to taste
Juice of ½ lemon
2 to 3 tablespoons extra-virgin olive oil (to taste)
1 recipe Crostini (page 19)
Softened unsalted butter for spreading (optional)
¼ cup coarsely chopped fresh Italian parsley

Place the green onions, anchovies, garlic, salt and pepper, lemon juice, and olive oil in a food processor with a steel blade. Process until smooth and thick. Spread the crostini lightly with butter if desired, then spread the anchovy purée on the toasts. Sprinkle with the chopped parsley. Serve immediately.

BROILED POLENTA CANAPÉS WITH MIXED SEAFOOD
CROSTINI DI POLENTA AI FRUTTI DI MARE

Serves 10

The tender, mealy texture of polenta is set off by toppings that include *besciamella*. Although not many of us normally associate this classic white sauce with Italian food, it is nevertheless an integral part of the Italian *cucina*. The crunch of the bread crumbs in this recipe adds texture to the creamy filling.

> 6 small clams, cleaned (see page 7)
> 6 mussels, cleaned (see page 8)
> ½ cup white wine
> 1 garlic clove, peeled and minced
> ½ cup boiled and shelled small shrimp
> ½ cup Besciamella (page 289)
> Salt and freshly ground black pepper to taste
> 4 tablespoons unsalted butter
> 1 cup fresh bread crumbs
> 1 recipe Polenta, poured into an oiled loaf pan and completely cooled (page 147)

In a medium saucepan, combine the clams, mussels, white wine, and garlic, cover, and cook over high heat until the shellfish open. Let cool slightly. Pick out the meat and discard the shells. If you wish to add a bit more flavor of the sea to the topping, strain the cooking liquid through a sieve lined with a paper towel, and reserve about 3 tablespoons. In a small bowl, combine the clams, mussels, shrimp, besciamella, the reserved cooking liquid if desired, and salt and pepper to taste. Set aside. (You can make the topping up to 1 day ahead. Cover and refrigerate.)

To prepare the bread crumbs, heat the butter in a small skillet until it is melted and begins to turn a deep golden brown. Add the bread crumbs and toss them until they are just crisp. Set aside. To make the polenta triangles, unmold the polenta and cut into ¼-inch-thick slices with a sharp knife. Then cut each slice in half diagonally and place on a cookie sheet.

Preheat the oven to 375°. Spread each polenta triangle with about a teaspoon of the seafood mixture. Sprinkle a few bread crumbs over each triangle and place the pan in the top third of the oven. Bake until the topping is bubbling hot and lightly spotted with golden dots. Serve immediately.

BROILED POLENTA CANAPÉS WITH CRABMEAT
TOAST DI POLENTA CON GRANCHI
Serves 10

In northern Italy, where polenta is often the grain of choice, crostini are made from leftover cooked polenta. The name *toast di polenta* derives from the practice of browning the topping, either in a hot oven or under a broiler. The warm slices of polenta have the comforting and familiar fragrance of corn, and the texture is yielding and tender. The golden yellow of the corn creates a beautiful palette for toppings of contrasting color. You can prepare the polenta up to three days before you plan to complete the recipe.

1 recipe Polenta, poured into an oiled loaf pan and completely cooled (page 147)

1½ cups cooked crabmeat, picked over and flaked

½ cup Besciamella (page 289)

½ garlic clove, peeled and minced

1 tablespoon fresh lemon juice

Salt and freshly ground black pepper to taste

Unmold the polenta and cut into ¼-inch-thick slices with a sharp knife. Then cut each slice in half diagonally. Set the polenta triangles aside. To prepare the topping, mix together the crabmeat, besciamella, garlic, lemon juice, and salt and pepper in a small bowl.

Preheat the broiler. Spread each polenta triangle with a tablespoon of the crabmeat mixture. Place the polenta toasts on a cookie sheet and broil until the topping is bubbling hot and lightly spotted with golden dots. Serve immediately.

FRIED SQUID

CALAMARI FRITTI

Serves 6

The most popular calamari dish in the United States—and deservedly so. There must be as many secret recipes for calamari fritti as there are Italian families. Some soak the calamari in milk, others think that would be heresy. Some cooks dredge calamari in bread crumbs, even in polenta. But the classic preparation is to soak them in milk and then dredge them in flour. This traditional recipe was perfected by Cynthia Brown, a very special woman who was the chef at Angeli Caffe for many years. Brown insists that the secret to good fried calamari is the care given to the act of dredging. So abandon your dislike for pasty flour stuck to your fingers, and think of modest Mediterranean seaside caffes as you give proper attention to massaging the flour into the squid.

> **3 pounds cleaned squid, tentacles trimmed and body sacs cut into rings (see page 10)**
> **2 cups half-and-half**
> **1 to 3 teaspoons coarsely ground black pepper (to taste)**
> **3 cups all-purpose flour**
> **Coarse salt to taste**
> **Olive oil for frying**
> **Lemon wedges**

Place the squid in a medium bowl. Add the half-and-half and black pepper and stir to mix. Marinate the squid for at least 1 hour, or refrigerate for up to 24 hours before frying.

In a shallow bowl, combine the flour with coarse salt to taste. Drain the squid in a colander. Add the squid to the seasoned flour and begin to "massage" them, rubbing the flour into the squid until every surface is thickly coated. Meanwhile in a deep heavy pan add oil to a depth of 3 inches. Heat until very hot but not smoking; the oil is ready when a squid ring added to the pan immediately begins to sizzle. Transfer the flour-coated squid a handful at a time to a dry sieve, and shake the sieve to get rid of excess flour. Fry the squid in small batches until a crisp, golden brown, using a long-handled metal spoon to gently move them around in the hot oil so they fry evenly. Use a slotted spoon to remove the squid, and drain on paper towels. Serve on a platter garnished with lemon wedges. Accompany with Salsa all'Arrabiata if you wish (page 287).

PAN-ROASTED SQUID
CALAMARI ARROSTO
Serves 4

This is a perfect dish for the calamari lover in a hurry. Quick to throw together, it vies with Calamari Fritti (page 24) as a favorite starter. Roasting is an unusual yet simple and effective method of cooking calamari. The high heat and quick cooking results in especially tender meat. Serve with plenty of good bread to soak up the garlic-and-rosemary-scented juices. Good as a light lunch with an Insalata Verde (page 281) and a bottle of chilled crisp white wine.

> 1 pound cleaned squid tentacles (see page 10), cut in half
>   lengthwise
> 1 large sprig fresh rosemary, leaves only, minced
> 2 tablespoons extra-virgin olive oil
> Salt and freshly ground black pepper to taste
> 2 to 3 garlic cloves, peeled and chopped
> ¼ cup coarsely chopped fresh Italian parsley
> Lemon wedges

Preheat the oven to 450°. Place the calamari in a small bowl. Sprinkle with the rosemary, oil, salt and pepper, and garlic, and toss until well coated. Place the seasoned calamari in a shallow baking dish. Roast for 25 minutes, or until tender, basting the squid with their juices several times. Remove from the oven, place in a shallow serving bowl, and sprinkle with the parsley. Serve immediately, with a generous squeeze of lemon juice.

FENNEL-CURED SALMON

SALMONE AL FINOCCHIO

Serves 20 as part of a cocktail buffet

Gravlax is a traditional Scandinavian dish that has crossed national boundaries. A delicate, elegant fish preparation, it is often found in the *altissima* of *alta cucina* restaurants in Italy. This recipe adds the Italian flavor of fennel and the Greek flavoring of ouzo to the cure. Try pairing the slightly sweet, transparent slices of this salmon with baby greens and Crostini (page 19) as a light appetizer. Or tuck a few slices into split foccacia and cut into finger sandwiches.

1 whole Norwegian salmon (about 3 pounds), filleted but skin left intact

2 tablespoons ouzo

Juice of 1 medium lemon

6 tablespoons coarse salt

¼ cup sugar

1 tablespoon fennel seeds

4 ounces (about 2 cups) white peppercorns, crushed

Green tops from 2 bulbs fennel

Extra-virgin olive oil

Use a pair of pliers, fish tweezers, or your fingers to remove the pin or "feather" bones from the fish. Lay the salmon fillets on a flat work surface or on a large platter, skin side down, and pour the ouzo over them. Let sit for 2 minutes. Pour the lemon juice over the fillets and let sit for another 2 minutes.

In a small bowl, mix together the salt, sugar, fennel seeds, and crushed white peppercorns. Pat the salmon fillets dry with paper towels and place them skin side down on a dry work surface. Sprinkle half the salt mixture evenly over the fillets. Spread half the fennel tops evenly over 1 fillet. Place the other fillet flesh side down on top of the first fillet. Wrap the fish in parchment paper and place in a pan that is long enough for the salmon to lie flat and has at least a

½-inch rim. Set a plate on top of the fish and weight with a heavy object (of about 2 pounds). Place the weighted fish in the refrigerator for 24 hours.

Drain the excess liquid from the pan, and unwrap the fillets. Discard the fennel tops and pat the salmon dry. Sprinkle the remaining salt mixture over the fillets, then spread the remaining fennel tops on top of 1 fillet, place the other fillet over it, wrap in fresh parchment, and refrigerate for 4 days. Once each day, drain the liquid from the pan and turn the fish, rewrapping it in fresh parchment.

To serve, unwrap the salmon and discard the fennel tops. Wipe the salmon to remove excess peppercorns. Drizzle lightly with oil. Slice the salmon very thin on a slight angle, starting at the tail end.

I RIPIENI

STUFFED FOODS

In every household in every region of Italy women create rustic delicacies by stuffing any food imaginable. The *ripieni* are a way for home cooks who deal with the same local ingredients day after day to vary the fare and make the most economical use of leftovers. Filling mussel or clam shells enriches a meal and makes everyday ingredients more festive.

Mussels Baked in Tomato Sauce

COZZE RIPIENE COLLA SALSA

Serves 4 to 6

24 large black or New Zealand mussels, cleaned (see page 8)

2 pinches of dried oregano

Freshly ground black pepper to taste

2 cups fresh bread crumbs

4 tablespoons melted unsalted butter

2 cloves garlic, peeled and minced

Small handful of chopped fresh Italian parsley

2 cups Fresh Tomato-Basil Sauce (page 286), plus extra if serving the mussels hot

Preheat the oven to 450°. Remove the upper shell from each mussel by carefully slipping an oyster knife or small wide knife between the two shells and jiggling it until the muscle relaxes and the shell opens. (If the mussels are very difficult to open, you can steam them in a covered skillet with a little white wine or water just until they open; do not overcook.) Scrape any meat adhering to the top shell onto the bottom shell. Sprinkle the mussels with the oregano and pepper.

In a small bowl, mix together the bread crumbs, melted butter, garlic, and parsley. Mound about 1 tablespoon of the seasoned bread crumbs onto each mussel, reserving the remaining crumbs. Arrange the mussels on a baking sheet and carefully spoon the tomato-basil sauce over them. Bake the mussels in the preheated oven for 10 minutes. Remove the pan from the oven and turn on the broiler. Sprinkle the remaining bread crumbs over the baked mussels. Place the pan under the broiler for 1 or 2 minutes to brown the crumbs. Serve hot and pass additional sauce, or serve as is at room temperature.

STUFFED MUSSELS FARMHOUSE STYLE
COZZE RIPIENE ALLA FATTORIA
Serves 4

In this recipe, mussels are topped with cooked sausage and sage leaves. Their top shells are held in place with blanched chives, resulting in beautiful shiny black bundles just waiting to be opened. This dish is best served as a sit-down appetizer.

> 1 bunch fresh chives
> 32 black mussels, cleaned (see page 8)
> 3 tablespoons extra-virgin olive oil
> 3 garlic cloves, peeled and minced
> 5 sweet Italian sausages, casings removed
> 32 fresh sage leaves, plus 2 to 3 bunches sage for garnish
> Lemon wedges

Preheat the oven to 375°. Blanch the chives by plunging them into boiling salted water for 10 seconds. Drain and immediately place in a bowl of ice water. When the chives are cool, lift out of the water and drain on a kitchen towel.

To open the mussels, place in a dry skillet large enough to hold them in one or two layers. Cover the pan and cook over high heat just until the shells pop open, 2 to 3 minutes. Set aside to cool. In a sauté pan, heat 2 tablespoons of the olive oil over medium heat. Add the garlic and cook just until its characteristic aroma is released. Crumble the sausage into the pan and sauté, stirring often and breaking up the lumps of meat, until cooked through. Place sausage in a colander to drain off the fat, transfer to a small bowl, and let cool.

Place a small amount of the cooled sausage mixture on top of each mussel and top with a sage leaf. Close the shells and tie each one with a blanched chive. Place the remaining 1 tablespoon olive oil in a baking pan and put the mussels in the pan. Bake the mussels for 12 to 15 minutes. Serve on a colorful platter garnished with bunches of sage and lemon wedges.

Mussels with Pesto Stuffing

Cozze al Pesto

Serves 4 to 6

The garlicky anise-like flavor of pesto and the delicately briny taste of mussels come together in this gusty dish of simple beauty. Prepare the bread crumbs and pesto in advance to make the final preparation a breeze.

For the bread crumbs

    5 slices day-old country bread

    3 tablespoons extra-virgin olive oil

    1 garlic clove, peeled and minced

    Salt and freshly ground black pepper to taste

    24 black mussels, cleaned (see page 8)

    2 tablespoons extra-virgin olive oil

    2 garlic cloves, peeled and sliced

    Juice of ½ lemon

    ½ cup white wine

    Handful of coarsely chopped fresh Italian parsley

    About ½ cup Basil Pesto (page 300)

    Lemon wedges

    1 bunch fresh basil

To make the bread crumbs, preheat the oven to 350°. Process the bread to coarse crumbs in a food processor with a steel blade. In a small bowl, mix the bread crumbs, oil, garlic, and salt and pepper to taste. Spread the seasoned bread crumbs on a cookie sheet and bake until golden brown, 10 to 15 minutes. Watch carefully to prevent them from burning. Remove from the oven and let cool. Stored in an airtight container, the crumbs will keep for up to 2 weeks.

continued

In a large sauté pan, combine the mussels, oil, garlic, lemon juice, wine, and parsley. Cover with a tight-fitting lid, and cook over moderately high heat until the mussels steam open, approximately 7 minutes. Let cool. Remove the top shell from each mussel. Top each mussel with a dab of pesto, then sprinkle with bread crumbs. The mussels may be prepared to this point and refrigerated for several hours.

To serve, slip under a hot broiler for a few seconds, or until the pesto is bubbling and the bread crumbs are crunchy. Serve on a platter garnished with lemon wedges and fresh basil.

Mussels with Spicy Tomato Sauce
COZZE ALL'ARRABIATA
Serves 6

There are two ways to prepare this recipe: the most deliciously messy is simply to steam open the mussels in the tomato sauce, and then to serve the sauced mussels in a shallow bowl at room temperature. The more elegant way, which I present here, is nearly as quick, can be prepared in advance, and is ideal for passing as an antipasto or as part of a buffet.

2 pounds mussels, cleaned (see page 8)

Splash of white wine or water

¼ cup olive oil

4 garlic cloves, peeled and minced

½ teaspoon dried red chile pepper flakes

4 tomatoes, peeled, seeded, finely chopped, and drained, or 1 cup canned Italian-style tomatoes, drained, seeded, and finely chopped

1 teaspoon fresh lemon juice

1 teaspoon grated lemon zest (optional)

Coarse salt to taste

1 small bunch fresh Italian parsley, coarsely chopped

Lemon wedges

Place the mussels in a skillet large enough to hold them in no more than two layers and add the wine, oil, and half the garlic. Cover and cook over high heat, shaking the pan occasionally, just until the mussels open, about 5 minutes. Remove from the heat, and use a slotted spoon or tongs to transfer the mussels to a bowl to cool. Strain the cooking juices through a sieve lined with a double thickness of paper towels into a small bowl.

To make the arrabiata sauce, return the strained pan juices to the skillet and reduce by half over high heat. Add the red chile pepper flakes, tomatoes, and the remaining garlic and cook over medium-high heat, stirring frequently, until the sauce begins to thicken, about 5 to 7 minutes. Add the lemon juice, zest, if using, and salt to taste, and spoon the sauce into a small bowl to cool.

To serve, remove the top shells from the mussels and discard. Arrange the mussels on the half-shell on a platter. Spoon a bit of the spicy sauce onto each mussel, and sprinkle the mussels with the chopped parsley. Serve at room temperature, with lemon wedges. The mussels may be made several hours ahead, covered with plastic wrap, and refrigerated. Bring to room temperature before serving.

LIGURIAN OLIVE-FILLED CLAMS
VONGOLE ALLE LIGURE
Serves 4 to 6

Cinque Terre is a unique collection of five tiny villages perched in narrow valleys that jut inward from Italy's Ligurian coast. Whether by train, boat, or by foot, arriving in these villages is like entering into a postcard. A small trattoria called Marina Piccola in the village of Manarola offers regional specialties in the hushed surround of olive trees. I put together this dish with the memory of an evening in this dreamy place.

½ cup homemade dried bread crumbs

1 anchovy fillet, minced

4 garlic cloves, peeled and minced

5 Kalamata or Gaeta olives, pitted and finely chopped, plus a handful of whole olives for garnish

½ tablespoon capers

¼ cup extra-virgin olive oil

24 clams, cleaned and soaked (see page 7)

Squeeze of lemon juice

Splash of white wine

Splash of fish stock (optional)

Handful of coarsely chopped fresh Italian parsley, plus several sprigs for garnish

Lemon wedges

In a small bowl, combine the bread crumbs, anchovy, half of the garlic, the olives, and capers and mix well. Set aside.

In a large sauté pan over medium heat, combine the oil, the remaining garlic, the clams, lemon juice, wine, fish stock if using , and the chopped parsley. Cover and let steam over medium heat until the clams open, approximately 5 to 7 minutes. Let cool. When the clams are cool enough, remove the top shell of each one. Place the clams in their half-shells on a serving platter. Strain the pan juices through a sieve lined with a double thickness of paper towels. Moisten each clam with a bit of the strained pan juices. Top each one with about a tablespoon of the bread crumb mixture. Garnish the serving platter with sprigs of parsley, lemon wedges, and whole olives. Serve immediately.

COOL CLAMS WITH PINE NUTS
VONGOLE AI PIGNOLI
Serves 4 to 6

Because of the controversy over eating uncooked shellfish in public places, the clams on the half-shell that we serve in the restaurants are often steamed and cooled, and then topped with a variety of marinades. In this dish, the chopped arugula in the dressing is strewn over the clams like an herb. The pine nuts add their oily pine flavor and a toasty crunch.

½ cup pine nuts

24 soft-shell clams, such as Manila, cleaned and soaked (see page 7)

Wine or water for steaming

1 recipe Arugula Dressing (page 293)

Preheat the oven to 375°. Spread the pine nuts on a baking sheet and toast in the oven for 3 to 5 minutes. Set aside to cool. When the nuts are cool, chop half of them coarsely. Set aside.

Place the clams in a skillet large enough to hold them in no more than two layers. Add enough wine or water to come ¼ inch up the sides of the pan, cover and cook over high heat, shaking the pan occasionally, just until the clams open, about 5 minutes. Let cool. When the clams are cool enough, remove and discard the top shell of each one. Transfer the clams in their half-shells to a serving platter.

Stir the toasted pine nuts into the dressing. Spoon the dressing over the clams. Serve immediately.

OREGANO-SCENTED BROILED CLAMS

VONGOLE ORIGANATE

Serves 4 to 6

For recipes that require you to broil clams or mussels on the half-shell, either start with raw mollusks, or, if you find opening raw shellfish too scary, first steam the shellfish briefly so that the shells open. If you choose the latter method, wait till they cool and merely pull off the top shells and discard—but remember that the seafood is already cooked. Broil only briefly so as not to toughen it.

I love this dish for its pure reductive simplicity. It's one of those recipes made by scraping the bottom of the pantry (and adding fresh clams, of course).

> 20 to 24 soft-shell clams, cleaned (see page 7)
> 2 garlic cloves, peeled and minced
> 2 sprigs fresh oregano, leaves only, finely chopped, or ½ teaspoon dried oregano
> 1½ cups fresh bread crumbs
> 1 tablespoon extra-virgin olive oil
> Salt and freshly ground black pepper to taste
> Juice of ½ lemon
> Lemon wedges

Prepare the clams on the half-shell by opening the raw clams and removing and discarding the top shells. Or, if you prefer, steam the clams in a covered pan over high heat just until they open. Then let cool and remove the top shells. Preheat the broiler. In a small bowl, mix together the garlic, oregano, bread crumbs, and olive oil. Place about 1 heaping teaspoon of the mixture on top of each clam, being careful to cover the tender meat, and lay the clams in a broiling pan. Slide the pan under the broiler and cook for about 3 minutes, or just until the clam juices are bubbling and the bread crumbs are golden. Remove from the broiler and arrange on a serving tray or individual appetizer plates. Sprinkle with salt and pepper to taste, and drizzle the lemon juice over the clams. Serve immediately, accompanied by lemon wedges.

CREAMY BAKED OYSTERS WITH CHIVES

OSTRICHE AL FORNO CON PANNA

Serves 4

I tasted these oysters on a wintry November night at a chic *nuova cucina* restaurant in Milano, La Corte de Regina. The setting was a stark but warm, almost medieval dining room with bare stone floors and a huge fireplace. The bubbling warmth of these pink-napped oysters was the beginning of a memorable meal.

24 oysters, preferably a variety with a deep shell
1 cup heavy cream
1 teaspoon tomato paste (optional)
Cayenne pepper to taste
1 small bunch fresh chives, finely chopped
2 tablespoons extra-virgin olive oil
¼ cup coarse fresh bread crumbs
Large handful of chopped fresh Italian parsley

Preheat the oven to 375°. Open the oysters with an oyster knife or can opener (see page 9), or have the fishmonger do it. Reserve the oysters in the deeper bottom shells, and discard the top shells. Pour the juices into a saucepan, and place the oysters in their shells in a baking pan. Add the cream, and the tomato paste if desired, to the juices in the saucepan, bring to a boil, and reduce by half. Remove from the heat and stir in the cayenne pepper and chives.

In a small bowl, mix together the oil, bread crumbs, and parsley. Spoon the reduced cream mixture over the top of the oysters, and sprinkle with the bread crumb mixture. Bake until golden brown and bubbly, about 8 minutes. Serve immediately.

Tuna Carpaccio with White Beans and Arugula Dressing

CARPACCIO DI TONNO AI FAGIOLI E RUCOLA

Serves 6

Carpaccio has acquired many faces since Harry Cipriani served his first plate of raw beef tenderloin in Venice. It was just a matter of time before the influence of Japanese sashimi infiltrated the Italian palate. Raw tuna has a rich smooth texture that mirrors the creaminess of cannellini beans.

1 pound sushi-quality Ahi tuna
2 bunches arugula
1 cup cooked cannellini beans
1 recipe Arugula Dressing (page 293)

Cut the tuna into 6 equal pieces. Gently pound each piece between two sheets of oiled parchment or waxed paper until very thin. (The tuna can be pounded several hours in advance, covered in plastic wrap, and refrigerated.)

When ready to serve, divide the arugula among six plates. Arrange the tuna slices over the arugula. Top with the cannellini beans and drizzle the arugula dressing over all. Serve immediately.

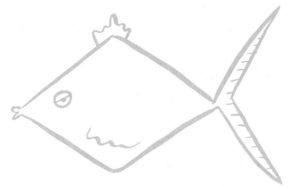

Salmon Carpaccio with Black Olive Paste

CARPACCIO DI SALMONE CON PESTO DI OLIVE

Serves 6

Few dishes are as visually striking as these peach-colored transparent petals of raw salmon drizzled with glossy black olive paste.

Juice of 2 lemons
2 tablespoons extra-virgin olive oil
Salt and freshly ground black pepper to taste
1½ pounds salmon fillet
1 recipe Black Olive Paste (page 298)
Lemon wedges
Small handful of Picholine or other tiny black olives

To make the marinade, in a small bowl combine the lemon juice, olive oil, and salt and black pepper to taste. Cut the salmon on a slight angle into very thin slices. Place the fish in a glass, stainless steel, or enamel baking pan and cover with the marinade. Refrigerate for at least 4 hours.

To serve, lift the salmon from the marinade and arrange on individual plates. Grind a bit of black pepper over each serving. Drizzle black olive paste over the carpaccio and garnish with lemon wedges and olives.

COLD SEAFOOD EXTRAVAGANZA ON ICE

FRUTTI DI MARE MISTI

Serves 10

This is the appetizer you present to people you really love when you are feeling quite flush. I've given amounts for ten because seafood platters seem to be most impressive when served abundantly to a largish group. If you really want to splurge, increase the quantities and serve the dish as a main course. It would be an elegant yet very simple centerpiece for a special buffet luncheon. Serve a first course of bruschetta topped with tomato and arugula or a simple salad of mixed field lettuces, and, for dessert, fresh fruit and a basket of biscotti. Here, I have suggested many types of seafood. Let your fish market be your guide.

20 medium shrimp, boiled but left in the shell

10 hard-shell clams, on the half-shell (see page 7)

20 oysters (10 each of 2 different types), on the half-shell (see page 9)

8 cooked crab claws (cocktail claws or Dungeness or King Crab claws)

5 rock lobster tails, broiled

10 sea scallops, blanched or grilled

20 black mussels, steamed open and top shells removed

Serve with one or more of the following sauces:

Cold Salsa all'Arrabiata (page 287)

Salsa Verde (page 288)

Parsley Pesto Dressing (page 295)

Black Pepper Dressing (page 297)

Garlic-Herb Mayonnaise (page 305)

SARDINES WITH TOMATOES AND HOT PEPPERS
SARDE CON POMODORI AL DIAVOLO
Serves 4 to 6

Few presentations show off the strength of flavor and the beautiful silvery color of canned sardines as this one does. *Olio santo* is such an easy condiment to make, yet it truly can exalt a dish as it does here. The sweet acid of the tomatoes and vinegar balances the pungent meaty flavor of the sardines, and the extra kick of spiciness from the oil provides the perfect finish.

2 large red-ripe round tomatoes or 4 red-ripe Roma tomatoes
½ small red onion, peeled and thinly sliced
2 cans high-quality sardines packed in olive oil
2 pinches of dried oregano
Pinch of red chile pepper flakes
Olio Santo (page 15) or extra-virgin olive oil
Drizzle of balsamic vinegar
Moroccan salt-cured black olives

Slice the tomatoes, discarding the ends, and arrange the slices in a slightly overlapping design on a serving platter. Scatter the onion slices over the tomatoes. Drain the sardines. Remove them carefully from the can so they remain intact, and arrange them over the onion and tomatoes. Sprinkle the oregano and red chile pepper flakes over the sardines, onions, and tomatoes. Dress the sardines, onions, and tomatoes by first drizzling generously with olio santo or extra-virgin olive oil, then with a bit of balsamic vinegar. Garnish the platter with a few Moroccan olives. Serve with good country bread.

Tuna Marinated in Sweet-and-Sour Saffron Vinaigrette

TONNO ALL'AGRODOLCE

Serves 4 to 6

This dish exemplifies the rich heritage of Italian cooking. Sicilian roots are apparent in the combination of saffron with tuna. It also combines the Italian tradition of *agrodolce,* or sweet and sour dishes, with the ancient technique of preserving fish in acidic marinades. The choice of red wine vinegar to match the deep flavor of tuna is further enhanced by the woodsy flavor of the rosemary. The saffron and sugar combine to create a glossy red-orange marinade that tints the tuna. Overall it's an awesome presentation. This dish is best made a day ahead. If you prefer, you can grill the tuna, then simply break it up into small pieces before marinating.

> 1 pound fresh tuna steaks
> Flour for dredging
> Salt and freshly ground black pepper to taste
> ½ cup extra-virgin olive oil
> 1 onion, peeled and thinly sliced
> 2 sprigs fresh rosemary, leaves only, minced
> ½ cup fish stock or water
> ¼ cup red wine vinegar, or more to taste
> 2 to 4 teaspoons sugar (to taste)
> 1 pinch of saffron threads, soaked in ¼ cup warm water

Cut the tuna steaks into pieces about 3 inches by 2 inches. Place the flour in a shallow baking dish and season with salt and pepper. Dredge the tuna in the flour and pat off the excess. Heat ¼ cup of the olive oil in a large sauté pan over medium heat. Add the tuna and sauté for approximately 2 minutes per side, or until just barely cooked through. Transfer the tuna to a glass, stainless steel, or enamel bowl.

In a small skillet, heat the remaining ¼ cup oil. Add the onion and rosemary and cook over medium heat until the onion is soft and translucent. Add the fish stock or water, vinegar, and 2 teaspoons sugar and cook, stirring, until the sugar dissolves. Taste the sauce for a sweet and sour character: If it needs more sweetness, add a bit more sugar; if it is too sweet, add a bit more vinegar. When the sweet and sour balance is right for you, add the saffron and its soaking liquid. Pour the hot sauce over the tuna. Cool, cover, and let marinate in the refrigerator overnight before serving.

WHITEFISH DROWNED IN LONG-COOKED ONIONS

PESCE IN CARPIONE

Serves 10

*I*n carpione, like the Venetian term *in saor* and the more common *sotto aceto,* refers to the technique of preserving food in vinegar. In Italy, the tradition of marinating sautéed fish in a mixture of oil, vinegar, herbs, and onion is associated particularly with freshwater fish. Here the extremely tender flesh of whitefish is prevented from falling apart in the marinade by a golden crust. Its characteristic texture becomes even more yielding after twenty-four hours in the marinade.

2 pounds whitefish fillet, skin on

Flour for dredging

Salt and freshly ground black pepper to taste

Vegetable oil for pan-frying

1¼ cups extra-virgin olive oil

1½ medium onions, peeled and thinly sliced

Small handful of coarsely chopped fresh Italian parsley

¼ cup golden raisins (optional)

⅓ cup champagne vinegar

1 teaspoon Dijon mustard

1 shallot, peeled and minced

Grated zest of 1 lemon

1 head radicchio or butter lettuce

¼ cup lightly toasted pine nuts

Remove the pin bones from the fish using tweezers, pliers, or your fingers. Cut the fish fillet crosswise into pieces about 1½ inches wide. Place the flour in a shallow dish and season with salt and pepper. In a large nonstick skillet, heat about ½ inch of vegetable oil until hot but not smoking. Lightly dust the fish with the seasoned flour, add to the pan, and fry until golden. Carefully remove the fish from the skillet and arrange it in a nonreactive baking pan.

In a medium skillet, heat ¼ cup of the olive oil and sauté the onions until very tender. Arrange the onions, chopped parsley, and the raisins, if desired, over the fish. To make the marinade, in a small bowl, whisk together the remaining 1 cup olive oil, the vinegar, mustard, shallot, lemon zest, and salt and pepper to taste. Pour over the fish and let marinate in the refrigerator for at least 24 hours.

Separate the radicchio or butter lettuce head into individual leaves, and arrange on serving plates. Lift the fish, topped with the onion mixture, out of the marinade and arrange on the lettuce leaves. Garnish with the pine nuts.

ANCHOVY-FILLED FRIED ZUCCHINI FLOWERS
FIORI DI ZUCCA RIPIENI
Serves 6

Fried zucchini flowers epitomize summer cooking to me. The addition of anchovy deepens the flavor. Sometimes I also tuck a cube of mozzarella into the flowers so that the crunchy treats are at once creamy and salty.

20 zucchini flowers
10 anchovy fillets, rinsed and cut in half
Olive oil for deep-frying
1 recipe Club Soda Batter (page 243)
½ bunch fresh Italian parsley, washed and thoroughly dried
Coarse salt (optional)
Edible flowers
Lemon wedges

Carefully wipe the zucchini flowers of any dirt or insects. Gently reach into the flowers and pinch out the stamens. Stuff each flower with 1 anchovy half.

Pour 2 to 3 inches of olive oil into a deep heavy-bottomed pan and heat until hot but not smoking. Hold a flower by the stem end and quickly dip it into the batter. Lift the coated flower to drain off excess batter and quickly drop it into the hot oil. (The oil should be hot enough that it begins sizzling immediately.) Add only as many flowers as will fit comfortably in the pan without crowding, and fry until a light golden brown. Lift the flowers out of the hot fat with a slotted spoon and let drain on paper towels. Repeat until all flowers are fried. Fry the parsley sprigs in the same manner, and drain. Place a cloth napkin on a large platter and arrange the fried zucchini flowers and parsley on it. Sprinkle coarse salt over them if desired. Serve immediately, garnished with edible flowers and lemon wedges.

MARINATED MIXED GRILL WITH VEGGIES AND ORANGE JUICE
CAPONATINA ALLA GRIGLIA
Serves 4 to 6

This *caponatina,* or little caponata, reveals the more baroque side of the Italian kitchen. Artichokes, eggplant, and peppers are combined with shrimp and scallops, then bathed in an orange juice–based dressing. Toasted almonds add the final touch to this homage to Sicily.

¼ pound baby artichokes

Juice of 2 lemons

1 medium eggplant

Salt

2 medium red bell peppers, cored, halved, and seeded

About 1 cup extra-virgin olive oil

1½ pounds medium shrimp, peeled and deveined (see page 9)

¾ pound sea scallops, tough side muscles removed

4 to 6 garlic cloves, peeled and minced

Small handful of coarsely chopped fresh Italian parsley, plus a few sprigs for garnish

1 bunch basil, leaves only, coarsely chopped, plus whole leaves for garnish

For the dressing

4 anchovy fillets, chopped to a paste

¾ cup extra-virgin olive oil

¼ cup white wine vinegar

¼ cup orange juice

1 tablespoon sugar

Salt and freshly ground black pepper to taste

¾ cup Garlicky Bread Crumbs (page 12)

6 ounces toasted slivered almonds

Trim the baby artichokes by stripping off the outer leaves until those remaining are pale green to yellow. Trim off the stem ends and cut off the tapered tips. Cut each artichoke in half lengthwise. As you work, place the trimmed artichokes in a bowl filled with water and the lemon juice to prevent discoloring. Set aside.

Slice off the stem and blossom ends of the eggplant. Cut the eggplant crosswise into slices about ¼ inch thick. Lay out the slices on paper towels, and salt generously. Let stand until beads of moisture appear on the surface, then dry the eggplant with paper towels.

Heat an outdoor grill or ridged stovetop griddle until very hot. Lightly brush the eggplant slices and pepper halves with olive oil, and place the vegetables on the grill oiled side down. Brush the tops with a bit of additional oil. Cook until grill marks are clearly visible and the vegetables are beginning to soften. Turn the vegetables and continue cooking until they are just soft and slightly charred, but not burned. Transfer to a platter and let cool.

Drain the artichokes and pat dry with a kitchen towel. Place in a bowl, lightly drizzle with olive oil, and toss to coat. Place the artichoke halves on the grill and cook, turning once, until they begin to soften. Place them in a large bowl. Cut the eggplant and peppers into thin strips about ¼ inch thick and add to the artichokes. Lightly brush the shrimp and scallops with oil, and briefly grill on both sides. (Remember that the seafood will continue to cook when it is removed from the heat.) Add the cooked seafood to the vegetables, along with the garlic and chopped parsley and basil.

In a bowl, mix together all the dressing ingredients. Pour over the seafood mixture, and mix well. Let marinate for 1 hour at room temperature or for several hours in the refrigerator; bring to room temperature before serving.

To serve, mound the caponatina on a platter and sprinkle with the bread crumbs and almonds. Garnish with sprigs of parsley and basil leaves.

SEAFOOD CAPONATA
CAPONATA AL MARE
Serves 4 to 6

I tasted this Palermitano specialty in a rustic trattoria in Taormina, where it stood out among the many choices on a huge antipasto table consisting only of eggplant dishes! The addition of seafood to the traditional vegetarian components of caponata transforms the dish into something that's very nearly a seafood jam. Use whatever summer vegetables or seafood are available to you to create your own version of this complex combination of tastes.

    ¾ cup olive oil
    1 large eggplant, cut into small cubes
    4 celery stalks, peeled and cut into ¼-inch-thick slices
    3 tablespoons extra-virgin olive oil
    1 large onion, peeled and cut into medium dice
    4 to 6 garlic cloves, peeled and minced
    1½ pounds medium shrimp, peeled and deveined (see page 9)
    1 pound black mussels, such as Prince Edward Island or Penn Cove,
        cleaned (see page 8)
    1½ pounds clams, preferably Manila, cleaned (see page 7)
    ¼ cup white wine
    ¼ cup Kalamata or Gaeta olives, pitted and cut in half lengthwise
    ¼ cup chopped fresh Italian parsley
    2 tablespoons capers
    2 tablespoons balsamic vinegar
    Salt and freshly ground black pepper to taste

Heat the ¾ cup olive oil in a deep pot or sauté pan over medium heat. Test the temperature of the oil by adding 1 cube of the eggplant to the oil; the oil is ready when it immediately starts to bubble around the eggplant cube. Use a skimmer, slotted spoon, or spatula to carefully lower the cubed eggplant into the oil; if the eggplant causes the oil to bubble up slightly as you are adding it, wait until the bubbling subsides before adding all the eggplant. Cook until golden brown. Transfer the cooked eggplant to a colander set over a bowl to drain off excess oil. Repeat the process to fry and drain the celery. Place the drained eggplant and celery in a large mixing bowl.

In a large sauté pan, heat 2 tablespoons of the extra-virgin oil. Add the onion and half the minced garlic and sauté until golden. Add the shrimp and sauté until cooked through but still tender. Transfer to the bowl containing the eggplant and celery. In another sauté pan, heat the remaining 1 tablespoon extra-virgin oil. Add the remaining garlic, the mussels, clams, and white wine, cover, and cook just until the shellfish open. Remove from the heat and let cool for a few minutes. Shell the mussels and the clams and add to the cooked vegetables. Add the olives, parsley, capers, and vinegar and carefully toss by hand to mix. Season with salt and pepper to taste.

DEEP-FRIED WHITEBAIT
BIANCHETTI FRITTI

The first time I saw Venice, I was sixteen, and because of a mixup in travel plans my friends and I spent our first night in an ancient convent on one of the canals. None of us recognized the tiny fish in the Venetian specialty that was served to us at dinner that evening. Not wanting to offend the nuns, we squelched our teenage sensibilities and plunged in anyway. We must have gone through a pound of fish apiece before we finally stopped.

1 pound whitebait
Flour for dredging
Salt and freshly ground black pepper to taste
Olive oil for deep-frying
Coarse salt
Lemon wedges

Rinse the whitebait in salted water and drain in a colander. Place the flour in a paper bag and season with salt and pepper. Add the whitebait a handful at a time, close the bag, and shake until the fish are covered with flour. Transfer to a plate. Pour 2 to 3 inches oil into a deep heavy-bottomed pan, and heat until hot but not smoking. Place the whitebait in a large strainer and remove excess flour by shaking the strainer. Carefully drop the floured fish into the hot oil a few at a time, being careful that they do not clump up into one large mass, and fry until a crunchy golden brown. Lift the fish out of the oil with a slotted spoon and drain briefly on paper towels. Serve immediately, sprinkled with coarse salt and garnished with lemon wedges.

Pizzas, Tarts, Bruschetta, and Panini

PIZZAS

I learned to make pizza dough by watching a young Neapolitan pizza maker who worked with me at Angeli for a few years. He taught me that dough is a living, changing entity, something that is affected by weather and especially humidity. Neapolitans like their pizza dough rather soft. In fact, the traditional way of buying pizza in Naples is from a small, hole-in-the-wall vendor who folds the whole pizza in quarters, wraps it in paper, and hands it to you. My pizza dough reflects the Napoli style. When you first sink your teeth into the crust, it is slightly crunchy, but beyond the outer layer, the dough is yielding and delicate. Both my pizza and foccacia doughs are fairly soft. The softer the dough, the more delicate and soft the finished product is. Doughs that seem tough and elastic make crunchy, brittle crusts.

Making pizza dough is very simple. However, although it is possible to describe what the texture of the dough should be, I urge you to take a pizza-making class at a local cooking school. There is no better learning experience than watching how an experienced pizza maker handles the dough and being able to feel the dough at different stages. And, I promise you, you can make pizza dough every day for a year and still learn something new.

That said, I'll give you some hints for teaching yourself. First of all, remember that the amount of flour you add on a hot, dry day will differ from what you need on a damp, cool day. Aim for a texture that is just a hair's breadth away from stickiness. If you rub your earlobe between your fingers, you will have an excellent idea of the ideal texture you are seeking.

Two indispensable tools for making pizza are available in many gourmet and hardware stores. The first is a pizza stone or unglazed tiles, which should be put onto the bottom shelf of a cold oven and preheated along with the oven. Baking the pizza on a stone cooks the dough quickly and most closely reproduces the slightly charred taste of a pizza baked in a wood-fired oven. The second tool is a wooden peel, a sort of giant wooden spatula, on which the pizza is formed and topped, and then slid from it onto the stone in the hot oven. The secret to sliding the pizza easily off the peel is to flour the peel well before you begin.

PIZZA DOUGH

Makes enough for four 8-inch pizzas

1 package active dry yeast
¼ cup lukewarm water
3¼ cups flour, plus more if necessary
1½ teaspoons salt
3 tablespoons extra-virgin olive oil
1 cup cold water

To make pizza dough using a food processor:

In a small bowl, sprinkle the yeast over the warm water. Let it fizz for about 5 minutes.

Put the flour, yeast mixture, salt, olive oil, and cold water into the bowl of a food processor fitted with the metal blade, and process until the dough forms a ball. The dough should be fairly soft. If not, add a bit more water. If it is too sticky, add a bit more flour. Process for another minute.

Sprinkle a work surface with a little flour, and transfer the dough to the floured surface. Knead for 2 to 3 minutes, or until smooth and elastic. Shape the dough into a ball.

Rub the inside of a large mixing bowl with a little cooking oil. Transfer the dough to the bowl, turn once to coat with oil, and cover tightly with plastic wrap. Let the dough rise in a warm place for about an hour, or until doubled in bulk.

To make pizza dough by hand:

In a small bowl, sprinkle the yeast over the warm water. Let it fizz for about 5 minutes.

In a large bowl, combine the yeast mixture, 2½ cups of the flour, the salt, olive oil, and cold water. Mix with a wooden spoon until you have a thick batter.

Sprinkle a work surface with a little flour, and transfer the dough to the floured surface. Knead the remaining flour, a little at a time, into the dough. The dough should be soft and elastic but not sticky. You may need a little less or a little more flour. Shape the dough into a ball.

continued

Rub the inside of a large mixing bowl with a little cooking oil. Transfer the dough to the bowl, turn once to coat, and cover tightly with plastic wrap. Let the dough rise in a warm place for about an hour, or until doubled in bulk.

To finish preparing the dough:
Sprinkle a work surface with flour. Divide the dough into quarters, and roll each piece into a tight smooth ball, kneading it to push the air out of it. Place the dough balls on a lightly floured surface, cover them with a clean kitchen towel, and let rest for an hour. Or place them on a floured towel on a cookie sheet, cover with a towel, and refrigerate overnight.

(The dough will keep in the refrigerator for approximately 2 days or in the freezer for up to 1 month; thaw overnight in the refrigerator before using.)

Place 1 of the balls of dough on a lightly floured work surface. Sprinkle a little more flour on top of the ball. Using your fingertips, press the ball down into a large flat disk about ½ inch thick. Lift the dough and lay it over the back of the fist of one hand. Place your other fist underneath the dough so your fists are almost touching. Now gently stretch the dough by moving your fists away from each other. Each time you perform this stretching move, rotate the dough. Continue stretching and rotating until the dough is about ¼ inch thick and measures about 9 inches across. The dough is now ready for whichever topping you choose. Repeat with the remaining dough balls.

UNCOOKED TOMATO SAUCE FOR PIZZA
SUGO CRUDO PER LA PIZZA

Makes enough for six 8-inch pizzas

This uncooked sauce makes a fresh, light topping.

1 28-ounce can Italian-style crushed tomatoes, drained
Salt and freshly ground black pepper to taste
2 tablespoons olive oil

Put the tomatoes, salt and pepper, and olive oil into the bowl of a food processor fitted with the metal blade, and blend for 1 minute. Or pass the ingredients through the medium disk of a food mill.

Pizza "Whore Style" with Mussels

PIZZA ALLA PUTTANESCA CON COZZE

Makes one 8-inch pizza

This pizza was inspired by the famous Roman pasta named for the ladies of the night. Garlic, hot peppers, capers, anchovies, and olives create a bold pizza that doesn't need the addition of cheese.

Dough for one 8-inch pizza (page 53), stretched out to a 9-inch round as directed on page 54

¼ cup Sugo Crudo per la Pizza (page 54)

2 to 4 garlic cloves, peeled and thinly sliced

10 black mussels, steamed open and meat removed

8 Kalamata or Moroccan oil-cured olives, pitted and torn in half

1 teaspoon capers

2 to 4 anchovies packed in salt (to taste), rinsed and broken apart

Red chile pepper flakes to taste

2 pinches of dried oregano

Extra-virgin olive oil for drizzling

Place a pizza stone or unglazed tiles on the lowest oven rack. Preheat the oven to 500°.

Sprinkle some flour onto a wooden pizza peel. Gently lift the stretched dough round onto it. Use the back of a large spoon to spread the tomato sauce over the pizza in a spiral motion, leaving a ½-inch border of dough. Scatter the garlic slices over the pizza. Cut the mussels in half crosswise and arrange them evenly on the pizza. Scatter the olives, capers, anchovies, hot pepper flakes, and oregano over the pizza. Drizzle on a bit of olive oil. Shake the wooden peel back and forth gently to make sure the pizza is not stuck to it. Then quickly slide the pizza onto the hot baking stone. Bake until the pizza edges are golden, about 6 to 8 minutes. Using a metal peel or spatula, remove the pizza from the oven.

FENNEL-SCENTED PIZZA WITH SARDINES

PIZZA ALLE SARDE

Makes one 8-inch pizza

The silvery skin of the sardines peeks out from beneath the red tomato slices in this fragrant, beautiful pizza.

Dough for one 8-inch pizza (see page 53), stretched out to a 9-inch round as directed on page 54

2 thin slices onion, separated into rings

1 ripe round tomato or 3 ripe Roma tomatoes, cut into ¼-inch-thick slices

5 canned boneless sardines packed in oil

1 tablespoon fennel seeds

Extra-virgin olive oil for drizzling

Place a pizza stone or unglazed tiles on the lowest oven rack. Preheat the oven to 500°.

Sprinkle some flour onto a wooden pizza peel. Gently lift the stretched dough round onto it. Scatter the onions over the pizza. Lay the tomato slices over the onions in a circular pattern, covering the dough but leaving a ½-inch border. Break the sardines into pieces as you lay them on the pizza. Sprinkle the fennel seeds over the pizza, and drizzle on olive oil to taste. Shake the wooden peel back and forth gently to make sure the pizza is not stuck to it. Then quickly slide the pizza onto the hot baking stone. Bake until the pizza edges are golden, about 6 to 8 minutes. Using a metal peel or spatula, remove the pizza from the oven.

PIZZA WITH SHRIMP AND GOAT CHEESE

PIZZA AL CAPRINO E GAMBERI

Makes one 8-inch pizza

Although goat cheese is definitely not a traditional Italian topping for pizza, I was overruled by my staff on this one. The sweet shrimp is offset by the tang of the creamy goat cheese and the nutty mellowness of the caramelized garlic.

Dough for one 8-inch pizza (page 53), stretched out to a 9-inch round as directed on page 54

Extra-virgin olive oil for drizzling

8 sun-dried tomatoes

20 cloves Caramelized Garlic (page 13)

10 medium shrimp, peeled and deveined (see page 9)

3 ounces fresh goat cheese, cut into thin slices

1 sprig fresh oregano, leaves only

Place a pizza stone or unglazed tiles on the lowest oven rack. Preheat the oven to 500°.

Sprinkle some flour onto a wooden pizza peel. Gently lift the stretched dough round onto it. Drizzle a liberal amount of oil over the dough. Tear the sun-dried tomatoes into bite-sized pieces, and scatter them over the dough. Scatter the garlic over the pizza. Arrange the shrimp evenly over the pizza, and then cover the pizza with the goat cheese slices. Sprinkle on the oregano and finish by drizzling a bit more oil over the pizza. Shake the wooden peel back and forth gently to make sure the pizza is not stuck to it, and then quickly slide the pizza onto the hot baking stone. Bake until the pizza edges are golden and the shrimp are cooked, about 8 minutes. Using a metal peel or spatula, remove the pizza from the oven.

Pesto Pizza with Shrimp

PIZZA AL PESTO CON GAMBERI

Makes one 8-inch pizza

Another unconventional yet felicitous combination. One bite makes apparent the special affinity shrimp and basil have for one another.

Dough for one 8-inch pizza (page 53), stretched out to a 9-inch round as directed on page 54

¼ cup Basil Pesto (page 300)

2 to 4 garlic cloves, peeled and thinly sliced

3 thin slices onion

8 medium shrimp, peeled, deveined, and cut in half lengthwise (see page 9)

2 teaspoons pine nuts

2 tablespoons grated imported Parmesan cheese

Place a pizza stone or unglazed tiles on the lowest oven rack. Preheat the oven to 500°.

Sprinkle some flour onto a wooden pizza peel. Gently lift the stretched dough round onto it. Use the back of a spoon to spread the pesto liberally over the pizza, leaving a ½-inch border of dough. Scatter the garlic and onion slices over the pesto and arrange the shrimp evenly over the pizza. Sprinkle the pine nuts over the pizza, and finish by sprinkling the Parmesan over all. Shake the wooden peel back and forth gently to make sure the pizza is not stuck to it, and quickly slide the pizza onto the hot baking stone. Bake until the pizza edges are golden and the shrimp are cooked, about 8 minutes. Using a metal peel or spatula, remove the pizza from the oven.

Pizza with Clams, Garlic, and Oregano

Pizza alle Vongole

Makes one 8-inch pizza

An absolutely traditional pizza from the deep south of Italy: The bread crumbs are used instead of cheese to add a contrast of textures to the pizza.

> **Dough for one 8-inch pizza (page 53), stretched out to a 9-inch round as directed on page 54**
>
> **¼ cup Sugo Crudo per la Pizza (page 54) or 1 ripe round tomato or 3 Roma tomatoes, cut into ¼-inch-thick slices**
>
> **3 garlic cloves, peeled and thinly sliced**
>
> **15 clams, steamed open and meat removed**
>
> **6 pitted green olives, torn in half**
>
> **2 teaspoons dried oregano**
>
> **¼ cup coarse fresh bread crumbs**
>
> **Extra-virgin olive oil for drizzling**
>
> **1 tablespoon chopped fresh Italian parsley**

Place a pizza stone or unglazed tiles on the lowest oven rack. Preheat the oven to 500°.

Sprinkle some flour onto a wooden pizza peel. Gently lift the stretched dough round onto it. If using the tomato sauce, spread it over the pizza with the back of a spoon; if using fresh tomatoes, arrange the tomatoes evenly over the dough. Arrange the garlic, clams, and olives evenly over the pizza. Finish by sprinkling on the oregano and bread crumbs. Drizzle a bit of olive oil over the pizza. Shake the wooden peel back and forth gently to make sure the pizza is not stuck to it, and quickly slide the pizza onto the hot baking stone. Bake until the pizza edges are golden, 6 to 8 minutes. Using a metal peel or spatula, remove the pizza from the oven. Scatter the parsley over the pizza, and serve.

Pizza Neapolitan Style

PIZZA ALLA NAPOLETANA

Makes one 8-inch pizza

The pizza of pizzas—the quintessential Italian treat. From Naples, where tomatoes, garlic, anchovies, and oregano are fed to every child practically at birth.

Dough for one 8-inch pizza (page 53), stretched out to a 9-inch round as directed on page 54

¼ cup Sugo Crudo per la Pizza (page 54)

2 to 4 garlic cloves, peeled and thinly sliced

4 anchovies packed in salt, rinsed and bones removed

2 pinches of dried oregano

Extra-virgin olive oil for drizzling

1 tablespoon chopped fresh Italian parsley (optional)

Place a pizza stone or unglazed tiles on the lowest oven rack. Preheat the oven to 500°.

Sprinkle some flour onto a wooden pizza peel. Gently lift the stretched dough round onto it. Use the back of a spoon to spread the tomato sauce over the pizza, leaving a ½-inch border of dough. Scatter the garlic slices over the pizza. Tear the anchovies in half and arrange evenly over the pizza. Sprinkle with the oregano and drizzle a liberal amount of oil over the pizza. Shake the wooden peel back and forth gently to make sure the pizza is not stuck to it, and quickly slide the pizza onto the hot baking stone. Bake until the pizza edges are golden, about 6 to 8 minutes. Using a metal peel or spatula, remove the pizza from the oven. Scatter the parsley over the pizza if desired, and serve.

TARTS

Although savory tarts are most often associated with the French kitchen, Italians share the tradition. Rather than the creamy, egg-rich fillings typical of classic French cuisine, Italian recipes focus on simple combinations of inexpensive ingredients and are leaner in nature. The tarts I've included range from the simple pizza relation called Sardenaira to the rather baroque Sicilian swordfish pie, Impanata di Pesce Spada, with a sweet dough that dates back to the Saracens. Well worth the extra trouble of making and rolling out the dough, these tarts are a sort of portable pizza. They are great to bring to a potluck dinner or as part of a picnic.

FLAKY TART DOUGH
PASTA FROLLA
Makes enough for a 10-inch tart

The Italian version of the French pâte brisée makes a buttery, flaky crust.

2½ cups all-purpose flour
1 teaspoon salt
8 tablespoons (1 stick) cold unsalted butter, cut into pieces
¼ cup ice water

To make the dough by hand:
In a large bowl, combine the flour and salt, and stir to mix. Add the butter pieces. With your fingertips or two knives, rapidly cut the butter into the flour until the mixture resembles coarse meal. Gradually add the ice water and mix the dough with a fork until it comes together. Gather the dough together into a ball, wrap in plastic wrap, and refrigerate for at least 1 hour.

continued

To make the dough using a food processor:

Place the flour, salt, and butter in the bowl of a food processor fitted with the metal blade. Process until the mixture forms small crumbs. While the machine is running, drizzle in the ice water and process until the dough forms a ball. Wrap in plastic wrap and refrigerate for at least 1 hour.

To roll out the dough:

Unwrap the dough, and place it on a lightly floured work surface. Pound the dough a few times with a rolling pin to soften it. Roll it out to a large round ⅛ inch to ¼ inch thick. Gently lift the dough up onto the rolling pin and ease into a 10-inch tart pan with a removable bottom. Firmly press the dough into the pan without stretching it. Trim the edges by rolling over the rim of the pan with the rolling pin. Refrigerate for at least 30 minutes.

To partially prebake the crust:

Preheat the oven to 400°. Line the tart shell with aluminum foil, and fill with pie weights, rice, or dried beans. Bake for 15 minutes. Remove from the oven, remove the aluminum foil and weights, and prick the bottom of the crust with a fork. Bake for 3 to 5 minutes longer to dry the pastry. Let cool before filling.

ORANGE-SCENTED SOFT TART DOUGH

PASTA ALL'ARANCIA

Makes enough to line a 12-inch springform pan

This is an extremely malleable and foolproof crust, perfect for moist fillings. I often use it for *torta rustica,* a layered savory tart. The orange flavor and subtle sweetness of the dough marries especially well to fish and seafood fillings.

4 cups all-purpose flour
¼ cup sugar
1 teaspoon salt
Grated zest of 1 orange
½ pound (2 sticks) cold unsalted butter, cut into pieces
2 large eggs, beaten
2 large egg yolks
About ⅓ cup milk

To make the dough by hand:

In a large bowl, combine the flour, sugar, salt, and orange zest. Make a well in the center, and add the butter, eggs, and yolks to the well. Lightly blend the egg mixture with your fingertips. With a knife or pastry blender, gradually cut the dry ingredients into the wet ingredients until the dough is crumbly. Slowly add the milk, tossing with a fork until the dough comes together. The dough will be soft. Gather into a ball, wrap in plastic wrap, and refrigerate for at least 1 hour, or up to 3 days.

To make the dough using a food processor:

Combine the flour, sugar, salt, orange zest, and butter in a food processor fitted with the metal blade. Pulse until the mixture is crumbly. Add the eggs and yolks and pulse just to blend; do not overmix. Add the milk gradually and pulse until the dough begins to clump together. Remove the dough from the processor and gather into a ball, wrap in plastic wrap, and refrigerate for at least 1 hour, or up to 3 days.

TOMATO-ANCHOVY TART WITH CARAMELIZED GARLIC

SARDENAIRA

Makes 1 10-inch tart

This hybrid of a French tart and an Italian pizza brings together the best of the Mediterranean coast. The caramelized garlic is our own touch—my chefs are constantly searching for ways to ward off vampires.

10-inch partially baked Pasta Frolla tart shell (page 61)
6 large red-ripe tomatoes, cored and thinly sliced
10 anchovy fillets
6 fresh basil leaves, julienned
¼ cup Caramelized Garlic with its oil (page 13)
½ cup fresh bread crumbs
2 tablespoons grated imported Parmesan cheese

Preheat the oven to 400°. Arrange the tomato slices in the tart shell. Lay the anchovies on top of the tomatoes. Sprinkle with the basil. Spoon on the caramelized garlic and its oil, and sprinkle with the bread crumbs and Parmesan. Bake for 15 minutes, or until the crust is golden brown.

MASHED POTATO TART
TORTA PUGLIESE
Makes one 9-inch or 10-inch tart

The warm comfort of mashed potatoes is layered with scarlet tomato sauce and given the punch of anchovies. I serve this tart both as an earthy luncheon dish accompanied by a crunchy romaine lettuce salad and also as a vegetable side dish.

8 large russet potatoes

Salt

2 tablespoons plus ¼ cup extra-virgin olive oil

4 eggs, beaten

Salt and freshly ground black pepper or red chile pepper flakes to taste

1 large onion, peeled and chopped

¼ cup dried bread crumbs

2 cups Fresh Tomato-Basil Sauce (page 286)

5 large anchovies packed in salt, rinsed and bones removed

Put the potatoes in a large pot with enough water to cover. Throw in a handful of salt. Bring to a boil, then turn the heat down and simmer until tender. Drain and let the potatoes cool until you can handle them. Peel and put through a ricer, or mash well in a mixing bowl. Stir in 2 tablespoons of the olive oil, the eggs, and salt and black or red pepper to taste. Meanwhile, sauté the onion in the remaining ¼ cup oil until soft. Remove from the heat.

Preheat the oven to 375°. Oil a 9- or 10-inch springform pan and coat the inside with the bread crumbs. Spoon half the potatoes into the pan. Top with the tomato-basil sauce and then with the cooked onion. Shred the anchovies and scatter them evenly over the onion. Top with the remaining potatoes and smooth the top. Bake for 1 hour, or until the potatoes are golden brown on top. Remove from the oven and let cool for 15 minutes. Carefully remove the springform ring and serve warm or at room temperature.

SICILIAN SWORDFISH PIE IN SWEET ORANGE PASTRY

IMPANATA DI PESCE SPADA

Makes 1 deep 10-inch tart

The Sicilian penchant for combining many flavors, textures, and colors is showcased in this intensely flavored tart. Delicious warm or at room temperature, it's the apotheosis of picnic food.

4 zucchini, cut lengthwise into thin slices

1 large onion, peeled and diced

3 celery stalks

½ cup extra-virgin olive oil

2 garlic cloves, peeled and minced

4 Roma tomatoes, finely diced

1½ pounds swordfish, cut into small dice

Grated zest of 1 lemon

Juice of 1 lemon

12 green olives, pitted and torn in half

1 tablespoon capers

2 pinches of dried oregano

Handful of coarsely chopped fresh Italian parsley

Salt and freshly ground black pepper to taste

1 recipe Orange-Scented Tart Dough (page 63)

2 cups dried bread crumbs

2 large eggs, beaten, for egg wash

Heat a charcoal or gas grill or a ridged stovetop griddle. Use a towel to rub oil onto the grids. Grill the zucchini slices, turning once, until grill marks are clearly visible on both sides. Let cool and cut crosswise into thin strips. Set aside.

In a large sauté pan, cook the onion and celery in the olive oil until wilted. Add the garlic and sauté briefly, until its aroma is released. Add the tomatoes and cook over moderate heat until they break down and begin to form a sauce. Add the swordfish, lemon zest and juice, olives, capers, oregano, parsley, and salt and pepper to taste. Cook until the fish is just cooked through and the sauce has thickened. Set aside.

Preheat the oven to 375°. Divide the dough in half. Roll out one half of the dough into a large circle and fit it into a 10-inch springform pan, leaving a 1-inch overhang. Sprinkle ½ cup of the bread crumbs over the crust. Arrange half the zucchini strips over the bread crumbs. Sprinkle an additional ½ cup bread crumbs over the zucchini, and top with the swordfish mixture. Sprinkle another ½ cup bread crumbs over the swordfish. Top with the remaining zucchini and the remaining ½ cup bread crumbs.

Roll the remaining dough into a ¼-inch-thick circle the size of the pan. Place the dough on top of the filling and brush the edges of the dough with some of the egg wash. Bring the overhanging dough up over the edges of the top crust, pressing it gently down to adhere. Use any leftover dough scraps to decorate the top crust if you wish. Bake the tart for 1 hour, or until the crust is a deep golden brown, brushing the crust with egg wash 2 or 3 times during cooking. Let the tart cool for at least 15 minutes before removing the springform ring. Serve warm or at room temperature.

BRUSCHETTA AND PANINI

Bruschetta and *panini,* or sandwiches, are always a surprise to Americans visiting Italy. The bruschetta is instantly recognizable as primal garlic bread, but to Americans used to Dagwood-style sandwiches, panini are at first disappointing because of the comparatively small amount of filling. The Italian panino is meant as a snack, usually eaten on the run. It is not intended to satisfy as a main meal, but the filling ingredients are unusual and serendipitous combinations. The recipes that follow are grounded in the Italian concern for quality, texture, and taste, but take more than a bow to our own Dagwood tradition. Many of these sandwiches are perfect for using leftover cooked fish.

BRUSCHETTA

The base preparation for this archetypal garlic bread is the same no matter which topping you plan to use. First, begin with a sturdy country loaf, then cut the bread into ½-inch slices. Toast the slices by any method you like—ideally, over a charcoal or gas grill or on a ridged stovetop griddle. If those are not options, toast the bread in a toaster or under a broiler; you can even hold it on a long fork over a gas burner. Grill until light ridge marks appear or toast until the bread is a light golden brown; the inside should remain soft. Have a couple of peeled garlic cloves handy, and as soon as the bread is done, rub the surface lightly with the garlic. Place the grilled, garlic-rubbed bread on a plate and drizzle with olive oil to your taste. Sprinkle lightly with salt and a few grindings of fresh black pepper. The toppings can be as varied as your imagination and available ingredients allow.

Sicilian Green Olive and Clam Salad with Bruschetta

AULIVI CUNSATI CON BRUSCHETTA

Serves 4 to 6

SHRIMP   SCALLOPS   MUSSELS

*A*ulivi cunsati is the Sicilian dialect expression for *olivi conditi,* seasoned olives. Here the green olives are paired with clams fennel, celery, and mint for a piquant treat.

4 pounds Manila clams, cleaned (see page 7)

½ cup white wine

½ teaspoon fennel seeds

15 green olives, pitted and quartered

½ fennel bulb, trimmed, cored, and finely chopped

3 inner celery ribs with leaves, finely chopped

4 garlic cloves, peeled and minced

20 fresh mint leaves, finely chopped

Handful of chopped fresh Italian parsley

¼ cup red wine vinegar

½ cup extra-virgin olive oil

Salt and freshly ground black pepper to taste

Salad greens for serving

Lemon wedges

4 to 6 pieces Bruschetta (page 68)

In a large sauté pan, combine the clams and white wine. Cover and steam over medium heat until the clams open. Remove the clam meat from the shells and place in a large bowl. Strain the cooking liquid through a sieve lined with cheesecloth, and reserve ¼ cup.

Add the fennel seeds, olives, chopped fennel, celery, garlic, mint, parsley, vinegar, olive oil, and reserved clam juice to the clams. Season to taste with salt and pepper. Place in the refrigerator to marinate for at least 2 hours.

To serve, mound the salad on a serving dish or on individual plates lined with greens. Garnish with lemon wedges and serve with the bruschetta to soak up the juices.

GRILLED FISH SALAD ON BRUSCHETTA

BRUSCHETTA CON INSALATA DI PESCE

Serves 4 to 6

TILAPIA   HALIBUT   SEA BASS

 A celebration of summer ingredents, this salad is vivid with color contrasts.

Olive oil for grilling

1½ pounds firm-fleshed whitefish fillet

1 large red bell pepper, stem, seeds, and white ribs removed, cut into quarters

2 zucchini, cut lengthwise into ¼-inch-thick slices

1 small eggplant, cut lengthwise into ¼-inch thick slices

1 bunch fresh basil, leaves only, roughly chopped

Small handful of coarsely chopped fresh Italian parsley

2 garlic cloves, peeled and minced, plus 1 whole peeled garlic clove

½ cup extra-virgin olive oil plus extra for drizzling

Juice of 1 lemon

Salt and freshly ground black pepper to taste

3 to 4 large ripe but firm tomatoes, cut in half

6 to 8 ½-inch-thick slices country bread

Handful of chopped fresh Italian parsley

Heat a charcoal or gas grill or ridged stovetop griddle until very hot. Use a towel dipped in oil to rub onto the grids. Lightly brush the fish fillet, bell pepper, zucchini, and eggplant with oil. Begin by grilling the fish fillet just until cooked through. (The flaky structure of the fillet will become apparent.) Remove the fish from the grill with a spatula and set aside to cool. Then grill the red pepper, zucchini, and eggplant until grill marks are clearly visible and the vegetables soften. Remove the vegetables from the grill with a spatula or tongs, and set aside to cool.

When the fish is cool enough to handle, pull it apart into small pieces, and remove any bones. Cut the pepper into thin strips. In a medium bowl, combine the fish, pepper strips, basil, parsley, minced garlic, extra-virgin oil, lemon juice, and salt and pepper to taste. Cover the bowl with a kitchen towel and set aside to marinate at room temperature. Cut the zucchini and eggplant into thin crosswise strips. Toss together in a small bowl and set aside.

Just before you are ready to serve, grill the tomatoes: Heat the grill until very hot, and brush the tomatoes lightly with oil. Start them cut side down on the grill. When grill marks appear, flip them over to the other side. When soft, transfer with a spatula to a plate. To make the bruschetta, grill the bread slices on both sides. As you remove the bread from the grill, rub one side of each slice with the whole garlic clove and drizzle with a bit of oil. Flatten a tomato half onto each slice of bread, rubbing it into the bread. Place the bruschetta on a large platter. Top each piece with some zucchini and eggplant strips and spoon on the fish salad. Garnish wish chopped parsley. Serve with lots of napkins.

SALMON SANDWICHES
PANINI DI SALMONE

Makes 4 sandwiches

TUNA OR SEA BASS

A delicious use for leftover grilled fish. If the mayonnaise is a bit rich for you, try tossing the salmon with a bit of oil and lemon juice for a lean treat.

1 pound salmon fillet, cut into 3 or 4 pieces

Salt and freshly ground black pepper to taste

1 cup Garlic-Herb Mayonnaise, plus extra for assembling the sandwiches (page 305)

1 celery stalk, finely diced

3 green onions, thinly sliced

6 sun-dried tomatoes, diced

Handful of chopped fresh Italian parsley

Juice of 1 lemon

8 slices good-quality bread, toasted

2 tomatoes, sliced

4 leaves Bibb lettuce

Season the salmon with salt and pepper and cook it on a hot grill or under a broiler until done. Let cool. Flake the salmon into a bowl. Add the 1 cup Garlic-Herb Mayonnaise, the celery, green onions, sun-dried tomatoes, parsley, lemon juice, and salt and pepper to taste. Mix well and adjust the seasoning if necessary.

To assemble the sandwiches, spread the toasted bread with additional mayonnaise. Spread the salmon salad onto 4 slices of the bread. Top with the sliced tomatoes and lettuce and the remaining bread.

ANCHOVY MELT
CROSTINO DI ACCIUGHE
Makes 1 sandwich

Across between bruschetta and an open-faced sandwich. In certain regions of Italy, this broiled open-faced sandwich is called a *crostino*. The bubbling creaminess of the mozzarella makes it a good foil for the salty anchovy. This combination also makes an ideal appetizer with cocktails served on small slices of toasted baguette.

1 medium red bell pepper
1 slice country bread, cut in half
1 garlic clove, peeled
Extra-virgin olive oil for drizzling
3 fresh basil leaves, chopped
Coarsely ground black pepper to taste
2 slices mozzarella cheese
4 anchovy fillets

Roast the pepper over a gas flame or under a broiler, turning occasionally, until lightly charred. Put in a bag, seal the bag, and set aside to steam for 20 minutes. Remove and discard the core and seeds. Cut the pepper into 4 strips.

Preheat the broiler. Lightly toast the pieces of bread under the broiler (or on a grill). Rub with the garlic clove and drizzle lightly with olive oil. Top each piece with 2 strips of roasted red pepper. Sprinkle with the basil and black pepper, place the cheese on the peppers, and crisscross the anchovies on top. Broil until the cheese is melted.

Seafood Club Sandwich

PANINO "CLUB"

Makes 2 sandwiches

For an especially elegant sandwich, use cooked lobster tail in place of the shrimp.

8 medium shrimp, peeled and deveined (see page 9)
1 garlic clove, peeled and minced
1½ to 3 tablespoons olive oil, plus extra for drizzling
Salt and freshly ground black pepper to taste
2 slices pancetta or bacon
4 slices country bread
2 tomatoes, sliced
1 small avocado, peeled and sliced
6 fresh basil leaves
1 bunch watercress, washed and trimmed

Sauté the shrimp and garlic in 1½ tablespoons olive oil until the shrimp are completely pink. Season with salt and pepper to taste, and set aside to cool. Cook the pancetta in 1½ tablespoons olive oil until done, but still slightly soft; if using bacon, do not add oil to the pan. Set aside to cool, then cut each slice in half. Slice the shrimp in half lengthwise.

To assemble, grill or toast the bread. Drizzle with olive oil. Layer the shrimp, pancetta, tomato, avocado, basil, and watercress on 2 slices of the bread, and top with the remaining bread.

GRILLED TUNA AND TAPENADE SANDWICH

PANINO AL TONNO FRESCO

Serves 1

Sicilian ingredients of tuna and olives combine in a panino that is definitely a cut above the ubiquitous tuna fish sandwich. The peppery arugula adds its bite to the mellow tuna.

1 thin slice tuna fillet (about 5 ounces)
Salt and freshly ground black pepper to taste
2 slices country bread
Extra-virgin olive oil
Handful of arugula or watercress leaves
¼ cup Pesto di Olive (page 298)

Season the tuna with salt and pepper and cook it on a hot grill or under a hot broiler until done. Grill or toast the bread lightly. Drizzle 1 slice of bread with olive oil, and top with the arugula and then the grilled tuna. Spread the other slice of bread with the pesto, and place it on top of the first slice. Cut in half.

PAN-FRIED FISH SANDWICH

PANINO DI PESCE FRITTO

Serves 1

SOLE   SNAPPER   TROUT

A sandwich to make when you feel like splurging with the satisfying crunchy tenderness of sautéed fish. In this case the fillet is dredged first in polenta, which adds its warm corn flavor and rough texture to the sandwich.

⅓ cup cornmeal
Handful of finely chopped fresh Italian parsley
1 cod fillet (about 5 ounces)
Salt and freshly ground black pepper to taste
2 tablespoons extra-virgin olive oil
Tomato-Herb Mayonnaise (page 304)
2 slices country or egg bread, lightly toasted
1 bunch watercress, washed and trimmed
1 ripe tomato, sliced
1 tablespoon fresh lemon juice

Mix the cornmeal and chopped parsley in a bowl. Season the cod fillet with salt and pepper, then dredge in the cornmeal mixture. Heat the olive oil in a sauté pan and sauté the fish over medium-high heat until golden brown on both sides and cooked through. Remove from the pan.

Generously spread the Tomato-Herb Mayonnaise on both slices of bread. Place a bit of watercress and tomato on top of 1 slice. Top with the fish and drizzle with the lemon juice. Place the other slice of bread on top and serve.

Soups and Braises

The old saying *Vive nel'acqua, affogato in salsa*—"lives in water, drowns in sauce"—beautifully describes this most familiar part of the Italian seafood repertoire. Many of us are introduced to this repertoire through cioppino, probably the most popular fish soup in America after the Provençal bouillabaisse. This comforting tomato-based soup may have its modern pedigree in San Francisco, but its roots are deeply embedded in Liguria, the Italian Riviera, where it is known as *ciuppin*. Its rich tomato broth, with deep winy overtones and plenty of herbs, is characteristic of most Italian fish soups and braises. The freshest fish available is teamed with water and wine, garlic, herbs, perhaps tomatoes, and other aromatic vegetables. From this inexpensive, catholic mélange comes a large repertory of variations on a theme. Braises naturally evolved from soups as the Italian population became more comfortable, allowing the luxury of a substantial portion of fillet for each person.

One tip to remember is that it is not necessary to make broth before assembling a soup. In traditional Italian recipes, water and wine bathe the fish as it cooks, and broth results naturally. However, I often use broth instead of water to intensify the flavor of the soup. If you keep some on hand in the freezer, it gives you the freedom to achieve maximum flavor quickly using boneless fillets and other quick cooking fish and shellfish instead of whole fish. Nearly all of the soup recipes in this chapter are prepared in this way, so that you can get the most flavor in the least amount of time. But remember that the Italian way with fish soups is often light and natural. The broths and resulting soup should taste clean—simple, with the flavors of each separate ingredient still apparent. Don't aim for heavy reductions or too strong a fish flavor in the final dishes.

The word *zuppa,* soup, is the stem of the Italian verb *inzuppare,* literally "to soak in soup," or, more loosely, "to dip one's bread into soup." The perfect finish to nearly any fish soup is a piece of toasted country bread rubbed with a garlic clove. The croûton adds texture and substance as it begins to melt into the broth as well as the welcome bite of garlic.

WHITE FISH BROTH

BRODO DI PESCE

Makes approximately 3 quarts

This is the ideal white fish broth, enriched with the flavors of fennel and leek with added depth from the initial sautéing of the vegetables. Good fish to use are halibut, whitefish, sea bass, and other mild-flavored lean fishes; include the head and tail to add body in the form of natural gelatin to the broth if you wish. This is the broth to choose when you want to make a real project of it and plan to freeze some for future use.

½ cup extra-virgin olive oil
1 onion, peeled and roughly chopped
1 fennel bulb with feathery top, chopped
1 celery stalk with leaves, chopped
1 large leek, washed and chopped
1 tomato, diced
2 garlic cloves, peeled
2 bay leaves
Handful of roughly chopped fresh Italian parsley, including stems
10 black peppercorns
5 pounds fish bones (from white-fleshed nonoily fish)
½ cup dry white wine
Juice of 1 lemon
3 quarts water
Salt to taste

Heat the olive oil in a large heavy stockpot. Add the vegetables, herbs, and peppercorns and sauté over moderate heat for approximately 5 minutes, or just until the vegetables begin to wilt. Add the fish bones and cook for about 8 minutes, or until any flesh remaining on the bones turns white. Make sure all the bones are cooked. Add the white wine to deglaze the pan, and cook over high heat until the alcohol evaporates. Add the lemon juice and water, bring to a simmer, and cook gently for 20 minutes. Add salt to taste, and strain the broth. If the broth is not for immediate use, let cool completely before refrigerating or freezing.

SPICY TOMATO BROTH
BRODO AL CIUPPIN

Makes about 3 quarts

This fish broth is full-bodied and spicy, with a strong tomato flavor. Because all the ingredients are put into the pot to simmer at once it is easy and quick to make. The broth is usable in as little as thirty minutes, but if you have the luxury of a little extra time, let it simmer for the full 1½ to 2 hours. The result will be heady with flavor. As with all the broth recipes in this book, straining will give you a thin, fairly clear broth. If you like the heartiness of a thicker base, simply lift out the fish bones and put the broth, with all the aromatic vegetables and fish bits that have fallen off the bones, through a food mill.

1 carrot, peeled and finely chopped

1 large onion, peeled and finely chopped

2 celery stalks, finely chopped

3 pounds fish bones (from white-fleshed nonoily fish)

2 bay leaves

2 teaspoons red chile pepper flakes

1 28-ounce can tomato purée

½ bunch fresh Italian parsley

1 tablespoon black peppercorns

2 cups white wine

3 cloves garlic, peeled

Water

Salt to taste

In a heavy large stockpot, combine all the ingredients except water and salt. Add water to cover, bring to a boil, and simmer over low heat for approximately 1½ to 2 hours. Add salt to taste, remove from the heat, and let sit for 10 minutes. Strain through a sieve, or remove the bones and put through the medium or coarse disk of a food mill.

RICH FISH BROTH

ZUPPA DI PESCE

Serves 6 to 8

FOR TRADITIONAL METHOD:

WHOLE SHEEPSHEAD   TILEFISH   ROCKFISH   PERCH

FOR MODERN METHOD:

FILLETS OF HALIBUT   SEA BASS   SWORDFISH

I give two methods for preparing this broth, traditional and modern. The traditional version results in more than a broth—a delicious *zuppa di pesce,* or fish soup. It can stand on its own, without the addition of any more fish or shellfish, and is especially savory if it is served over crostini. When made according to the quick modern method, it results in a thick broth that is an ideal base for the addition of any shellfish you wish. Add pasta and it is a great first course. This broth is even better when made ahead, chilled overnight, and reheated.

¼ cup extra-virgin olive oil

1 large onion, peeled and chopped

2 cups chopped celery stalks and leaves

4 to 6 garlic cloves, chopped

Large handful of chopped fresh Italian parsley

2 to 3 large sprigs fresh rosemary, leaves only, chopped fine

3 pounds whole white fish (for traditional method), cut crosswise into manageable pieces, or 1 pound fillets of white-fleshed nonoily fish (for modern method)

8 cups fish stock, water, or a combination

2 cups white wine

Salt and cayenne or freshly ground black pepper to taste

Traditional Method for Broth:

Heat the olive oil in a large soup pot over medium heat. Sauté the onion and celery until soft. Add the garlic and sauté until its characteristic aroma is released.

continued

Add the parsley, rosemary, and cut-up whole fish. Cover with the liquid and bring to a boil. Reduce the heat and simmer for 30 minutes. Add salt and cayenne or black pepper to taste. Remove the fish bones and put the soup through the medium disk of a food mill.

Quick Modern Method for Broth:

Heat the olive oil in a large soup pot over medium heat. Sauté the onion and celery until soft. Add the garlic and sauté until its characteristic aroma is released. Add the parsley and rosemary and the liquid, and bring to a boil. Reduce the heat and simmer until the broth is slightly reduced, about 10 minutes. Add salt and pepper to taste. Add the fish fillets and poach in the simmering liquid until done, about 6 to 8 minutes. Put the soup through the medium or coarse disk of a food mill.

LIGURIAN CABBAGE SOUP
ZUPPA DI CAVOLO

Serves 4 to 6

This is more a stew than a soup, as it is thick with cabbage and has very little broth. It's unusual in that the flavor of fish comes solely from the broth. Best of all, it's simple yet very satisfying. Like all zuppe it gets its name because it is served over toasted bread.

1 medium red onion, peeled and finely chopped

4 celery stalks with leaves, finely chopped

¼ cup extra-virgin olive oil

4 garlic cloves, peeled and finely chopped, plus 1 to 2 whole peeled garlic cloves

1 small head Savoy cabbage, shredded

6 to 8 cups White Fish Broth (page 79) or Spicy Tomato Broth (page 80)

Salt and freshly ground black pepper to taste

Generous handful of chopped fresh Italian parsley

4 to 6 slices toasted or grilled country bread

In a large soup pot over very low heat, sauté the onion and celery in the olive oil until they are very soft and sweet and just beginning to color. Add the chopped garlic, and sauté for 1 minute. Add the cabbage and cook slowly over low heat for about 20 minutes, or until the cabbage is completely wilted. Add just enough fish broth to cover the cabbage. Bring to a boil, then reduce to a simmer and cook for about 45 minutes. Near the end of the cooking process, add salt and pepper to taste.

Add the chopped parsley to the broth. Rub the grilled or toasted bread with the whole garlic cloves and place in individual bowls. Ladle the soup over the bread, and serve.

Fish Soup Livornese Style

CACCIUCCO ALLA LIVORNESE

Serves 4

MONKFISH   SEA BASS   HALIBUT   SNAPPER

According to tradition, this most famous Tuscan fish soup is made with five kinds of fish and/or seafood, equal in number to the number of c's in its name. The characteristic supporting ingredients of a true *cacciucco* are onions, hot pepper, garlic, and red wine. Use Spicy Tomato Broth that has been passed through a food mill rather than a strainer and is thick with fish bits and aromatic vegetables.

¼ cup extra-virgin olive oil

2 onions, peeled and chopped

6 garlic cloves, peeled and sliced, plus 1 to 2 whole peeled garlic cloves

3 tomatoes, cut into medium dice

1 bunch fresh basil, leaves only, roughly chopped

½ teaspoon red chile pepper flakes

6 cups Spicy Tomato Broth (page 80)

½ cup red wine

1 pound fish fillets, cut crosswise into 1-inch slices

¼ pound bay or sea scallops, tough side muscles removed if necessary

¼ pound medium shrimp, deveined but shells left on (see page 9)

¼ pound cleaned squid, tentacles trimmed and body sacs cut into ½-inch rings (see page 10)

Salt and freshly ground black pepper to taste

12 soft-shell clams, such as Manila, cleaned (see page 7)

16 black mussels, cleaned (see page 8)

Handful of chopped fresh Italian parsley

½ lemon

Toasted or grilled country bread

In a large soup pot, heat the olive oil over medium heat. Add the onions and cook until soft. Add the sliced garlic and cook until it releases its characteristic aroma. Add the tomatoes, basil, and red chile pepper flakes and cook for about 1 minute. Add the broth and wine and bring to a simmer. Add the fish, scallops, shrimp, squid, and salt and pepper to taste. Cover and simmer for about 2 minutes. Add the clams and mussels, cover, and cook over moderately high heat until the shellfish have opened. Add the chopped parsley and a squeeze of lemon juice. Rub the toasted or grilled bread with the whole garlic cloves and place in individual bowls. Ladle the soup over the bread, and serve.

SICILIAN FISH SOUP WITH FENNEL AND POTATOES

ZUPPA DI PESCE ALLA TRAMEZZINA

Serves 4 to 6

TUNA   SWORDFISH   SHARK   MAHIMAHI

In this unusual dish from Sicily, sautéed fish is added to a finished broth. An intriguing and beautiful combination, especially with the inclusion of scarlet saffron threads and feathery fennel tops. For a more elegant, if nontraditional, presentation, sauté the fish until completely cooked, then serve in wide shallow bowls with the "stew" spooned over it.

½ cup extra-virgin olive oil

2 medium onions, peeled and chopped

2 small fennel bulbs, trimmed (reserve tops), cored, and thinly sliced

4 to 5 celery stalks, chopped

4 leeks, white part only, washed and sliced crosswise

3 large potatoes, peeled and diced

6 to 8 garlic cloves, peeled and chopped

Generous handful of chopped fresh Italian parsley

1 bunch fresh basil, leaves only, chopped

12 fresh sage leaves

½ cup white wine

8 cups Spicy Tomato Broth (page 80)

3 bay leaves

Salt to taste

1½ pounds firm boneless fish steaks or fillets, cut into portions

About 2 cups milk

Flour for dredging

½ teaspoon saffron threads, dissolved in 1 cup hot water

Large pinch of red chile pepper flakes

½ cup chopped reserved fennel tops (see above)

Heat ¼ cup of the olive oil in a large soup pot over medium heat. Cook the onions, sliced fennel, and celery until crisp-tender, about 10 minutes. Add the leeks, potatoes, garlic, parsley, basil, and sage leaves, and cook for 5 minutes. Add the white wine, broth, bay leaves, and salt to taste. Bring to a boil, then reduce the heat and simmer until the potatoes are just tender, 10 to 15 minutes.

Meanwhile, dip the fish fillets in milk, then in flour. Heat the remaining ¼ cup olive oil in a nonstick skillet over medium heat. Add the fish and sauté until golden on both sides, but not completely cooked.

Carefully transfer the fish to the soup. Simmer for 3 to 4 minutes longer, until the fish just begins to flake. Add the saffron and its soaking water, the chile pepper flakes, and the chopped fennel tops, and simmer for about 1 minute. Serve immediately.

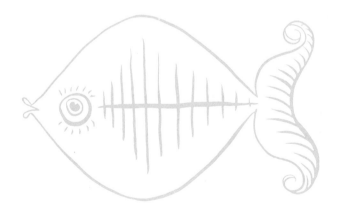

LIGURIAN STEW WITH PINE NUTS AND MUSHROOMS
BURIDDA
Serves 4 to 6

SNAPPER   HALIBUT   SEA BASS   MONKFISH

This regional soup showcases the unexpected combination of fish, nuts, and porcini mushrooms—the best from the juxtaposition of *bosco mare,* ''woods and sea.'' To further enrich the soup, add shiitake or portobello mushrooms for their earthy flavor. This dish is especially delicious made only with monkfish rather than a combination of fish. Its unique lobsterlike taste and texture stand up to the strong flavors of mushrooms and nuts.

2 ounces dried porcini mushrooms

6 anchovy fillets

¼ cup pine nuts or walnuts

¼ cup white wine

2 medium onions, peeled and chopped

3 celery stalks with leaves, finely chopped

½ cup extra-virgin olive oil

4 to 6 garlic cloves, peeled and chopped, plus 1 to 2 whole peeled garlic cloves

¼ pound shiitake or portobello mushrooms, cleaned, trimmed, and sliced

1 ripe tomato, roughly chopped

6 cups White Fish Broth (page 79) or water

2 pounds fish fillets, cut into small pieces

Generous handful of chopped fresh Italian parsley

Toasted or grilled country bread

Soak the porcini mushrooms in hot water to cover for at least 20 minutes. Drain well. In a food processor or blender, purée the softened porcini, anchovies, and pine nuts or walnuts with the wine.

In a large saucepan or stockpot, sauté the onions and celery in the olive oil until soft. Add the garlic and shiitake or portobello mushrooms and sauté until the mushrooms are a bit limp and the garlic is golden. Add the tomato and cook over medium heat until the liquid is released, 5 to 10 minutes. Add the porcini-nut purée and cook until the liquid evaporates. Add the broth or water and bring to a boil. Reduce the heat to a simmer, add the fish, and poach until done, about 6 to 8 minutes. Add the chopped parsley. Rub the toasted or grilled country bread with the whole garlic cloves, and place in individual bowls. Ladle the soup over, and serve.

Mussels with Shallots, Garlic, and Parsley
COZZE ALLE SCALOGNE
Serves 4

Shallots are not associated with the Italian kitchen as often as they are with French cuisine. However, their subtle sweet bite is often used in Ligurian cooking, as in this savory dish of mussels.

¼ cup extra-virgin olive oil
6 shallots, peeled and minced
3 garlic cloves, peeled and minced
48 mussels, cleaned (see page 8)
2 cups white wine or 1 cup wine and 1 cup water
Generous handful of chopped fresh Italian parsley
½ tablespoon grated lemon zest
Salt and freshly ground black pepper to taste
Generous handful of Garlicky Bread Crumbs (page 12)

Heat the olive oil in a sauté pan over medium heat. Add the shallots and garlic, and sauté until golden. Add the mussels and wine, or wine and water, cover, and cook until the mussels open. Add the parsley, lemon zest, and salt and pepper to taste. Transfer the mussels and their juices to a serving platter or individual plates and sprinkle with the bread crumbs.

Steamed Mussels with Saffron

COZZE ALLO ZAFFERANO

Serves 4

Along Italy's coast and throughout its islands that were conquered by Arabs, saffron is a traditional addition to many dishes, especially fish soups. The brilliant gold-orange threads suffusing a rich broth or staining the white flesh of a fish fillet enhance the pleasure of these dishes.

¼ cup extra-virgin olive oil
½ small onion, peeled and minced
1 fennel bulb, trimmed, cored, and minced
1 carrot, peeled and minced
2 celery stalks, minced
48 black mussels, cleaned (see page 8)
¼ cup White Fish Broth (page 79) or water
¼ cup white wine
Generous pinch of saffron, soaked in ½ cup warm water
Salt and freshly ground pepper to taste
Crusty bread

Heat the olive oil in a skillet large enough to accommodate the mussels in one or two layers. Add the onion, fennel, carrot, and celery and cook over low heat until soft. Add the mussels, fish broth or water, wine, saffron with its soaking liquid, and salt and pepper to taste. Cover and steam over medium heat until the mussels open, approximately 8 minutes. If any mussels do not open, discard them. Serve in wide shallow bowls with plenty of crusty bread.

STEAMED CLAMS WITH FENNEL AND ROSEMARY
VONGOLE IN PORCHETTA
Serves 4

When Italian dishes are named *in porchetta,* the reference is usually to the seasonings used for the traditional *porchetta,* or whole roast pig. In Tuscany and Lazio the pigs are rubbed and stuffed with garlic and either fennel or rosemary. They are usually served at large outdoor festivals and the aroma travels for miles. This traditional seafood rendition of the classic flavors is made a bit more modern by the addition of sautéed fennel.

¼ cup extra-virgin olive oil

2 garlic cloves, peeled and minced

2 medium fennel bulbs, trimmed, cored, and thinly sliced, tops reserved and chopped

48 soft-shell clams, such as Manila, cleaned (see page 7)

1 sprig fresh rosemary, leaves only, finely minced

1 teaspoon fennel seeds, lightly crushed with a rolling pin

¼ cup white wine

Crusty bread

Heat the olive oil in a large sauté pan over medium heat. Add the garlic and cook until it releases its characteristic aroma. Add the sliced fennel and sauté until it begins to wilt. Add the clams, rosemary, fennel seeds, and white wine, cover, and cook until the clams open, approximately 5 to 7 minutes. Garnish with a small handful of the reserved chopped fennel tops, and serve in wide shallow bowls with crusty bread.

STEAMED CLAMS IN WHITE WINE
VONGOLE IN BIANCO
Serves 4

The Italian seafood dish. Made with either clams or mussels, this simple dish is lavish with the flavors of olive oil, garlic, wine, and parsley, the classic underpinnings of nearly all Italian food. Four hungry people could conceivably eat double this amount, the clams are so addictive. Accompany this with lots of bread to dip into the broth and scoop up every bit of garlic, a light white wine, and finish with insalata verde dressed only with coarse salt and the best olive oil you have. (All it takes to change this dish from *in bianco* to *al pomodoro* is a couple of tablespoons of tomato sauce or a bit of tomato paste diluted with water.)

¼ cup extra-virgin olive oil

6 to 8 garlic cloves, peeled and sliced

48 soft-shell clams, such as Manila, cleaned (see page 7) or
   48 black mussels, cleaned (see page 8)

½ to 1 teaspoon red chile pepper flakes (to taste)

1 cup white wine

Squeeze of lemon juice

2 handfuls of chopped fresh Italian parsley

Lemon wedges (optional)

Heat the olive oil in a large sauté pan over medium heat. Add the garlic and cook over low heat until it releases its characteristic aroma. Add the clams, red chile pepper flakes, white wine, lemon juice, and half the parsley. Cover and steam until the clams open, approximately 5 to 7 minutes. Transfer to individual serving bowls, and garnish with the remaining chopped parsley. Serve with lemon wedges if desired.

Moroccan Clams via Sicily

VONGOLE CON CHARMOULA

Serves 4

After experimenting for a week or so with Sicilian couscous recipes, I finally combined my memories with advice (via their excellent cookbooks) from Joyce Goldstein and Paula Wolfert and came up with this dish. One fundamental ingredient is the *charmoula*, or Moroccan spice mixture, which continues to sneak its way into various other dishes at the restaurants. If you are concerned some of your guests may be timid about highly spiced food, serve the charmoula on the side.

¼ teaspoon cayenne pepper

½ teaspoon ground cumin

1 teaspoon paprika

6 to 8 garlic cloves, peeled and minced

½ small bunch fresh cilantro, leaves only, chopped

2 tablespoons chopped fresh Italian parsley

Juice of ½ lemon

¼ cup extra-virgin olive oil

48 soft-shell clams, such as Manila, cleaned (see page 7)

½ cup white wine

To prepare the charmoula, mix together in a small bowl the cayenne, cumin, paprika, about two thirds of the garlic, the cilantro, parsley, lemon juice, and 3 tablespoons of the olive oil.

Heat the remaining 1 tablespoon olive oil in a large sauté pan and sauté the remaining garlic over medium heat until it releases its characteristic aroma. Add the clams and white wine. Cover and cook until the clams open, approximately 4 minutes. Remove from the heat and drizzle the charmoula over all. Serve immediately.

CLAMS AND MUSSELS IN TOMATO BROTH
VONGOLE E COZZE AL POMODORO
Serves 4 to 6

f you prefer a more rustic look, don't bother to put the tomato
broth through the food mill. I, for one, enjoy the look of flecks of
tomato skin in the broth, and they do add a bit more fullness to the final flavor of the dish.

For the tomato broth
¼ cup extra-virgin olive oil
4 large garlic cloves, peeled and chopped
4 to 5 large ripe tomatoes, diced
Small handful of chopped fresh basil
Small handful of chopped fresh Italian parsley
½ cup white wine
4 cups White Fish Broth (page 79) or water
Salt and freshly ground black pepper to taste

¼ cup extra-virgin olive oil
2 large red onions, peeled and chopped
4 to 5 tender celery stalks with leaves, chopped
2 garlic cloves, peeled and chopped
3 pounds clams, cleaned and soaked (see page 7)
2 pounds black mussels, cleaned (see page 8)
3 sprigs fresh oregano, leaves only, or 1 teaspoon dried oregano

To make the broth:
Heat the olive oil in a large saucepot over medium heat. Add the garlic and sauté
until its characteristic aroma is released. Add the tomatoes, basil, and parsley and
cook over high heat until the tomatoes release their liquid. Add the wine and
cook about 1 minute. Add the fish broth or water, and bring to a boil. Reduce
the heat until the broth is at a vigorous simmer and cook, stirring occasionally,

for about 30 minutes. Season with salt and pepper. Let cool slightly, then pass through a food mill, or process in a food processor until smooth.

Meanwhile, heat the olive oil in a large saucepot over medium heat. Sauté the onions and celery until soft. Add the garlic and sauté until its characteristic aroma is released. Add the tomato broth and bring to a boil. Add the clams, mussels, and oregano. Reduce the heat to a simmer, cover, and cook until all the clams and mussels have opened. Remove the shellfish to serving bowls and pour the hot broth over them.

Braised Baccalà with Onions, Tomatoes, Raisins, and Pine Nuts

Baccalà alla Silvana

Serves 4 to 6

HALIBUT   TILEFISH   MONKFISH

As soon as the combined aroma of raisins, onions, and tomatoes rises up out of the pot I am back in the narrow winding streets of the Jewish section of Rome. There, this dish taught me to enjoy the salty intensity of baccalà. The slightly sweet and sour flavor reminds me of traditional Ashkenazi dishes my mother serves.

½ cup extra-virgin olive oil

2 pounds prepared baccalà (see page 6), cut into portions

Flour for dredging

2 large onions, peeled and chopped

8 garlic cloves, peeled and chopped

8 sprigs fresh thyme

3 large ripe tomatoes, peeled, seeded, and chopped, or 1 28-ounce can Italian-style tomatoes

½ cup dark raisins, soaked in hot water until plumped, and drained

¾ cup toasted pine nuts

2 dashes of balsamic vinegar

Salt and freshly ground black pepper to taste

2 handfuls of chopped fresh Italian parsley

In a large skillet, heat ¼ cup of the olive oil. Dredge the fish in flour, shake off the excess, and place the fish fillets in the skillet. Cook over moderate heat, turning once, until the fillets have a lightly golden crust. Transfer to a plate and set aside.

Heat the remaining ¼ cup oil in the same skillet, and sauté the onions until they are soft. Add the garlic and sauté briefly over low heat just until it gives off its characteristic aroma. Add the thyme sprigs, tomatoes, and raisins; if using canned tomatoes, crush them with your fingers as you add them to the pan. Cook until the tomatoes release their liquid, about 10 minutes. Add the pine nuts, balsamic vinegar, and salt and pepper, and reduce the heat to medium low. Gently place the fish fillets in the pan, adding any accumulated juices from the fish. Spoon some of the sauce over the fish and sprinkle with half of the chopped parsley. Cover and cook at a gentle simmer until the fish begins to flake, about 6 to 8 minutes. Transfer the fish to a platter. Add the remaining parsley to the sauce and reduce the sauce over high heat for about 2 minutes. Spoon the sauce over the fish and serve.

Tuna Braised with Tomato Sauce, Peas, and Pancetta

TONNO AI PISELLI

Serves 4 to 6

SWORDFISH   CORVINA   BONITO

The pairing of fresh peas with fish or seafood is a long-standing Italian culinary tradition that takes advantage of the sweet intensity of the legume. The Italian way is to braise the peas thoroughly until they are very tender. Here their flavor merges with that of the tuna for a truly unique taste.

¼ cup extra-virgin olive oil

1 large red onion, peeled and chopped

6 to 8 garlic cloves, peeled and chopped

¼ pound pancetta, diced

A large pinch of red chile pepper flakes

¼ cup dry vermouth or white wine

8 Roma tomatoes, chopped, or 1 28-ounce can Italian style-tomatoes in juice

12 fresh sage leaves, julienned, or ¾ tablespoon dried whole sage

2 cups fresh of frozen peas

Salt to taste

4 to 6 tuna fillets (approximately 6 ounces each)

Handful of chopped fresh Italian parsley

In a large skillet, heat the olive oil over medium heat. Sauté the onion until soft, about 10 minutes. Add the garlic and sauté over low heat just until it gives off its characteristic aroma. Add the pancetta and cook until it renders its fat and begins to brown. Add the chile pepper flakes and dry vermouth, increase the heat to high, and deglaze the pan, stirring up all the browned bits that are stuck to the bottom. Add the tomatoes, sage, and peas: If using fresh tomatoes, cover and cook over high heat for 5 minutes, then uncover and cook over moderately low heat until the peas are very soft and the tomatoes have formed a sauce, about 15 minutes. If using canned tomatoes, crush them with your fingers as you put them into the pan, and cook, uncovered, over moderately low heat for 15 to 20 minutes. If the sauce needs more liquid, add a bit of water (or fish broth if you have it on hand). Add salt to taste.

Gently set the tuna steaks into the sauce and spoon some sauce over them. Reduce the heat to a slow simmer and cook, occasionally agitating the pan to bathe the fish in the braising juices, until the fish is cooked, about 10 minutes. Using a wide spatula, carefully transfer the fish to a platter. Add the parsley to the sauce and heat through. Spoon over the fish and serve.

TUNA WITH TOMATO, MINT, AND CAPERS

TONNO ALLA MATALOTTA

Serves 4 to 6

SWORDFISH   SHARK   STURGEON

This recipe, with slight variations, is prepared all over the Mediterranean. Tomatoes, capers, and olives combine with mint to produce a robust, extremely fragrant, sauce. It calls for a fish that can stand up to it, one with an assertive flavor all its own. Tuna meets all the necessary requirements.

¼ cup extra-virgin olive oil
2 medium onions, peeled and chopped
4 to 6 large garlic cloves, peeled and chopped
15 fresh mint leaves, chopped
3 sprigs fresh oregano, leaves only, or ½ teaspoon dried oregano
4 large round or 8 Roma tomatoes, peeled, seeded, and chopped
1½ cups green olives, pitted and cut lengthwise into quarters
¼ cup capers
1 tablespoon sugar (optional)
4 to 6 tuna steaks (about 6 ounces each)
½ cup white wine (optional)
Sprigs of fresh mint and oregano

In a large deep skillet, heat the olive oil over medium heat. Sauté the onions until soft. Add the garlic, chopped mint, and oregano and sauté briefly until fragrant. Add the tomatoes and cook until their liquid is released, about 10 minutes. Add the olives and capers. For a hint of a sweet-and-sour taste, stir in the sugar. Carefully place the fish steaks in the sauce, and spoon some of the sauce over the tops. If you wish, moisten the braise with the wine. Reduce the heat to a slow simmer and cook, occasionally agitating the pan to bathe the fish in the braising juices, until the fish is cooked, about 10 minutes. To serve, use a wide spatula to transfer the fish to a large serving platter. Spoon the sauce over and garnish with sprigs of mint and oregano.

TUNA ROAST BRAISED WITH ANCHOVY AND AROMATIC VEGETABLES

TONNO AL BATTUTO

Serves 6 to 8

SWORDFISH   BONITO

A wonderful recipe that treats a large cut of tuna like a beef roast. The fish is "larded" with an herb-garlic paste and then braised with finely chopped aromatic vegetables to produce an intensely flavorful sauce. The simplest way to most impressive results, the larger cut of fish needs less tending than smaller fillets and steaks.

10 to 12 canned anchovy fillets, rinsed and roughly chopped

10 fresh mint or basil leaves, chopped fine, plus additional herb sprigs for garnish

8 garlic cloves, peeled and chopped

3 pounds tuna in one piece

Flour for dredging

¼ cup extra-virgin olive oil

1 large red onion, peeled and finely chopped

2 celery stalks, finely chopped

2 large carrots, peeled and finely chopped

1 cup white wine

2 to 3 cups White Fish Broth (page 79) or water or a combination

Salt and freshly ground pepper to taste

Handful of chopped fresh Italian parsley, plus additional sprigs for garnish

Lemon wedges

In a small bowl, mash together the anchovies, chopped mint or basil, and half the garlic to a paste. Use a sharp paring knife to make 1-inch-deep incisions all over the tuna. Stuff the anchovy-garlic paste into the slits; if you have any remaining paste, rub it all over the tuna. Dredge the tuna lightly in flour, and shake off any excess. Heat the oil in a Dutch oven or casserole over high heat and sear the tuna on all sides until it has a lightly golden crust. Remove from the casserole and set aside on a platter. Add the onion, celery, and carrots to the pot and sauté until soft. Add the remaining garlic and cook until it releases its characteristic aroma. Return the tuna to the casserole. Add the wine and enough fish broth or water to come 2 inches up the sides of the pan, and bring just to a simmer. Reduce the heat to low. Taste for salt and pepper, and add the chopped parsley. Cover and slowly braise the tuna, basting occasionally, until tender, about 20 to 25 minutes.

To serve, lift the tuna onto a serving platter. Purée the aromatic vegetables and the cooking juices in a food processor. If you like, simmer the puréed sauce until slightly reduced. Spoon the sauce around the tuna. Garnish with lemon wedges and herb sprigs, and slice like a roast.

TUNA IN THE STYLE OF THE PIZZA MAKER
TONNO ALLA PIZZAIOLA
Serves 4 to 6

The traditional pizza tastes of tomato and oregano are combined in a simple but rich sauce. Crushing the tomatoes with your fingers results in a coarser sauce, while the food mill makes a beautifully smooth purée.

¼ cup extra-virgin olive oil

2 garlic cloves, peeled and minced

1 teaspoon red chile pepper flakes

2 28-ounce cans Italian-style peeled tomatoes in juice

½ cup Barolo or other full-bodied red wine

2 teaspoons dried oregano

Salt and freshly ground black pepper to taste

4 to 6 tuna steaks (approximately 6 ounces each)

Grated zest of ½ lemon

Juice of ½ lemon

Lemon wedges

Heat the oil in a skillet large enough to accommodate the fish in one layer. Add the garlic and sauté over low heat just until it gives off its characteristic aroma. Add the red chile pepper flakes and tomatoes: Either crush the tomatoes with your fingers as you add them or put them through the coarse disk of a food mill directly into the pan. Then add the red wine and oregano and cook the tomato sauce over high heat, stirring frequently, for 5 minutes. Season with salt and pepper. Gently add the tuna steaks to the pan. Spoon some of the sauce over the fish, then sprinkle the lemon zest and juice over the fish. Reduce the heat to a very gentle simmer, cover the pan, and braise the tuna slowly, basting every few minutes to help keep it moist, for approximately 12 minutes, or until the fish is done. With a spatula, carefully lift the fish out of the sauce and transfer it to a serving platter. If the sauce seems too thin, cook it down over high heat for a few minutes. It should be thick enough to have some body, but still run out of the spoon. Spoon the sauce over the fish. Garnish with lemon wedges. Serve hot or at room temperature.

FISH SOUP WITH COUSCOUS, CHICKPEAS, AND RAISINS

CUSCUSÙ ALLA TRAPANESE

Serves 4 to 6

GROUPER   HAKE   TUNA   SWORDFISH   MONKFISH

Couscous, a grain that is traditionally associated with Morocco, has its own history in Sicily, especially in Trapani, where it is a legacy of the Arab conquest. This dish marries the favorite Italian technique of braising with Moroccan spices and couscous—a striking modern lesson on the intermingling of cultures. Harissa is the classic Moroccan hot sauce.

For the harissa

½ cup ground caraway seeds

1 tablespoon ground cayenne pepper

2 tablespoons ground coriander

2 tablespoons ground cumin

2 tablespoons ground fennel

Juice of ½ lemon

Extra-virgin olive oil

Salt and freshly ground black pepper to taste

1½ to 2 pounds fish fillets or boneless steaks, preferably 2 or 3 different varieties of fish

½ cup extra-virgin olive oil

1 large onion, peeled and chopped

2 bay leaves

3 garlic cloves, peeled and sliced

Handful of chopped fresh Italian parsley

3 Roma tomatoes, diced

2 to 3 cups White Fish Broth (page 79) or water or a combination

For the couscous

> 2 boxes (4 cups) instant couscous
>
> 1 15-ounce can chickpeas, drained
>
> 1 cup dark or golden raisins
>
> 1 cinnamon stick, smashed with hammer or mallet
>
> **White Fish Broth (page 79) (optional)**

Tomato wedges
Lemon wedges

To make the harissa, combine the spices and the lemon juice in a small bowl. Drizzle in olive oil, stirring until the mixture has a syrupy consistency. Add salt and pepper to taste. Use a pastry brush to slather the fish with a bit of the harissa. Place in a dish and marinate in the refrigerator for at least 2 hours.

In a deep medium skillet, heat the olive oil. Add the onion, bay leaves, garlic, and parsley, and cook over moderate heat until the onion is soft. Add the tomatoes and cook until they break down. Lay the fish fillets or steaks side by side in the pan. Add enough fish broth, water, or a combination to come 1 inch up the sides of the pan, cover, and braise the fish over low heat until done, about 7 to 10 minutes.

Meanwhile, prepare the couscous according to the package directions, adding the chickpeas, raisins, and smashed cinnamon stick.

To serve, mound the couscous in large shallow pasta bowls. Top with the fish and spoon a bit of the broth over. Garnish with tomato and lemon wedges. Pass the remaining harissa on the side.

Baccalà with Tomatoes and Olives

BACCALÀ AL SUD

Serves 4 to 6

HALIBUT   SEA BASS   GROUPER   COD

In nearly all these braising recipes, you can either briefly sauté the fish fillets first before braising as I've done here or simply start them in the sauce or braising liquid. The initial sauté enriches the final dish and helps delicate, flaky fish to hold its shape.

> **2 pounds prepared baccalà (see page 6), cut into portions**
> **Flour for dredging**
> **½ cup extra-virgin olive oil**
> **1 red onion, peeled and diced**
> **2 garlic cloves, peeled and minced**
> **1 bunch fresh oregano, leaves only**
> **2 pinches of dried oregano**
> **10 fresh basil leaves**
> **Generous handful of chopped fresh Italian parsley**
> **4 ripe tomatoes, chopped**
> **½ cup white wine**
> **1 to 2 cups White Fish Broth (page 79) or water**
> **1 cup pitted black or green olives, torn in half**

Lightly dredge the baccalà in flour, shaking off the excess. In a large deep pan, heat the oil and sauté the baccalà until golden. Remove from the pan and add the onion and garlic. Sauté over moderate heat until the onion is soft. Add the herbs and sauté briefly to bring out their flavor. Add the tomatoes, wine, and 1 cup of the fish broth or water and cook until the tomatoes begin to break down and form a sauce. Add the olives. Gently lay the sautéed fish in the sauce. Add additional broth or water if necessary so that the liquid comes halfway up the fish. Bring to a bare simmer, cover, and braise the fish for about 10 minutes or until done.

Pastas

In my previous books, *Cucina Fresca, Pasta Fresca,* and *Cucina Rustica,* space considerations were such that we could only include a few fish pastas. What a pleasure to be able to devote the proper attention to this most popular of all fish categories. From thin linguine bathed in a garlicky tomato-scented broth and topped with small sweet clams to a tangle of pasta, clams, mussels, shrimp, calamari, and scallops all in one dish, pasta cookery embraces the abundance of fish and seafood available in all parts of the seas that surround Italy and the lakes and rivers within her boundaries. There are few ingredients that can't find their way into a pasta recipe. Even as simple a combination as golden fettuccine with butter, garlic, and anchovies can become a satisfying meal. In these days of health concerns, fish is often the focal point of the meal, and fish pastas are probably the best way to introduce an avowed ''fish hater'' to the delicious riches of the lakes and seas. And since just a small amount of fish is needed for a recipe that incorporates pasta, the dishes are economical as well.

The first three pastas that follow are somewhat enriched versions of the popular *spaghetti alla checca,* that simplest of pastas with an uncooked sauce of chopped ripe tomato, fragrant basil, garlic, olive oil, and milky mozzarella. These recipes substitute seafood for the cheese and add appropriate flavors such as lemon to enhance the shellfish. The fourth is a savory combination of mussel meat out of the shell and creamy white beans.

FUSILLI WITH SCALLOPS

FUSILLI CON CAPE SANTE

Serves 4 to 6

I give instructions for blanching the scallops, but if you want to save time and trouble, go ahead and purchase already cooked seafood, substituting the same amount of cooked shrimp for the scallops. The idea is to get you in and out of the kitchen quickly, deliciously, and without trauma.

1 lemon, cut in half

3 bay leaves

8 ounces bay scallops or sea scallops, tough side muscles removed if necessary, sea scallops cut into quarters

5 large red-ripe tomatoes, cored and cut into small dice

1 to 2 garlic cloves, peeled and minced

6 leaves fresh basil, coarsely chopped

Small handful of coarsely chopped fresh Italian parsley

Grated zest of 1 lemon

Salt and freshly ground black pepper to taste

1 to 1½ cups extra-virgin olive oil

1 pound imported fusilli or cavatappi

½ cup Pesto di Olive (page 298) (optional)

Lemon wedges

Bring a large saucepan of water to a boil. Salt the water and add the lemon halves and bay leaves. When the water returns to the boil, add the scallops. Cook just until the scallops turn opaque and firm, 2 to 3 minutes. Immediately drain the scallops in a colander, then gently scoop them into a bowl of ice water. When the scallops are completely cold, drain them well, making sure no ice remains to dilute your sauce. In a medium bowl, combine the tomatoes, garlic, basil, parsley, lemon zest, and salt and pepper. Add enough of the extra-virgin olive oil to just cover the mixture. Add the cooled scallops and toss gently. Marinate in the refrigerator for at least 1 hour, preferably 2 or 3.

continued

Remove the tomato-scallop mixture from the refrigerator and place it in a serving bowl to come to room temperature while you cook the pasta. Cook the pasta in abundant boiling salted water until al dente. Drain and immediately add the hot pasta to the sauce in the serving bowl. Toss gently. If you wish, garnish the pasta with the pesto di olive. Serve with lemon wedges.

PASTA WITH TUNA FOR EATING ON THE TERRACE

PASTA AL TONNO PER LA TERRAZZA

Serves 4 to 6

SWORDFISH   BONITO

My best friend in Italy, Carol Fabi, and I concocted this dish while on vacation in Tuscany. We were staying in a house with an enormous deep terrace that completely encircled the house. One evening we dragged out some chairs and a small table for an impromptu meal al fresco. In this dish, the meaty flavor of tuna unites well with the sharp flavors of the green olives and green onions. If you wish, you may use about half a cup of Pesto di Olive Verde (page 299) as a garnish rather than adding whole olives to the pasta. This is the perfect way to turn leftover fish into another meal.

Olive oil for grilling

1 pound tuna steaks or 2 6½-ounce cans tuna in oil or water, drained

5 large red-ripe tomatoes, cored and cut into small dice

½ cup pitted green olives, cut in quarters lengthwise

1 to 2 garlic cloves, peeled and minced

2 sprigs fresh oregano, leaves only, or a healthy pinch of dried oregano

Small handful of coarsely chopped fresh Italian parsley

6 green onions, trimmed and thinly sliced

Grated zest of 1 lemon

Salt and freshly ground black pepper to taste

1 to 1½ cups extra-virgin olive oil

1 pound imported penne

Lemon wedges (optional)

If using fresh tuna, heat a charcoal or gas grill or a ridged stovetop griddle until very hot. Lightly rub the grill with a towel dipped in a bit of oil to prevent the fish from sticking. Grill the fish, turning once, until it is barely cooked through, approximately 10 minutes per inch of thickness. Let cool, then cut into 1-inch pieces.

Meanwhile, in a medium bowl, combine the tomatoes, olives, garlic, oregano, parsley, green onions, lemon zest, and salt and pepper. Add enough of the extra-virgin olive oil to just cover the tomato mixture. Stir the mixture until the tomatoes release their juices. Add the tuna; if using canned tuna, flake it into the mixture and stir to mix. Marinate in the refrigerator for at least 1 hour, preferably 2 or 3.

Remove the tomato-tuna mixture from the refrigerator and place it in a serving bowl to come to room temperature while you cook the pasta. Cook the penne in abundant boiling salted water until al dente. Drain and immediately add the hot pasta to the sauce in the serving bowl. Toss gently and, if you wish, garnish with lemon wedges.

SUMMER SHELLS WITH SHRIMP
CONCHIGLIE DELL'ESTATE
Serves 4 to 6

A fresh uncooked sauce that can be thrown together in minutes if you buy ready-cooked shrimp. This dish is also great as a pasta salad or first course served in scooped-out tomato halves.

1 lemon, cut in half

1 pound medium shrimp, peeled and deveined (see page 9)

5 large red-ripe tomatoes, cored and cut into small dice

12 fresh basil leaves, julienned

4 garlic cloves, peeled and minced

¼ cup extra-virgin olive oil

Dash of red wine vinegar

Salt and freshly ground black pepper to taste

1 pound imported medium conchiglie

Lemon wedges (optional)

Squeeze the lemon juice into a large pot and fill it with water. Bring to a boil. Add the shrimp and cook just until they begin to turn pink. Drain and place in a bowl of ice water. When the shrimp are completely cold, drain and place in a mixing bowl. Add the tomatoes, basil, garlic, olive oil, red wine vinegar, and salt and pepper to taste. Let marinate in the refrigerator for at least 1 hour, preferably 2 or 3.

Remove the shrimp mixture from the refrigerator and place it in a serving bowl to come to room temperature while you cook the pasta. Cook the conchiglie in abundant boiling salted water until al dente. Drain and immediately add the hot pasta to the sauce in the serving bowl. Toss gently and, if you wish, garnish with lemon wedges.

SHELLS WITH MUSSELS AND WHITE BEANS
CONCHIGLIE CON COZZE E FAGIOLI
Serves 4 to 6

The traditional combination of mussels and white beans is tossed with pasta shells, tomatoes, and herbs for an unusual pasta salad. I first came across the pairing of mussels and beans in Forte dei Marmi, a chic Tuscan sea resort. My friend Grazia took me to a tiny *locale* that served us a hot dish of small shells, perfectly cooked creamy beans, and briny mussel meat.

1 pound imported small conchiglie
Olive oil for drizzling
¼ cup extra-virgin olive oil
5 garlic cloves, peeled and minced
Pinch of red chile pepper flakes
36 mussels, cleaned (see page 8)
1 cup white wine or White Fish Broth (page 79)
1 small red onion, peeled and minced
3 celery stalks, minced
5 Roma tomatoes, cored and diced
2 15-ounce cans white beans
Small handful of chopped fresh Italian parsley
½ cup chopped fresh sage or thyme leaves
Juice of 1 lemon

Cook the pasta shells in abundant boiling salted water until al dente. Drain and cool under running water. When cool, drain well and place in a serving bowl. Drizzle with a little olive oil and toss to keep the pasta from sticking together.

In a skillet large enough to accommodate all the mussels in one or two layers, combine the extra-virgin olive oil, 3 of the minced garlic cloves, the red chile pepper flakes, mussels, and wine or fish broth. Cover and steam the mussels over high heat until the shells open, approximately 6 to 8 minutes. If any mussels do not open, discard them. Strain and reserve the cooking juice. Set aside 12 mussels and remove the cooked meat from the remaining mussels, discarding the shells. Add the mussel meat and the remaining ingredients, including the reserved garlic, to the pasta. Moisten with the reserved cooking juices and a drizzle of olive oil, and toss. Garnish with the reserved mussels in the shell, and serve at room temperature.

Fettuccine with Anchovy, Butter, and Parmesan

FETTUCCINE BURRO E PARMIGIANO NEL MARE

Serves 4 to 6

The anchovies add their meaty, salty, flavor to deepen the familiar pasta with *burro e parmigiano*.

1½ pounds fresh fettuccine
8 tablespoons (1 stick) unsalted butter
2 to 3 anchovy fillets (to taste), finely minced
Juice of ½ lemon
Handful of chopped fresh Italian parsley
½ cup freshly grated imported Parmesan cheese
Salt and freshly ground black pepper to taste

Cook the fettuccine in abundant boiling salted water until al dente. Meanwhile, melt the butter in a small sauté pan. Add the anchovies and cook over low heat to allow the flavor to be absorbed by the butter, about 2 minutes. Remove from the heat and add the lemon juice and parsley.

Drain the fettuccine and transfer to a serving bowl. Pour the anchovy butter over the pasta and add the cheese. Season with salt, if necessary, and pepper, toss until the pasta is well coated, and serve immediately.

FETTUCCINE NEAPOLITAN STYLE
FETTUCCINE ALLA NAPOLITANA
Serves 4 to 6

An unusual dish in that it combines a meatless tomato sauce with egg pasta, a taboo for many Italians. The anchovies turn the sauce a deep rich color, much as if a beef broth had been added. The butter serves as the liaison to link the sauce to the richness of the egg pasta. A great last-minute dish that can be thrown together with items from the pantry.

4 garlic cloves, peeled and minced

½ cup chopped fresh Italian parsley

8 anchovies, finely chopped

¼ cup extra-virgin olive oil

6 red-ripe tomatoes, peeled, seeded, and finely chopped, or 1 28-ounce can imported Italian tomatoes, drained, seeded, and finely chopped

Salt and freshly ground black pepper to taste

1 pound fresh fettuccine

4 tablespoons unsalted butter, at room temperature

Combine the garlic, parsley, anchovies, and olive oil in a medium skillet and heat until the garlic releases its characteristic aroma and the anchovies dissolve into the oil. Add the tomatoes and cook over medium heat for 15 to 20 minutes, or until the sauce begins to thicken. Season with salt and pepper.

Meanwhile, cook the fettuccine in abundant boiling salted water until al dente. Drain and transfer to a serving dish. Add the butter and toss until well coated. Pour the sauce over the pasta and toss to mix. Serve immediately.

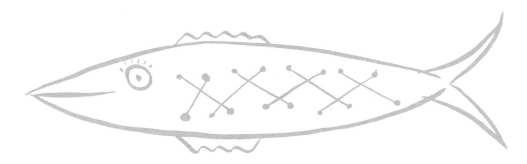

SICILIAN SAFFRON-TINTED PASTA
WITH SARDINES

ZITI ALLE SARDE

Serves 4 to 6

The best *pasta alle sarde* I ever ate was in Taormina at a rough trattoria called Il Botte, where I was served a gargantuan portion laden with the fresh silvery sardines stewed with handfuls of wild fennel. That distinctive dish has never left my memory. However, even this most tradition-bound of all Sicilian pasta dishes has its variations. One of my favorites is to add fennel tops and a bit of saffron to the pasta cooking water to imbue the pasta with the scent of anise and a brilliant yellow color.

1 pound fresh sardines or 2 cans boneless sardines in olive oil

1 cup extra-virgin olive oil

1 onion, peeled and minced

1 small fennel bulb, trimmed, cored, and thinly sliced, tops reserved
   and coarsely chopped

2 anchovy fillets, minced

¼ cup pine nuts

2 tablespoons currants or raisins, plumped in hot water for 15
   minutes and drained

Pinch of saffron threads, soaked in ½ cup hot water for 15 minutes

1 pound imported ziti

Salt and freshly ground black pepper to taste

Handful of Garlicky Bread Crumbs (page 12)

To prepare fresh sardines, clean and scale them, detach and remove the backbones, and cut off the heads. Cut the sardines in half lengthwise, then again crosswise. To prepare canned sardines, drain off the oil and remove any bones.

In a large skillet, heat the oil and cook the onion and sliced fennel until soft and translucent. Add the anchovies and cook until they disintegrate into the vegetables. Add the pine nuts and stir until they begin to turn golden. Immediately add the sardines, chopped fennel tops, and currants or raisins. Gently stir to mix. Add the saffron and its soaking liquid. If the sauce seems dry, add a bit of the pasta cooking water. Cook over low heat for a minute or so, until the flavors mingle.

Meanwhile, cook the ziti in abundant boiling salted water until al dente; drain. Season the sauce with salt and pepper, and add the pasta. Toss over low heat for a few seconds to allow the pasta to absorb the sauce. Transfer the pasta to a serving dish and top with the toasted bread crumbs. Serve immediately.

ORRECHIETTE WITH MARSALA-SCENTED TOMATO SAUCE

PASTA ALLA MARSALA

Serves 4 to 6

WHITEFISH   TILAPIA   ORANGE ROUGHY

Dry Marsala has a nutty flavor with an ephemeral sweetness that is never cloying. It adds an indefinable depth to this simple tomato sauce.

½ cup extra-virgin olive oil

1 large onion, peeled and chopped

1 teaspoon ground nutmeg

1 cup dry Marsala wine

¾ cup Fresh Tomato-Basil Sauce (page 286) or crushed Italian-style peeled tomatoes

10 fresh basil leaves, chopped

Salt and freshly ground black pepper to taste

¾ to 1 pound sole fillets, cut into 1-inch pieces

1 pound imported orrechiette

Heat the olive oil in a large sauté pan over low heat. Add the onion and cook until translucent, about 20 minutes. Add the nutmeg and Marsala and cook over high heat until the Marsala has reduced by a third. Add the tomato sauce or tomatoes, basil, and salt and pepper to taste, and bring to a simmer. Add the fish, and cook just until tender, about 4 minutes. Remove from the heat.

Meanwhile, cook the orrechiette in abundant boiling salted water until al dente. Drain and transfer to a serving platter. Pour the fish sauce over the pasta and toss until coated. Serve immediately.

Farfalle with Tuna, Porcini Mushrooms, and Tomato

FARFALLE AL TONNO E PORCINI

Serves 4 to 6

A simple pantry ingredient, tuna packed in oil has a rich mellow flavor. When joined with the woodsy taste of porcini mushrooms and sweet tomatoes it becomes the centerpiece for a special everyday pasta.

1 ounce dried porcini mushrooms

½ cup extra-virgin olive oil

3 garlic cloves, peeled and minced

6 ripe tomatoes, coarsely chopped, or 1 28-ounce can imported Italian tomatoes

2 6½-ounce cans tuna in oil, drained and flaked

Juice of ½ lemon

Small handful of chopped fresh Italian parsley

Salt and freshly ground black pepper to taste

1 pound imported farfalle

Soak the porcini mushrooms in hot water until softened, about 20 minutes. Drain, discard any hard bits, and chop finely. Set aside.

In a large sauté pan, heat the olive oil over medium heat. Add the garlic and mushrooms and cook until the garlic releases its characteristic aroma. Add the tomatoes; if using canned tomatoes, lift them from the can and squeeze between your fingers directly into the pan. Cook until the sauce thickens, about 10 to 15 minutes. Add the tuna, lemon juice, parsley, and salt and pepper to taste, and cook for about 3 minutes.

Meanwhile, cook the farfalle in abundant boiling salted water until al dente. Drain and transfer to a serving platter. Pour the sauce over the pasta and toss until well coated. Serve immediately.

WHITEFISH RAGÙ

SUGO DI PESCE

Serves 4 to 6

CARP   PERCH   CATFISH

The literal translation of the word *ragù* is "gravy." The classic Neapolitan ragù is a one-pot dish of braised beef that becomes a two-course meal. First a pasta is dressed with the gravy or cooking juices of the meat, then the meat itself is served with vegetables as the second course. In this variation, fish fillets, usually of freshwater fish, are braised with aromatic vegetables, herbs, wine, and tomatoes until they fall apart and become one with the "gravy." Because fish cooks in so little time, the dish achieves the complexity and depth of a ragù very quickly.

1 large onion, peeled and minced

4 to 5 celery stalks, minced

1 carrot, minced

¼ cup extra-virgin olive oil

4 garlic cloves, peeled and minced

Generous handful of chopped fresh Italian parsley

1 bunch fresh basil, leaves only, chopped

2 bay leaves

½ cup white wine

6 round or 12 Roma tomatoes, peeled, seeded, and chopped, or 1 28-ounce can Italian-style tomatoes, puréed with their juice in a food processor

1½ pounds whitefish fillets

3 to 4 cups White Fish Broth (page 79) or water

Grated zest of 1 lemon (optional)

1 pound imported spaghetti

In a large skillet, cook the onion, celery, and carrot in the olive oil until soft. Add the garlic, parsley, basil, and bay leaves, and cook just until the garlic gives off its characteristic aroma. Add the wine and cook over high heat until the alcohol evaporates. Add the tomatoes and cook until they break down and form a sauce. Lay the fish fillets in the sauce and add just enough broth or water to barely cover the fish. If desired, add the lemon zest. Bring the liquid to a bare simmer and cook until the fish begins to flake apart and the liquid has reduced, about 20 minutes. Vigorously stir the ragù mixture so that the fish breaks apart completely.

Meanwhile, cook the spaghetti in abundant boiling salted water until al dente. Drain the spaghetti and add to the ragù. Stir over low heat for 1 minute. Transfer to pasta bowls and serve immediately.

"Dressed-Up" Linguine with Tuna

LINGUINE AL TONNO ALLA FESTIVA

Serves 4 to 6

A simple Sicilian-inspired pasta of tuna, capers, and olives is given a festive air with a scarlet border of sweet tomato sauce. The preparation of the tuna is a good example of how Italian sauces often are made saucy from a simple mélange of a few carefully chosen ingredients bound together with olive oil and a bit of the pasta water. This dish has been my "demonstration" dish for over a year. Audiences are astonished by the earthy elegance achieved with so little strain.

For the bread crumbs

3 thick slices day-old country bread

2 garlic cloves, peeled and minced

2 tablespoons extra-virgin olive oil

Salt and freshly ground black pepper to taste

½ cup extra-virgin olive oil

Pinch of red chile pepper flakes

3 garlic cloves, peeled and sliced

½ pound fresh tuna, cut into ½-inch dice, or 2 6½-ounce cans tuna, drained

Juice of ¼ lemon

Small handful of coarsely chopped fresh Italian parsley

2 teaspoons capers

¼ cup pitted Moroccan olives, cut in quarters (optional)

1 pound imported linguine

1 recipe Fresh Tomato-Basil Sauce (page 286) or 2 cups good-quality prepared tomato sauce

Heat the oven to 350°. Tear the bread up, place in a food processor with a steel blade, and process until the bread crumbs are very coarse. Transfer the crumbs to a small bowl and add the garlic, olive oil, and salt and pepper to taste.

Stir to mix. Spread the bread crumbs on a cookie sheet and bake until golden brown, approximately 20 minutes. Be careful not to let them burn! Set aside.

In a medium sauté pan, combine the olive oil, red chile pepper flakes, and garlic and heat over medium heat. When the oil begins to bubble, add the fresh tuna and sauté, stirring, just until it cooks through and is firm to the touch; if using canned tuna, add it to the pan and stir until heated through. Remove from the heat and let the tuna and garlic steep briefly in the oil. Add the lemon juice, parsley, capers, and olives.

Cook the linguine in abundant boiling salted water until al dente. Meanwhile, heat the tomato sauce. Drain the pasta and transfer to a shallow serving dish. Pour the warm tuna-garlic mixture over the pasta and gently toss. Spoon the hot tomato sauce around the edge of the pasta. Top the pasta with the bread crumbs. Serve immediately.

Linguine with Shrimp, Black Olive Paste, and Fennel

LINGUINE AI GAMBERI E PESTO DI OLIVE

Serves 4 to 6

The sweetness of fennel and shrimp adds a mellowing note to the pungent flavor of the pesto di olive. Black olive paste has a striking, dense, glossy look that adds a touch of earthy elegance whenever it is used.

1 fennel bulb, with feathery tops
¼ cup extra-virgin olive oil
1 pound medium shrimp, peeled and deveined (see page 9)
Juice of ½ lemon
2 tablespoons Pesto di Olive (page 298)
¼ cup White Fish Broth (page 79) or water
Salt and freshly ground black pepper to taste
1 pound imported linguine

Trim the fennel, and reserve the green tops. Core the fennel bulb, cut in half lengthwise, and thinly slice. Coarsely chop the reserved tops. In a medium sauté pan, heat 2 tablespoons of the olive oil and sauté the sliced fennel until soft. Remove the fennel from the pan and set aside. Add the remaining 2 tablespoons oil to the pan and heat until hot. Sauté the shrimp until pink. Add the lemon juice, pesto, and fish broth or water and stir until blended. Add the reserved fennel tops to the pan, and season with salt and pepper.

In the meantime, cook the pasta in abundant boiling salted water until al dente. Drain and transfer to a shallow serving bowl. Pour the sauce over the pasta and mix thoroughly. Serve immediately.

Linguine with Angry Shrimp

LINGUINE CON GAMBERI ARRABIATI

Serves 4 to 6

 favorite tomato sauce is combined with the most popular crustacean for an assured success at the table.

½ cup extra-virgin olive oil
2 to 3 teaspoons red chile pepper flakes (to taste)
1 28-ounce can imported Italian tomatoes
5 garlic cloves, peeled, 3 left whole and 2 minced
Salt to taste
1 pound medium shrimp, peeled and deveined (see page 9)
1 pound imported linguine
Handful of chopped fresh Italian parsley

Heat ¼ cup of the olive oil in a sauté pan over medium heat. Add the chile pepper flakes. As soon as the flakes begin to release their color, add the tomatoes, crushing them between your fingers as you carefully add them to the pan. (Or set a food mill over the pan and purée the tomatoes directly into it.) Stir the tomatoes, mixing well with the oil and chile pepper flakes. Put the 3 whole garlic cloves through a press directly into the sauce, and season with salt to taste. Cook over moderately high heat until the tomatoes begin to break down and the sauce thickens, approximately 15 minutes.

Meanwhile, in a medium sauté pan, heat the remaining ¼ cup olive oil. Add the minced garlic and cook until it releases its characteristic aroma. Add the shrimp and cook just until pink. Set aside. Cook the linguine in abundant boiling salted water until al dente. Drain and place in a shallow serving bowl.

Add the shrimp, tomato sauce, and parsley, and mix thoroughly. Serve immediately.

Fettuccine with Shrimp, Artichokes, and Leeks
FETTUCCINE AL CARCIOFO NEL MARE
Serves 4 to 6

A light, modern dish that is a simple sauté of shrimp and spring-time vegetables. Roughly chopping the shrimp before cooking allows its flavor to permeate the sauce and gives a chunky ragù-like texture to the dish.

20 baby artichokes

1 lemon, cut in half

¼ cup extra-virgin olive oil

5 garlic cloves, peeled and minced

Pinch of red chile pepper flakes

4 bay leaves

2 leeks, washed, halved lengthwise, and cut into thin slices

12 fresh sage leaves, cut into julienne

2 cups white wine or White Fish Broth (page 79)

1 tablespoon grated orange zest

Juice of 1 orange

1½ pounds medium shrimp, peeled, deveined, and roughly chopped (see page 9)

8 tablespoons (1 stick) unsalted butter or any of the flavored butters on pages 307 to 310, cut into tablespoons

Generous handful of chopped fresh Italian parsley

Salt and freshly ground black pepper to taste

1 pound imported fettuccine

Trim the artichokes and cut in half lengthwise. Rub the cut edges with the lemon and set aside. Heat the oil in a large skillet and add the garlic, red chile pepper flakes, and bay leaves. Sauté briefly, until the garlic releases its characteristic aroma. Add the leeks and sage and cook over moderate heat until the leeks begin to wilt. Add the wine or broth, orange zest, juice, and artichokes. Bring to a simmer, cover, and steam for 5 to 7 minutes to soften the artichokes a bit. Uncover and cook until the liquid is reduced by half. Add the shrimp, butter, and parsley and cook just until the shrimp is done. Season with salt and pepper to taste.

Meanwhile, cook the fettuccine in abundant boiling salted water until al dente. Drain and add to the shrimp sauce. Cook, stirring, over low heat for 1 minute. Transfer to a serving bowl and serve immediately.

LINGUINE WITH SHRIMP AND PESTO
LINGUINE CON GAMBERI E PESTO
Serves 4 to 6

An unconventional combination once requested by a customer at Trattoria Angeli, this sneaked its way into the greater Angeli repertoire. Shrimp and garlic have a great affinity for one another, and the contrasting colors of pink shrimp on forest-green pesto please the eye.

> 3 tablespoons extra-virgin olive oil
> 1 pound medium shrimp, peeled and deveined (see page 9)
> Salt and freshly ground pepper to taste
> 1 pound imported linguine
> ¼ cup Basil Pesto (page 300)

In a medium sauté pan, heat the olive oil. Add the shrimp and sauté until completely pink. Season with salt and pepper to taste. Remove from the pan and set aside. Set the pan aside.

In the meantime, cook the linguine in abundant boiling salted water until al dente. Drain, reserving about 1 cup of the cooking water, and transfer the pasta to a shallow serving bowl. Add the pesto to the pan the shrimp were cooked in. Slowly stir in enough of the reserved pasta water until the pesto has the consistency of a sauce. Pour over the pasta and toss well. Arrange the cooked shrimp on top of the pasta. Serve immediately.

Linguine Fini with Lemon, Butter, and Scallops

CAPE SANTE AL LIMONE E BURRO

Serves 4 to 6

This luscious dish gives a nod to the traditional scampi flavors of butter, garlic, and lemon. Scallops briefly sautéed in butter have a sensual velvet texture.

> 1 pound sea scallops, tough side muscles removed
> ½ pound (2 sticks) unsalted butter
> 2 garlic cloves, peeled and minced
> Juice of 2 lemons
> ¼ cup White Fish Broth (page 79) (optional)
> Salt and coarsely ground black pepper to taste
> 1 pound imported linguine fini
> Small handful of coarsely chopped fresh Italian parsley

If the scallops are very thick, slice them in half horizontally. In a large sauté pan, melt the butter. Add the garlic and scallops and sauté until the garlic gives off its characteristic aroma and the scallops turn firm and opaque. Add the lemon juice, the fish broth, if desired, and salt and pepper to taste. Remove from the heat and cover the pan.

Meanwhile, cook the pasta in abundant boiling salted water until al dente. If you wish, add about ¼ cup of the pasta cooking water to the sauce to moisten it. Drain the pasta and immediately add it to the sauce. Add the parsley and cook over low heat for a minute or so to allow the linguine to absorb the sauce. Serve immediately.

Penne with Scallops in a Baked Tomato Sauce

PENNE AL CAPE SANTE AL FORNO

Serves 4 to 6

Layered and baked tomatoes result in a sweeter-than-usual tomato sauce. As the tomatoes cook, the top layer roasts, giving the resulting sauce an undertone of ''sun-dried'' tomato flavor. The sauce can either be served piping hot or prepared in advance and presented at room temperature with the hot pasta.

8 ripe Roma tomatoes, cored and cut into thin wedges
6 large fresh basil leaves, chopped
2 to 3 garlic cloves, peeled and minced
¼ cup extra-virgin olive oil
Salt and freshly ground black pepper to taste
1 pound sea scallops, tough side muscles removed
1 pound imported penne

Preheat the oven to 400°. Place half the tomatoes in a small ovenproof baking dish. Scatter half the basil and garlic over them, drizzle 2 tablespoons of the olive oil over, and season with salt and pepper. Lay the scallops atop the tomatoes and repeat with another layer of tomatoes, basil, and garlic, the remaining 2 tablespoons olive oil, and salt and pepper to taste. Bake for approximately 30 minutes, or until the tomatoes are very soft.

About 10 minutes before the sauce is done, cook the penne in abundant boiling salted water until al dente. Drain and transfer to a serving dish. Top with the baked tomato-scallop mixture and toss well. Serve immediately.

THE DEVIL'S PENNE WITH FRIED CALAMARI
PENNE ALL'ARRABIATA CON CALAMARI FRITTI
Serves 4 to 6

An untraditional combination of two of the most requested dishes at my restaurants, penne all'arrabiata and calamari fritti. The easiest way to prepare this dish is to marinate the squid and make the tomato sauce a day ahead. The next day, simply fry the calamari, heat up the sauce, and cook the pasta. A time-consuming dish becomes a breeze to make! The texture of the al dente pasta against the crunchy calamari is incredibly satisfying, and the look of the golden rings atop the red tinted pasta is especially enticing.

> **2 pounds cleaned squid, tentacles trimmed and body sacs cut into rings (see page 10)**
>
> **2 cups milk or half-and-half**
>
> **¼ cup extra-virgin olive oil**
>
> **1 to 2 teaspoons red chile pepper flakes (to taste)**
>
> **1 28-ounce can Italian-style tomatoes**
>
> **3 garlic cloves, peeled**
>
> **Salt to taste**
>
> **Olive oil for frying**
>
> **Flour for dredging**
>
> **Coarse salt to taste**
>
> **1 pound imported penne**
>
> **Handful of chopped fresh Italian parsley**
>
> **Lemon wedges**

Place the squid in a small bowl. Add the milk or half-and-half and stir well. Place in the refrigerator to marinate for at least 1 hour, or up to 24 hours.

In a skillet, heat the olive oil over moderate heat. Add the red chile pepper flakes. As soon as the flakes begin to add some color to the oil, add the tomatoes, crushing them between your fingers into the skillet. (Or set a food mill over the skillet and purée the tomatoes directly into it.) Stir the tomatoes, mixing well with the oil and chile pepper flakes. Squeeze the garlic cloves through a press directly into the sauce, and add salt to taste. Cook the sauce over moderately high heat until the tomatoes begin to break down and the sauce thickens, approximately 15 minutes. Set aside. (The sauce can be prepared up to 24 hours in advance and refrigerated; reheat over medium heat before serving.)

Pour 3 inches of oil into a deep heavy saucepan and heat until hot but not smoking over medium-high heat. Meanwhile, season the flour with coarse salt and place in a shallow bowl. Drain the squid in a colander and add to the seasoned flour. Massage the flour into the squid, rubbing until every bit of surface is thickly coated. Place a squid ring in the hot oil. If it immediately begins to sizzle, the oil is ready. Lift up the dredged squid a handful at a time and place in a dry sieve. Shake the sieve to get rid of excess flour. Fry the squid in small batches until a crisp golden brown, using a long-handled metal spoon to gently move the squid around in the hot oil so it will fry evenly. Use a slotted spoon to transfer the crispy squid to paper towels to drain.

Meanwhile, cook the penne in abundant boiling salted water until al dente. Drain. Add the chopped parsley to the tomato sauce. Toss the pasta with the sauce, and spoon into individual pasta bowls. Top each serving of pasta with a generous handful of calamari. Serve with lemon wedges. Yum!

Linguine with "Drowned" Squid

LINGUINE CON CALAMARI AFFOGATI

Serves 4 to 6

The secret to cooking squid is to either cook it quickly, for less than five minutes, or to stew it for a good while. This long-cooked dish results in a deeply flavorful squid stew rich with wine, aromatic vegetables, and herbs. This recipe is perfect for older, larger calamari that need long cooking to become tender.

½ cup extra-virgin olive oil

1 medium onion, peeled and roughly chopped

4 celery stalks, roughly chopped

1 large carrot, roughly chopped

4 to 6 garlic cloves, peeled and minced

10 sprigs fresh thyme

10 sprigs fresh oregano

Generous handful of coarsely chopped fresh Italian parsley, plus additional for garnish

3 bay leaves

15 medium Roma tomatoes, quartered

3 cups fruity white wine

3 cups White Fish Broth (page 79) or water

2 pounds cleaned squid, tentacles trimmed and body sacs cut in half lengthwise (see page 10)

Salt and freshly ground black pepper to taste

1 pound imported linguine

In a large deep skillet, heat the oil over medium-low heat, and cook the onion, celery, and carrot until soft. Add the garlic, thyme, and oregano and stir until the garlic begins to give off its characteristic aroma. Add the handful of chopped parsley, the bay leaves, tomatoes, wine, and broth or water. Stir and bring to a boil over high heat. Boil for a minute or so, then lower the heat so the mixture simmers. Add the calamari and salt and pepper to taste, and simmer until the calamari is tender and the sauce is thickened and reduced, approximately 40 minutes.

Meanwhile, cook the linguine in abundant boiling salted water until al dente; drain. Remove the herb sprigs from the pasta sauce, if desired. Add the pasta to the sauce, and toss over low heat for a few seconds to allow the pasta to absorb the sauce. Serve immediately, garnished with chopped parsley.

Spaghetti with Crabmeat and Herbs

Spaghetti ai Granchi

Serves 4 to 6

Crab is a particularly Venetian specialty, rarely seen farther south in Italy. It is truly a regional dish. Here crabmeat is tossed into a fresh tomato sauce with herbs and briefly stewed. Bottarga is the pressed and salted egg sac of gray mullet (found in Italian markets and gourmet specialty stores). It is shaved into ultra-thin slices (much like truffles) to give an intense briny caviar-like flavor to dishes.

¼ cup extra-virgin olive oil

1 medium onion, peeled and diced

4 to 6 garlic cloves, peeled and minced

1 to 2 teaspoons red chile pepper flakes (to taste)

1 cup loosely packed fresh oregano leaves

2 teaspoons dried oregano

1 bunch fresh thyme

Generous handful of coarsely chopped fresh Italian parsley

1 bunch fresh basil, leaves only, coarsely chopped

15 medium Roma tomatoes, cored and cut into small dice

½ cup white wine

2 cups fish broth, preferably Spicy Tomato Broth (page 80)

1½ pounds lump crabmeat, picked over

Salt to taste

1 pound imported spaghetti

2 tablespoons bottarga (optional)

Lemon wedges

In a large skillet, heat the oil. Add the onion and sauté until soft and translucent, approximately 7 minutes. Add the garlic, chile pepper flakes, and herbs, stir, and sauté for 2 minutes, or until the garlic releases its characteristic aroma. Add the tomatoes, wine, and fish broth, bring to boil over high heat, and boil for 2 minutes. Add the crabmeat, reduce the heat for about 10 minutes, and cook until the sauce is thickened and reduced. Season with salt.

In the meantime, cook the spaghetti in abundant boiling salted water until al dente. Drain and add to the sauce. Toss over low heat for a few seconds to allow the pasta to absorb the sauce. Serve immediately. Grate the bottarga over the pasta at the table if desired, and garnish with lemon wedges.

VERMICELLI WITH RED CLAM SAUCE
VERMICELLI ALLE VONGOLE
Serves 4 to 6

The classic Neapolitan dish of sweet, tender clams loaded with garlic, oil, and wine, with just enough tomato purée to turn the juices a deep orange. Three quarters of a cup of oil may seem like a lot, but the flavor of the oil is crucial to the success of the dish.

¾ **cup extra-virgin olive oil**

6 to 8 garlic cloves, peeled and minced

3 pounds soft-shell clams, such as Manila, cleaned (see page 7)

1½ cups dry white wine

1 4-ounce can tomato purée

2 handfuls of chopped fresh Italian parsley

1 pound imported vermicelli

In a large sauté pan, heat the olive oil. Add the garlic and cook over low heat until it releases its characteristic aroma. Add the clams, white wine, tomato purée, and half the parsley. Stir well, cover the pan, and turn the heat up to medium high. Cook until the clams are open, about 5 minutes.

Meanwhile, cook the vermicelli in abundant boiling salted water until al dente; drain. Remove the clams from the sauce and set aside. Add the pasta to the sauce and toss over low heat so that the pasta absorbs the sauce. Transfer the pasta to a large serving platter. Arrange the clams in their shells on top of the pasta and pour any remaining sauce on top. Top with the remaining parsley, and serve immediately.

LINGUINE WITH "FRUITS OF THE SEA"

LINGUINE AI FRUTTI DI MARE

Serves 4 to 6

The ever-poetic Italians dub crustaceans "fruits of the sea," and no dish showcases them as beautifully as *linguine ai frutti di mare*. The choice of seafood depends on regional availability, so those listed here are only suggestions. The sauce should be more broth-like than thickly saucy so that the star of the dish is the heap of varied shellfish.

½ cup extra-virgin olive oil

2 to 3 garlic cloves, peeled and minced

6 ripe tomatoes, chopped, or 1 28-ounce can imported Italian tomatoes

Handful of chopped fresh Italian parsley

Salt and freshly ground black pepper to taste

20 Manila clams, cleaned (see page 7)

20 black mussels, cleaned (see page 8)

20 medium shrimp, peeled and deveined (see page 9)

⅓ pound bay scallops

⅓ pound squid, cleaned and cut into ¼-inch-thick rings (see page 10)

1 cup dry white wine

1 pound imported linguine

In a heavy medium sauté pan, heat ¼ cup of the olive oil. Add the garlic and cook over medium heat until it gives off its characteristic aroma. Add the tomatoes; if using canned, lift the tomatoes out of their juice and crush them between your fingers into the pan. Add the parsley and cook until the tomatoes break down and thicken into a sauce. Add salt and pepper to taste. Set aside.

In a medium sauté pan, heat the remaining ¼ cup olive oil. Add all the seafood and sauté for 1 minute. Add the white wine, cover, and let steam until the clams and mussels open. Stir in the tomato sauce.

In the meantime, cook the linguine in abundant boiling salted water until al dente; drain. Remove the mussels and clams from the sauce and set aside. Add the pasta to the tomato sauce and toss until it is well coated. Transfer the pasta to a large serving platter or to individual plates. Arrange the clams and mussels in their shells on top of the pasta, and pour any remaining sauce on top. Serve immediately.

LINGUINE WITH DOUBLE CLAMS
LINGUINE AL DOPPIO VONGOLE
Serves 4 to 6

For those who can't get enough clams atop their pasta, the most requested dish at Angeli Mare provides a double hit of the crustaceans. Half of the clams are first steamed open, chopped, and incorporated into the sauce; the remaining clams are steamed and served whole in the shell on top of the pasta. The butter mixed with the wine in the sauce adds a rich touch as it helps the clam juices coat the pasta. Be sure to let the cooked linguine stew in the sauce for a few seconds so it absorbs the fragrant juices.

5 pounds soft-shell clams, such as Manila, cleaned (see page 7)
1 cup extra-virgin olive oil
2 cups dry white wine
12 garlic cloves, peeled and minced
1 teaspoon red chile pepper flakes
1 cup White Fish Broth (page 79) or pasta cooking water
4 tablespoons unsalted butter
½ cup chopped fresh Italian parsley
Salt to taste
1 pound imported linguine

Place half the clams in a large sauté pan and add ¼ cup of the oil, 1½ cups of the wine, and half the garlic. Cover and steam over medium heat until the clams open. Strain the cooking juices through a fine sieve and reserve. Pull the clam meat out of the shells, coarsely chop, and set aside.

continued

In a large sauté pan, heat the remaining ¾ cup olive oil over medium heat. Add the remaining chopped garlic, the red chile pepper flakes, chopped clams, and the remaining uncooked clams, and cook until the garlic releases its characteristic aroma. Add the remaining ½ cup white wine, the fish broth, and the reserved clam juices. Cover and cook until the clams are open. Add the butter and parsley. Season with salt to taste.

Meanwhile, cook the linguine in abundant boiling salted water until al dente; drain. Remove the whole clams from the sauce and set aside. Add the pasta to the clam sauce and toss over low heat until it absorbs a bit of the sauce. Transfer the sauced pasta to a large serving platter. Arrange the clams in their shells on top of the pasta, and pour any remaining sauce on top. Serve immediately.

Linguine with Mussels Puttanesca Style
LINGUINE CON COZZE ALLA PUTTANESCA
Serves 4 to 6

Mussels, capers, olives, and hot pepper have a natural affinity for one another, so it isn't unusual that they turn up together all over southern Italy. Few dishes are as visually pleasing as this one with its glistening black mussel shells against a scarlet sauce bedecked with black olives and capers. I was treated to an enriched version of this dish in Apulia. An inspired home cook threw in a couple of roughly torn sun-dried tomatoes to add an unforgettable intensity of flavor.

¼ cup extra-virgin olive oil

4 to 5 garlic cloves, peeled and minced

3 anchovy fillets, finely chopped

½ to 1 teaspoon red chile pepper flakes (to taste)

12 Roma tomatoes or 6 ripe round tomatoes, peeled, seeded, and chopped

1 tablespoon capers

¼ cup pitted Moroccan or Kalamata olives, cut into quarters lengthwise

1½ pounds black mussels, cleaned (see page 8)

1 pound imported linguine

Handful of chopped fresh Italian parsley

In a large sauté pan, heat the olive oil over medium heat. Add the garlic, anchovies, and red chile pepper flakes. Cook until the garlic releases its characteristic aroma and the anchovies begin to ''melt.'' Add the tomatoes and cook over high heat, stirring frequently, until the tomatoes begin to break down and give off their juices. Add the capers and olives, lower the heat, and cook until the sauce begins to thicken. Just before the sauce is done, add the mussels to the pan. Cover the pan and cook just until the mussels are open.

Meanwhile, cook the linguine in abundant boiling salted water until al dente; drain. Remove the mussels from the sauce and set aside. Add the linguine and parsley to the sauce, and toss until the pasta is well coated. Transfer to a serving platter. Top with the mussels and serve immediately.

SPAGHETTI WITH MUSHROOMS AND MUSSELS

SPAGHETTI AL BOSCO MARE

Serves 4 to 6

The woodsy flavor of mushrooms is often paired with mussels in Liguria, where both are available in abundance.

2 cups sliced mushrooms
3 tablespoons extra-virgin olive oil
24 mussels, cleaned (see page 8)
2 tablespoons fish broth, white wine, or water
½ teaspoon finely chopped fresh thyme
Juice of ½ lemon
Salt and freshly ground black pepper to taste
1 pound imported spaghetti
1 tablespoon unsalted butter
Lemon wedges

Cook the mushrooms in the oil in a large sauté pan over high heat until they are a bit crusty. Add the mussels, fish broth, thyme, lemon juice, and salt and pepper, cover, and cook until the mussels have opened. Remove from the heat.

In the meantime, cook the spaghetti in abundant boiling salted water until al dente. Reheat the mussels if necessary, add the butter, and toss over low heat until the butter melts and the sauce is smooth. Remove the mussels from the sauce and set aside. Drain the spaghetti, add it to the sauce, and toss until well coated. Place the pasta in a shallow serving bowl. Arrange the cooked mussels in their shells on top of the pasta. Garnish with lemon wedges and serve immediately.

SURF-AND-TURF ZITI

ZITI ONDE E TERRA

Serves 4 to 6

An Italian version of surf and turf, this dish makes a hearty meal. The combination of sausage and mussels may seem strange, but it is often on the table in Italian seaside communities. It well illustrates the adage that no matter how close Italians are to the sea, their roots remain firmly planted in the countryside.

1 pound mild Italian sausages, casings removed
1 large onion, peeled and minced
4 garlic cloves, peeled and minced
4 medium tomatoes, chopped
½ cup dry white wine
Handful of chopped fresh Italian parsley
Salt and freshly ground black pepper to taste
3 pounds mussels, cleaned (see page 8)
1 pound imported ziti

Place the sausage and minced onion in a large sauté pan and cook over medium heat, breaking up the sausage with a spoon, until the meat is no longer pink and the onion is soft, about 15 minutes. Add the garlic and sauté until it releases its characteristic aroma. Add the tomatoes, wine, parsley, and salt and pepper to taste, and bring to a boil. Lower the heat to medium so that the sauce cooks at a moderate simmer. Arrange the mussels on top of the sausage mixture, cover, and steam just until the mussels open.

Meanwhile, cook the ziti in abundant boiling salted water until al dente. Drain the pasta and transfer to a shallow serving bowl. Remove the mussels from the sauce and set aside. Pour the sauce over the pasta and toss well. Arrange the mussels on top of the sauced pasta. Serve immediately.

RAVIOLI STUFFED WITH FISH AND GREENS

RAVIOLI AL MAGRO

Serves 4 to 6 (makes about 60 ravioli)

CATFISH   SNAPPER   SEA BASS

The meatless combination of greens and fish makes this dish *al magro,* or Lenten-style, one of those dishes allowed to be eaten on religious days when meat is forbidden. I serve these special ravioli topped with fresh sage leaves stewed in butter. Yes, you are allowed a sprinkle of Parmesan cheese on this one.

2½ cups day-old country bread torn in large pieces, plus extra if necessary

About 2 cups milk

1 medium onion, peeled and finely chopped

¼ cup extra-virgin olive oil

5 large Swiss chard leaves, ribs trimmed out and discarded, chopped

6 garlic cloves, peeled and minced

1½ pounds boneless fish fillets cut into small pieces

¾ cup White Fish Broth (page 79) or water, plus extra if necessary

½ cup white wine or ¼ cup brandy

Juice of 1 lemon

Generous handful of chopped fresh Italian parsley

1 bunch fresh basil, leaves only, chopped

Salt and freshly ground black pepper to taste

2 eggs, beaten

⅓ cup grated imported Parmesan cheese

1 recipe Pasta all'Uovo (page 146)

8 tablespoons (1 stick) unsalted butter

1 bunch fresh sage, leaves only

In a small bowl, soak the bread in 2 cups milk. In a large skillet, cook the onion in the olive oil over medium heat until soft. Add the Swiss chard and cook just until it wilts. Add the garlic and cook until its characteristic aroma is released. Add the fish, broth or water, wine or brandy, lemon juice, parsley, basil, and salt and pepper. Cover and cook over low heat for about 8 minutes, or until the fish is completely cooked. Transfer to a bowl and let cool.

When the fish mixture is cool enough to handle, flake the fish apart with your fingers and return it to the same bowl. Squeeze the milk from the bread and add it to the fish mixture, along with the eggs and Parmesan. Stir vigorously until the mixture has a smooth consistency. If necessary, adjust the consistency by adding either more soaked bread or more broth or water. The mixture should hold together without being dry. Correct the seasoning if necessary. The filling can be made up to 2 days ahead, covered, and refrigerated.

Roll out the pasta dough and stuff the ravioli as described on page 146. Cook the ravioli in abundant boiling salted water until done, 2 to 5 minutes; drain. Meanwhile, combine the butter and sage leaves in a small saucepan and heat over low heat until the butter is melted. Transfer the ravioli to a serving platter and pour the melted sage butter over them.

Shrimp-Filled Ravioli

RAVIOLI DI GAMBERI

Serves 4 to 6 (makes about 60 ravioli)

For a truly baroque taste experience, top these shrimp-filled ravioli with whole clams steamed with tomato (page 135). For a simpler dish, pair them with melted butter and sage as in the previous recipe or with Fresh Tomato-Basil Sauce (page 286).

1 medium red onion, peeled and finely chopped

¼ cup extra-virgin olive oil

5 large Swiss chard leaves, ribs trimmed out and discarded, finely chopped

2 large pinches of dried sage

½ bunch fresh thyme, leaves only

Pinch of ground celery seed

5 garlic cloves, peeled and minced

¾ pound peeled shrimp, roughly chopped

1 pound boneless fish fillets such as whitefish, sole, or perch

1 cup White Fish Broth (page 79) or water, plus extra if necessary

1 cup white wine

Salt and freshly ground black pepper to taste

About ½ cup grated imported Pecorino Romano cheese

1 cup dried bread crumbs

1 recipe Pasta all'Uova (page 146)

In a large skillet, cook the onion in the olive oil over medium heat until soft. Add the chard, sage, thyme, and celery seed and cook just until the chard wilts. Add the garlic and cook until its characteristic aroma is released. Add the shrimp, fish, broth or water, wine, and salt and pepper. Cover and cook over low heat for about 8 minutes, or until the fish is completely cooked. Transfer to a bowl and let cool.

When the fish mixture is cool enough to handle, flake the fish apart with your fingers, and return it to the same bowl. Add the Pecorino Romano and enough bread crumbs to make a fairly smooth mixture. If necessary, adjust the consistency by adding more bread crumbs or more broth or water. The mixture should hold together without being dry. Correct the seasoning if necessary.

Roll out the pasta dough and stuff the ravioli as described on page 146. Cook the ravioli in abundant boiling salted water until done, 2 to 5 minutes; drain. Top with the sauce of your choice and serve immediately.

Fresh Egg Dough for Ravioli

PASTA ALL'UOVO

Makes about 60 ravioli

2 cups unbleached all-purpose flour
3 large eggs, beaten

To make the dough, put the flour in a food processor with the steel blade. With the machine running, gradually add enough of the beaten eggs so that the flour and eggs come together and the mixture forms pellets the size of coffee beans. Turn the rough mixture out onto a board and knead firmly into a stiff dough. Form into a ball, cover with a kitchen towel, and allow the dough to rest for at least 15 minutes. Or wrap the dough in plastic wrap and refrigerate for up to 24 hours.

To roll out the pasta, unwrap the dough, carefully cut off a slice 1 inch thick, and rewrap the remaining pasta. Flatten the pasta slice with the heel of your hand. If the dough feels a little tacky, coat each side lightly with flour. Set the pasta machine rollers at the widest point and feed the pasta through the rollers. Fold the sheet of pasta in thirds, and feed it through the rollers 4 or 5 more times, each time folding it as you roll it, with just enough flour to keep it from sticking. Be careful not to use too much! Then continue to roll the sheet of pasta through the machine to the thinnest setting. Cut the sheet into manageable lengths, lay out on a lightly floured surface, and cover with a towel to prevent drying. Repeat the process with the remaining dough. Stuff the pasta as soon as all of it is rolled out.

To shape and stuff the ravioli, position one sheet of the pasta dough horizontally in front of you on a work surface. Make a row of generous teaspoonfuls of your filling 1 inch apart down the center of the pasta sheet. Carefully fold the sheet in half, matching the edges of the dough. With your fingertips, gently pat the filling down. Then press down the dough between each mound of filling to seal it. Use a pasta cutter to trim the edges of the dough and cut apart the ravioli. Gently crimp the edges of the ravioli with a fork. Lay the ravioli on a lightly floured tea towel, and repeat with the remaining pasta and filling. Set the ravioli aside to dry for at least 5 minutes before cooking.

POLENTA

Makes 6 servings soft polenta or 1 loaf firm polenta

Polenta, or coarse corn meal, is the grain of choice in Northern Italy. Its slightly grainy texture and light corn flavor work as a perfect foil to many savory dishes, and its bright yellow color adds a rustic sunny touch to all food with which it is paired.

Polenta is served in three different ways. It can be poured directly out of the saucepan into a bowl, and presented soft and buttery with a fragrant topping. Or it can be poured into a loaf pan and allowed to firm, then sliced and grilled or sautéed to add a crunchy contrast as an accompaniment to a main dish. Or, as in Baked Polenta Lasagna with Shrimp and Scallops (page 148), it can be used much like pasta, as a base for a variety of baked dishes.

6 ½ cups water
2 teaspoons salt
4 tablespoons unsalted butter
1½ cups imported polenta or coarse yellow corn meal

Bring the water to a boil in a large pot over high heat, and add the salt and butter. As soon as the water returns to the boil, whisk in the polenta in a slow, steady stream. Reduce the heat to medium and, with a whisk or a wooden spoon, cook, stirring constantly for 30 to 40 minutes, or until the polenta is thick enough to grab the whisk yet still soft.

For soft polenta, serve immediately. For baked, grilled, or fried polenta, pour the hot polenta into a loaf pan or a baking dish. Smooth the polenta with a rubber spatula, and let cool. Polenta can be made up to 3 days ahead, covered, and refrigerated. Then it can be sliced and grilled, fried, or baked in a casserole.

BAKED POLENTA LASAGNA WITH SHRIMP AND SCALLOPS

LASAGNE DI POLENTA AL FORNO

Serves 6 to 8

Polenta ''lasagnas'' can be thrown together in minutes using ingredients on hand. Let your imagination be your guide. This dish finds its patrimony in *polenta pasticciata,* a creamy layered dish of polenta slices, tomato-basil sauce, besciamella, and mozzarella. Few dishes satisfy so completely on a cold, rainy evening.

> **2 cups Fresh Tomato-Basil Sauce (page 286)**
> **1 recipe Polenta (page 147), poured into a lasagna pan and cooled**
> **¾ pound small shrimp, peeled and deveined (see page 9)**
> **½ pound bay scallops**
> **1 recipe Besciamella (page 289)**

Preheat the oven to 375°.

To assemble the lasagna, spoon the tomato sauce evenly over the cooled polenta. Scatter the shrimp and scallops over the tomato sauce. Finish by topping with the besciamella. Bake uncovered until the sauce is bubbly and the besciamella is dotted with golden spots, approximately 30 minutes.

ew foods complement the delicate flavor of Italian Arborio rice as do fish and shellfish. In some of the following recipes the fish is added to the rice halfway through the cooking time so it cooks along with the porridgelike risotto, lending a great deal of flavor to the rice itself. In others, a savory fish sauté or braise is served atop a completed risotto, adding an explosion of flavor to each biteful of the comfortingly bland rice as well as a contrast of texture.

Please don't feel you must prepare every risotto in this chapter with fish broth, or even chicken broth. Often Italian cooks use only water if the ingredients are especially flavorful. The broths add flavor, but can sometimes overpower the flavors of the other ingredients in the risotto if not diluted. In general, I prefer to use either equal parts fish broth and water or all water.

MIXED SEAFOOD RISOTTO

RISOTTO FRUTTI DI MARE

Serves 4 to 6

Prepared tomato sauce gives a uniform color and deep, rich flavor to this dish, while fresh chopped tomatoes result in a sweet, light risotto. The choice is up to you. The look of pink shrimp, black mussels, and white squid submerged in creamy red-orange rice is voluptuous and enticing.

2 tablespoons unsalted butter

3 tablespoons extra-virgin olive oil

1 small onion, peeled and chopped

4 garlic cloves, peeled and minced

6 Roma tomatoes, peeled, seeded, and chopped, or 1 cup prepared tomato sauce

10 fresh basil leaves, coarsely chopped

2 cups Arborio rice

½ cup dry white wine

2 handfuls chopped fresh Italian parsley

4 cups combined White Fish Broth (page 79) or chicken broth and water or water

12 medium shrimp, peeled and deveined (see page 9)

½ pound squid, cleaned and body sacs cut into rings (see page 10)

12 mussels, cleaned (see page 8)

12 clams, cleaned (see page 7)

Salt and freshly ground black pepper to taste

In a heavy 2-quart saucepan, melt the butter with the olive oil. Add the onion and cook slowly over low heat until it is softened. Add the garlic and cook briefly until it releases its characteristic aroma. Add the fresh tomatoes if using and the basil, and cook over moderate heat until the tomatoes break down and form a sauce. Add the rice, reduce the heat, and cook slowly, stirring constantly, until the rice has absorbed all the liquid. Add the white wine and cook slowly, stirring constantly, until it is completely absorbed. If using prepared tomato sauce, add it now and cook slowly, stirring, until the liquid is absorbed. Add half of the parsley.

Meanwhile, heat the broth and/or water until very hot. Add the hot liquid to the rice one ladleful at a time, and cook over low heat, stirring frequently; wait until all the liquid is absorbed each time before adding the next ladleful. Continue cooking, adding as much liquid as necessary. After about 10 minutes of cooking time, add the shrimp. After about 20 minutes of cooking, when the rice is nearly done, add the squid, mussels, and clams. Cover and cook just until the clams and mussels open. Add salt and pepper to taste. Serve in individual shallow pasta bowls, garnished with the remaining parsley.

RISOTTO FROM THE WOODS AND SEA
RISOTTO AL BOSCO MARE
Serves 4 to 6

We've been making this dish at Angeli Caffè for years, and it is still in the top five of our most popular risotti.

1 ounce dried porcini mushrooms

½ cup extra-virgin olive oil

6 tablespoons unsalted butter

2 garlic cloves, peeled and minced

¼ pound shiitake mushrooms, stems removed, thinly sliced

½ pound fresh domestic mushrooms, stems trimmed, thinly sliced

1 onion, peeled and diced

2 cups Arborio rice

½ cup dry white wine

6 to 7 cups combined chicken broth and water

1 pound medium shrimp, peeled and deveined (see page 9)

½ bunch fresh thyme, leaves only

Salt and freshly ground black pepper to taste

½ cup grated imported Parmesan cheese (optional)

Soak the porcini mushrooms in a small bowl of warm water for at least 20 minutes. Carefully drain the porcini, straining out any sand, and strain and reserve the soaking liquid.

In a large skillet, heat ¼ cup of the olive oil and 2 tablespoons of the butter. Add the garlic, and cook until it has released its characteristic aroma. Add the mushrooms—first add the shiitakes, which take longer to cook, then add the domestic mushrooms and the porcini, and sauté over high heat just until wilted. Do not overcook the mushrooms; they will continue to cook in the risotto. Remove from the heat and set aside.

In a heavy saucepan, heat the remaining ¼ cup olive oil and 2 tablespoons of the butter. Add the onion and cook over low heat until tender. Add the rice and sauté, stirring constantly, until the grains of rice are opaque and make a clicking sound against the sides of the saucepan, about 1 to 2 minutes. Add the white wine and cook slowly, stirring constantly, until it is completely absorbed. Meanwhile, heat the broth and water until very hot. Add the hot liquid to the rice mixture one ladleful at a time, and cook over low heat, stirring frequently. Wait until all the liquid is absorbed each time before adding the next ladleful.

Three quarters of the way through the cooking time (after about 18 to 20 minutes), add the sautéed mushrooms with all their accumulated juices, the reserved porcini soaking liquid, the shrimp, thyme, and salt and pepper to taste. When the rice is just barely tender, add the remaining 2 tablespoons of butter and, if you wish, the Parmesan cheese. Remove from the heat and stir vigorously until the butter and cheese are absorbed. Spoon the risotto into individual bowls and serve immediately.

Springtime Risotto with Sautéed Fish Fillet

RISOTTO PRIMAVERA CON FILLETTI

Serves 4 to 6

TILAPIA   SOLE

A tender fish fillet sautéed until golden brown and served atop a "primavera" risotto of leeks, asparagus, peas, and arugula makes a striking presentation. Start cooking the fish about five minutes before the risotto is done. It is important to choose a thin white-fleshed fillet that will cook quickly and whose delicate flesh will underscore the tenderness of the rice.

8 tablespoons unsalted butter (6 tablespoons if sautéing fish in clarified butter)

1 medium onion, peeled and finely chopped

1 large carrot, peeled and finely chopped

1 celery stalk, finely chopped

1 leek, white part only, washed and cut into thin strips

2 cups Arborio rice

½ cup dry white wine

6 to 7 cups combined chicken broth and water

¼ pound medium asparagus, tips only (reserve stalks for another use)

1 cup fresh peas

1 bunch spinach or arugula, washed and chopped

Handful of chopped fresh Italian parsley, plus extra for garnish

10 leaves fresh basil, chopped

Salt and freshly ground black pepper to taste

1¼ pounds John Dory fillets, cut into portions

Flour for dredging

2 tablespoons olive oil or ¼ cup clarified butter (see page 14)

¾ cup grated imported Parmesan cheese, plus additional for the table

Lemon wedges

In a heavy 2-quart saucepan, melt 4 tablespoons of the butter. Add the onion, carrot, and celery, and cook slowly over low heat until the vegetables are softened and nearly tender. Add the leek and rice and sauté, stirring constantly, until the grains of rice are opaque and make a clicking sound against the sides of the saucepan, about 1 to 2 minutes. Add the white wine and cook slowly, stirring constantly, until it is completely absorbed. Meanwhile, heat the broth and water until very hot. Add the hot liquid to the rice one ladleful at a time and cook over low heat, stirring frequently. Wait until all the liquid is absorbed each time before adding the next ladleful.

Midway through the cooking time (after about 12 minutes), add the asparagus tips, peas, greens, parsley, basil, and salt and pepper to taste.

Then prepare the fish, while continuing to stir the risotto, adding as much liquid as necessary. Rinse the fish fillets and dry well with a kitchen towel. Season the flour with salt and pepper to taste. Lightly dredge the fillets in the seasoned flour, shaking off any excess. In a nonstick skillet, heat 2 tablespoons of the oil and 2 tablespoons of the butter, or heat the clarified butter, until very hot but not smoking. Add the fish fillets and cook until golden, approximately 1 to 2 minutes per side. Remove from the heat and set aside while you finish the risotto.

When the rice is just barely tender, add the remaining 2 tablespoons butter and the Parmesan cheese. Remove from the heat and stir vigorously until the butter and cheese are absorbed. Spoon the risotto into individual bowls. Top each portion with a sautéed fish fillet. Garnish with a bit of chopped parsley. Serve immediately, accompanied with lemon wedges, and pass Parmesan cheese at the table.

Chianti-Stained Risotto with Squid

RISOTTO AI CALAMARI CON CHIANTI

Serves 4 to 6

MUSSELS

Once, after visiting vineyard after vineyard in Tuscany, I went through a period where I put red wine in nearly everything. I really enjoy cooking with Chianti. With its light, grapey flavor it seems more a food to me than a beverage. In this dish the wine stains the rice with its color while providing an acidic foil for the earthy taste of the squid.

> 6 tablespoons unsalted butter
> 2 tablespoons olive oil
> 1 medium onion, peeled and finely chopped
> 1 large carrot, peeled and finely chopped
> 1 celery stalk, finely chopped
> 2 cups Arborio rice
> 1 cup Chianti
> 6 to 7 cups combined White Fish Broth (page 79) and water
> Handful of chopped fresh Italian parsley
> Salt and freshly ground black pepper to taste
> 2 pounds squid, cleaned and cut into rings (see page 10)

In a heavy 2-quart saucepan, melt 4 tablespoons of the butter with the oil. Add the onion, carrot, and celery, and cook slowly over low heat until the vegetables are softened and nearly tender. Add the rice and sauté, stirring constantly, until the grains of rice are coated with fat and make a clicking sound against the sides of the saucepan, about 1 to 2 minutes. Add the Chianti and cook slowly, stirring constantly, until it is completely absorbed. Meanwhile, heat the broth and water until very hot. Add the hot liquid to the rice mixture one ladleful at a time, and cook over low heat, stirring frequently. Wait until all the liquid is absorbed each time before adding the next ladleful.

Midway through the cooking time (after about 12 minutes), add the parsley and salt and pepper to taste. After about 20 minutes of cooking time, stir in the squid rings. When the rice is just tender, remove the saucepan from the heat and vigorously beat in the remaining 2 tablespoons butter. Spoon the risotto into individual bowls and serve immediately.

RISOTTO WITH SQUID AND PEAS

RISOTTO AI CALAMARI E PISELLI

Serves 4 to 6

I first became enamored of things Italian when I was in college majoring in Italian literature. My studies took me often to Italy, where I was able to practice my avocation—cooking. Who knew? I was amazed to see peas paired with squid, a combination that seemed absolutely bizarre at the time. But in fact this dish is considered a classic for the perfect way each ingredient complements the other. Adding pea purée as well as whole peas intensifies the pea flavor and gives a lovely celadon hue to the dish.

> 2 cups fresh or frozen peas
>
> 2 cups water
>
> 6 tablespoons unsalted butter
>
> 2 tablespoons olive oil
>
> 1 medium onion, peeled and finely chopped
>
> 2 pounds squid, cleaned and cut into rings (see page 10)
>
> 2 cups Arborio rice
>
> 1 cup dry white wine
>
> 6 to 7 cups combined White Fish Broth (page 79) and water
>
> Handful of chopped fresh Italian parsley
>
> Salt and freshly ground black pepper to taste

Cook 1 cup of the peas in the 2 cups water until very tender. In a food processor with a steel blade or in a food mill fitted with a medium disk, purée the cooked peas with all the cooking liquid. Set aside.

In a heavy 2-quart saucepan, melt 4 tablespoons of the butter with the oil. Add the onion, and cook slowly over low heat until softened and nearly tender. Add the squid rings and sauté briefly until they just begin to firm up. Add the rice and sauté, stirring constantly, until the grains of rice are coated with fat and make a clicking sound against the sides of the saucepan, about 1 to 2 minutes. Add the white wine and cook slowly over low heat, stirring constantly, until the wine is completely absorbed. Meanwhile, heat the broth and water until very hot. Add the pea purée and one ladleful of the hot liquid to the rice and cook over low heat, stirring frequently, until all the liquid is absorbed. Continue to add the hot liquid to the rice mixture one ladleful at a time, and cook over low heat, stirring frequently. Wait until all the liquid is absorbed each time before adding the next ladleful. Three quarters of the way through the cooking time (after about 15 minutes), add the 1 cup uncooked peas, the parsley, and salt and pepper to taste. When the rice is just tender, remove the saucepan from the heat and vigorously beat in the remaining 2 tablespoons of butter. Spoon the risotto into individual bowls and serve immediately.

Risotto with Mussels and Porcini

Risotto con Cozze e Porcini

Serves 4 to 6

In this risotto, the tomatoes and their juices become a sauce that is the primary cooking medium for the rice. The grains soak up the sweet juices and turn a deep red-orange. Peeking through the creamy rice, the glossy black mussels add the contrast of color and briny taste.

1 cup dried porcini mushrooms

3 tablespoons olive oil

4 tablespoons unsalted butter

1 small onion, peeled and chopped

4 garlic cloves, peeled and finely chopped

6 large ripe tomatoes, peeled, seeded, and chopped

2 cups Arborio rice

¼ cup red wine

2 cups combined White Fish Broth (page 79) and water

Handful of chopped fresh Italian parsley

Salt and freshly ground black pepper to taste

30 black mussels, cleaned (see page 8)

¾ cup freshly grated imported Parmesan cheese (optional)

Soak the porcini mushrooms in a small bowl of warm water for at least 20 minutes. Carefully drain the porcini, straining out any sand, and strain and reserve the soaking liquid.

In a heavy 2-quart saucepan, heat the oil and 2 tablespoons of the butter. Add the onion and cook, stirring frequently, until it is soft. Add the garlic and cook for 1 minute. Add the tomatoes and cook until they break down and form a sauce. Add the rice, and cook slowly, stirring constantly, over low heat until all the tomato sauce is absorbed. Add the wine to the rice and cook slowly over low heat, stirring constantly, until it is completely absorbed. Meanwhile, heat the broth and water until very hot. Add the reserved mushroom liquid and a ladleful of the broth and water to the rice and cook over low heat, stirring frequently. When all the liquid is absorbed, continue to add the hot broth and water one ladleful at a time, and cook over low heat, stirring frequently. Wait until all the liquid is absorbed each time before adding the next ladleful. About three quarters through the cooking time (after about 18 to 20 minutes), add the parsley and salt and pepper to taste. Stir in the mussels, and cover the pan to steam them. When the mussels are open and the rice is just tender, remove the saucepan from the heat and vigorously stir in the remaining 2 tablespoons butter and, if desired, the Parmesan cheese. Spoon the risotto into individual bowls and serve immediately.

RISOTTO WITH SHRIMP AND SUN-DRIED TOMATO PESTO

RISOTTO CON GAMBERI ALLE PUMATE

Serves 4 to 6

The shrimp in this dish are sautéed separately and served in a pool of their cooking juices atop the finished risotto. The presentation adds another dimension to the risotto. The intensity of the pure shrimp flavor against the creamy blandness of the rice is especially delicious.

For the risotto

> 3 tablespoons olive oil
>
> 4 tablespoons unsalted butter
>
> ½ medium onion, peeled and chopped
>
> 1 garlic clove, peeled and minced
>
> 6 Roma tomatoes, peeled, seeded, and chopped
>
> 2 cups Arborio rice
>
> 6 cups combined White Fish Broth (page 79) or chicken broth and water
>
> Salt and freshly ground black pepper to taste
>
> ¼ cup Sun-Dried Tomato Pesto (page 302)

For the shrimp

> 2 garlic cloves, peeled and minced
>
> 2 tablespoons olive oil
>
> 24 medium shrimp, peeled and deveined (see page 9)
>
> ½ cup white wine
>
> Small handful of chopped fresh Italian parsley
>
> 10 fresh basil leaves, chopped
>
> Salt and freshly ground black pepper to taste
>
> ¾ cup grated imported Parmesan cheese (optional)

In a heavy 2-quart saucepan, heat the oil and 2 tablespoons of the butter. Add the onion and cook, stirring frequently, until it is soft. Add the garlic and tomatoes and cook until the tomatoes begin to break down and form a sauce, about 10 minutes. Add the rice and cook, stirring constantly, until the rice absorbs all of the tomato juices. Meanwhile, heat the broth and water until very hot. Add 2 ladlesful of the hot broth and water to the rice and cook over low heat, stirring frequently. When all the liquid is absorbed, begin to add the hot broth and water to the rice one ladleful at a time, and cook over low heat, stirring frequently. Wait until all the liquid is absorbed each time before adding the next ladleful. About halfway through the cooking time (after about 15 minutes), add the sun-dried tomato pesto.

When the risotto is nearly done, prepare the shrimp topping: In a medium skillet, cook the garlic in the oil until it releases its characteristic aroma. Add the shrimp and cook over high heat for a minute or so. Add the wine and cook until the alcohol evaporates. Lower the heat and add the parsley, basil, and salt and pepper. Remove from the heat and set aside. When the rice is barely tender, remove the saucepan from the heat and vigorously stir in the remaining 2 tablespoons butter and, if desired, the Parmesan cheese. Spoon the risotto into individual bowls, top with the sautéed shrimp, and serve immediately.

RISOTTO WITH SCALLOPS AND TOMATO CREAM

RISOTTO ALLE CAPE SANTE

Serves 4 to 6

An elegant dish, rich with cream and the silken texture of barely cooked scallops. The scallops are sautéed separately and served bathed in a silky tomato sauce over the finished risotto.

For the scallops

2 tablespoons unsalted butter

2 tablespoons olive oil

2 shallots, peeled and minced

1 garlic clove, peeled and minced

3 Roma tomatoes, peeled, seeded, and chopped, or ¼ cup prepared tomato sauce

6 sprigs fresh thyme

⅓ cup white wine

1 pinch of saffron threads, soaked in 2 tablespoons hot water

For the risotto

2 tablespoons extra-virgin olive oil

4 tablespoons unsalted butter

½ medium onion, peeled and minced

2 cups Arborio rice

6 to 7 cups combined White Fish Broth (page 79) or chicken broth and water

20 sea scallops, tough side muscles removed

Grated zest of ½ lemon

½ cup cream

Salt and freshly ground black pepper to taste

To prepare the topping, heat the butter and oil in a medium skillet. Add the shallots and garlic and sauté until the shallots soften, about 2 minutes. Add the tomatoes or tomato sauce and thyme sprigs. Cook until the fresh tomatoes just begin to break down and form a sauce, or until the prepared sauce is heated through. Add the wine and saffron with its soaking liquid and cook until the liquid evaporates. Set aside.

To prepare the risotto, heat the oil and 2 tablespoons of the butter in a heavy 2-quart saucepan. Add the onion and cook, stirring frequently until it is soft. Add the rice and sauté, stirring constantly, until the grains of rice are coated with fat and make a clicking sound against the sides of the saucepan, about 1 to 2 minutes. Meanwhile, heat the broth and water until very hot. Add 2 ladlesful of the hot broth and water to the rice. When all the liquid is absorbed, continue to add the hot broth and water one ladleful at a time and cook over low heat, stirring frequently. Wait until all the liquid is absorbed each time before adding the next ladleful.

Just before the risotto is finished, reheat the tomato sauce. Add the scallops and lemon zest and cook over high heat for about 2 minutes. Add the cream and salt and pepper and simmer until the cream reduces slightly and the scallops are just cooked. Do not overcook the scallops! When the rice is barely tender, remove the saucepan from the heat and vigorously stir in the remaining 2 tablespoons butter. Spoon the risotto into individual shallow pasta bowls and top with the scallop mixture. Serve immediately.

Spicy Risotto with Grilled Artichokes and Squid

RISOTTO AI CARCIOFI E CALAMARI

Serves 4 to 6

A great way to use any combination of leftover grilled fish, seafood, or vegetables you might have on hand, this rustic dish is filled with the flavors of the grill.

½ pound calamari steaks

Oil for grilling

4 garlic cloves, peeled and minced

6 baby artichokes

1 lemon, cut in half

For the risotto

¼ cup extra-virgin olive oil

½ medium onion, peeled and chopped

1 garlic clove, peeled and minced

2 cups Arborio rice

¼ cup white wine

6 to 7 cups combined White Fish Broth (page 79) or chicken broth and water

Handful of chopped fresh Italian parsley

1 teaspoon red chile pepper flakes

Salt and freshly ground black pepper to taste

2 tablespoons olive oil or unsalted butter

Heat an outdoor charcoal grill or a ridged stovetop griddle until very hot. Rub two calamari steaks with oil and the minced garlic and grill quickly over high heat. Cut the grilled steaks into thin strips. Set aside.

Trim the artichokes of their tough outer leaves. Cut a slice off the stem end of each one and cut off the sharp points of the leaves. Cut the artichokes in half, rub with the lemon, and then with oil. Grill for about 3 to 5 minutes. Cut each grilled artichoke half lengthwise into eighths and set aside.

In a heavy-bottomed 2-quart saucepan, heat the extra-virgin oil. Add the onion and cook, stirring frequently, until it is soft. Add the garlic and cook until it releases its characteristic aroma. Add the rice, and sauté, stirring constantly, over low heat until the grains of rice are coated with fat and make a clicking sound against the sides of the saucepan, about 1 to 2 minutes. Add the wine and cook, stirring constantly, until it has been absorbed. Meanwhile, heat the broth and water until very hot. Add 2 ladlesful of the broth and water to the rice. When all the liquid is absorbed, continue to add the hot broth and water one ladleful at a time, and cook over low heat, stirring frequently. Wait until all the liquid is absorbed each time before adding the next ladleful. About 15 minutes into the cooking time, add the grilled calamari and artichokes, the parsley, and red pepper flakes, and season with salt and pepper. When the rice is barely tender, remove the saucepan from the heat and vigorously stir in the olive oil or butter. Spoon the risotto into individual bowls and serve immediately.

PINK RISOTTO WITH CRABMEAT
RISOTTO ROSA CON GRANCHE
Serves 4 to 6

The elegant richness of this delicate Venetian dish belies its quick preparation. The sumptuous result of the addition of crab to a risotto seems like cheating, it's so easy.

4 tablespoons unsalted butter

2 tablespoons extra-virgin olive oil

1 small onion, peeled and finely chopped

3 garlic cloves, peeled and minced

3 Roma tomatoes, peeled, seeded, and chopped, or ¼ cup prepared tomato sauce

2 cups Arborio rice

½ cup white wine

6 to 7 cups combined White Fish Broth (page 79) or chicken broth and water

1 pound lump crabmeat, picked over

Juice of ½ lemon

Handful of chopped fresh Italian parsley

¼ cup minced fresh chives

Salt and freshly ground black pepper to taste

In a heavy 2-quart saucepan, melt 2 tablespoons of the butter with the olive oil. Add the onion and cook slowly over low heat until it is tender. Add the garlic and cook briefly until it gives off its characteristic aroma. Add the tomatoes, or sauce, and cook over moderate heat until the fresh tomatoes give off their juice and begin to form a sauce, or until the prepared sauce is heated through. Add the rice and cook over low heat, stirring constantly, until the rice has absorbed all the juices of the tomatoes. Add the white wine and cook, stirring constantly, until it has been absorbed.

Meanwhile, heat the broth and water until very hot. Add 2 ladlesful of the broth and water to the rice and cook, stirring, over low heat. When all the liquid is absorbed, continue to add the hot broth and water to the rice mixture one ladleful at a time and cook over low heat, stirring frequently. Wait until all the liquid is absorbed each time before adding the next ladleful. After about 20 minutes of cooking time, add the crabmeat, lemon juice, parsley, and 2 tablespoons of the chives. Season with salt and pepper to taste. When the rice is just tender, remove from the heat and beat in the remaining 2 tablespoons butter. Spoon into individual shallow pasta bowls and serve immediately, garnished with the remaining 2 tablespoons chives.

CLAM RISOTTO WITH TOMATOES
RISOTTO ALLE POVERACCE
Serves 4 to 6

A dish with a loyal following at Trattoria Angeli. The rice is bathed in red wine, then allowed to absorb the pungent juices of the clams as they steam open in the rice.

2 tablespoons unsalted butter

¼ cup extra-virgin olive oil

1 small onion, peeled and finely chopped

4 garlic cloves, peeled and minced

4 Roma tomatoes, peeled, seeded, and chopped

2 cups Arborio rice

½ cup red wine

6 to 7 cups combined White Fish Broth (page 79) or chicken broth and water

24 soft-shell clams, cleaned (see page 7)

Handful of chopped fresh Italian parsley

Salt and freshly ground black pepper to taste

continued

In a heavy 2-quart saucepan, melt the butter with 2 tablespoons of the olive oil. Add the onion and cook over low heat until it is tender. Add the garlic and cook briefly until it gives off its characteristic aroma. Add the tomatoes and cook over moderate heat until they give off their juice and begin to form a sauce. Add the rice and cook over low heat, stirring constantly, until the rice has absorbed all the juices of the tomatoes. Add the red wine and cook slowly over low heat, stirring constantly, until it is completely absorbed.

Meanwhile, heat the broth and water until very hot. Add 2 ladlesful of the broth and water to the rice. When all the liquid is absorbed, continue to add the hot broth and water one ladleful at a time and cook over low heat, stirring frequently. Wait until all the liquid is absorbed each time before adding the next ladleful. After about 18 minutes of cooking time, add the clams and parsley, and cover the pan to steam the clams open. When the clams are open and the rice is just tender, remove the saucepan from the heat and vigorously stir in the remaining 2 tablespoons oil. Season with salt and pepper to taste. Spoon into individual shallow pasta bowls and serve immediately.

RISOTTO WITH OYSTERS AND CREAM
RISOTTO ALLE OSTRICHE
Serves 4 to 6

Oysters are dipped in fresh bread crumbs, sautéed in butter, and served atop creamy risotto for an unusual contrast of textures. I was once served sautéed oysters as an antipasto and when my *primo* of risotto arrived, I ended up finishing the oysters with the rice. This presentation was the logical next step.

24 oysters, cleaned (see page 9)

For the risotto
2 tablespoons unsalted butter
2 tablespoons extra-virgin olive oil
3 green onions, minced

1 garlic clove, peeled and minced

2 cups Arborio rice

½ cup white wine

6 to 7 cups combined White Fish Broth (page 79) or chicken broth and water

Handful of chopped fresh Italian parsley

¼ cup heavy cream

Salt and freshly ground black pepper to taste

3 eggs, beaten

Fresh bread crumbs for coating (see page 12)

Clarified butter (see page 14) or a combination of melted unsalted butter and oil for panfrying

Shuck the oysters and reserve the juices. Set aside.

In a heavy 2-quart saucepan, melt the butter with the extra-virgin olive oil. Add the green onions and cook slowly over low heat until wilted and tender. Add the garlic and cook briefly until it gives off its characteristic aroma. Add the rice, and sauté, stirring constantly, until the grains of rice are coated with fat and make a clicking sound against the sides of the saucepan, about 1 to 2 minutes. Add the wine and cook slowly, stirring constantly, until it is completely absorbed.

Meanwhile, heat the broth and water until very hot. Add 2 ladlesful of the broth and water to the rice. When all the liquid is absorbed, continue to add the hot broth and water to the rice mixture one ladleful at a time and cook over low heat, stirring frequently. Wait until all the liquid is absorbed each time before adding the next ladleful. After about 20 minutes of cooking time, add the reserved oyster juices and the parsley. When the rice is just tender, remove the saucepan from the heat and vigorously beat in the cream. Season with salt and pepper to taste.

Meanwhile, just before the risotto is ready, dip the oysters into the beaten eggs, then roll in the fresh bread crumbs. Pour enough clarified butter, or melted butter and oil, into a small skillet to cover the bottom by at least ¼ inch and heat until very hot. Add the breaded oysters and sauté until golden brown. Serve the risotto in individual shallow pasta bowls topped with the fried oysters.

Grilled and Broiled Fish

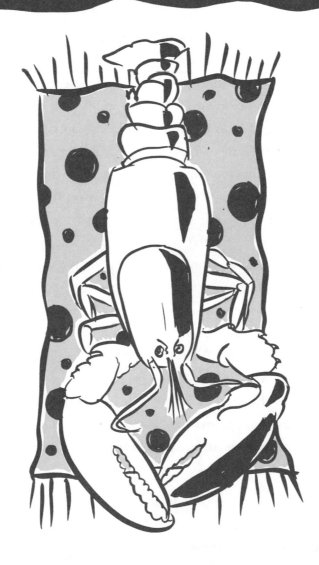

Grilling is probably the most fundamental technique of Italian fish cookery. Fresh fish needs little more than to be barely brushed with oil, grilled over a hot fire, and served with a dusting of salt and a spritz of lemon. Any additional ingredients are merely embellishments. Austere marinades that either bathe the fish in moisture and add flavor before cooking or are brushed on after the fish has come off the fire and immediately absorbed into the hot flesh add succulence and more flavor. Herb and vegetable pastes go one step beyond marinades. They tend to be more pungent and often help the delicate skin or flesh of the fish to form a protective crust.

Americans are often surprised when they see the thinness of the tuna and swordfish steaks served in Italian restaurants. We who are used to "bigger is better" are taken aback by these seemingly meager cuts. Unlike proponents of the new California cuisine, however, Italians prefer their fish cooked through, or medium. When you grill a thick piece of fish, the outer portions are invariably tough and dry by the time the center is cooked. By portioning fish into relatively thin slices, Italians are able to cook fish steaks quickly while retaining tenderness.

There are many grill accessories on the market that help even a sometime outdoor cook achieve outstanding results. The most essential are a good grill brush, a grill fork, and a spatula. A product that I now find indispensable has recently appeared in gourmet stores and catalogs. It is a simple grid of metal with narrower openings than those of the usual barbeque grate. The grid, which sits atop the regular grate, allows you to grill small items that would otherwise fall through. It makes grilling shrimp, scallops, and small vegetables a pleasure instead of an exercise in frustration. Always remember to preheat the additional grate along with the grill. Many people have great success with hinged fish holders. They come in sizes that accommodate fish both small and large. I use these holders mostly when cooking over an open fire with no grate. At home I prefer to cook directly on the grate of the grill. Try them, though, and see if you find them a comfortable way to cook.

It's a good idea to keep a squirt bottle filled with water near the grill to tame unwanted flare-ups. However, you can prevent flare-ups by allowing as much of the oily marinade as possible to drain off the fish before laying it on the grill.

Sometimes we are just not in the mood to grill—either the weather is not conducive to lighting a fire outside or we're simply too lazy—and nearly all of these recipes are as delicious broiled as grilled. Always remember to preheat the broiler for proper cooking.

SWORDFISH WITH LEMON-OREGANO BATH
PESCE SPADA AL SALMORIGLIO
Serves 4 to 6
TUNA   SHARK   MAHIMAHI

Whenever I open my faithful dog-eared copy of Marcella Hazan's *The Classic Italian Cookbook* and see the 1979 date on the inscription my mother wrote, I am reminded of the length of my fascination with this *cucina*. I still remember how intrigued I was by Marcella's savory idea of brushing a steaming hot fillet with a highly flavored yet simple marinade. In fact, I think I can point to her recipe for *salmoriglio* as a touchstone for the simplicity of my culinary palette.

Olive oil for grilling
1½ pounds swordfish, cut into ½-inch-thick steaks
Salt and freshly ground black pepper to taste
1 recipe Salmoriglio (page 290)
Lemon wedges

Heat a charcoal or gas grill, ridged stovetop griddle, or broiler until very hot. Lightly rub the grill with an oil-soaked towel to prevent the swordfish from sticking. Season the swordfish steaks with salt and pepper. Grill or broil until done, about 2 minutes on each side. Transfer to a serving platter and drench with the salmoriglio. Garnish with lemon wedges. Serve immediately.

WHOLE FISH BATHED IN WARMED HERBAL MARINADE

PESCE IN OLIO ALL'ERBE

Serves 4 to 6

SALMON   PERCH   SNAPPER

The success of this dish lies in the quality of the oil and the freshness of the herbs. Cook the herbs gently so that their flavors are brought out to the fullest. To avoid a conflagration, remember to allow as much oil as possible to drain off the fish before laying it on the grill. If you broil the fish, set the broiler pan on the middle rather than the highest shelf so that the fish cooks evenly.

½ cup olive oil

1½ tablespoons finely chopped fresh rosemary, plus additional whole sprigs for garnish

1½ tablespoons finely chopped fresh oregano

1½ tablespoons coarsely chopped fresh Italian parsley

1½ tablespoons finely chopped fresh basil

Salt and freshly ground black pepper to taste

1 large fish (approximately 4 pounds), scaled and cleaned (see page 5)

Lemon wedges

Heat the olive oil in a sauté pan over low heat. Add the chopped herbs and salt and pepper and sauté until the herbs release their flavor into the oil, about 2 to 3 minutes. Let cool completely.

Make 2 diagonal slashes on each side of the fish to allow it to absorb the marinade. Place the fish in a baking dish and pour the cooled herb oil over it. Let the fish marinate for at least 20 minutes.

Heat a charcoal or gas grill, ridged stovetop griddle, or broiler until very hot. Transfer the fish to the hot grill or broiler, reserving the marinade, and cook for approximately 10 minutes per inch of thickness, turning the fish once halfway through the cooking process. Transfer the fish to a serving dish. Reheat the reserved marinade and pour it over the fish. Garnish with lemon wedges and rosemary sprigs.

FISH IN GRAPE LEAVES
PESCE NELLE VIGNE
Serves 1 to 2

TILAPIA   SEA BASS   MULLET

This rustic presentation of a whole fish wrapped in grape leaves has come to be my signature fish dish at the Angeli restaurants. When cooked, the charred vine leaves turn khaki, and the fish head and tail peek out on both ends. Fillets of fish wrapped in grape leaves are also delicious, especially when the fillets are first slathered with an herb paste. They are easy to serve to a large group.

1 whole snapper (about 1½ pounds), scaled and cleaned
   (see page 5)
Salt and freshly ground black pepper to taste
3 lemon slices
2 garlic cloves, peeled and thinly sliced
2 sprigs fresh rosemary
Extra-virgin olive oil
1 small jar grape leaves (available in some supermarkets and in
   Middle Eastern grocery stores)

Prepare a fire in a charcoal grill. Rinse the fish under cold running water and pat dry. Season the fish cavity with salt and pepper. Stuff the fish with the lemon slices, sliced garlic, and rosemary sprigs. Drizzle a little olive oil inside the cavity. Wrap the fish in grape leaves, completely covering the body of the fish but leaving the head and tail exposed. (Use the remaining grape leaves to decorate the serving platter.) When the coals are medium-hot, brush the wrapped fish with olive oil, and place it on the grill. Cook for about 10 minutes, then turn carefully with a long spatula. Cook for another 10 minutes, or until done.

SWORDFISH WITH CAPERS, PARSLEY, AND OREGANO

PESCE SPADA ALL'ISOLA

Serves 4

TUNA   SHARK   MAHIMAHI

During my youthful traveling days I found myself in Sardinia after the traditional all-night voyage in steerage from Civitavecchia to Olbia. My friend and I hitched a ride to the beach and promptly passed out from exhaustion on the sand. Upon awakening on an empty, idyllic beach we discovered that we had fallen into the rich world of the Hotel Cala di Volpe. They were kind enough to feed two wide-eyed teenagers with this great dish before sending us on our way.

2 pounds swordfish, cut into steaks
¼ cup extra-virgin olive oil
Juice of 2 lemons
3 tablespoons chopped fresh oregano
3 tablespoons chopped fresh Italian parsley
1 tablespoon capers

Heat a charcoal or gas grill, ridged stovetop griddle, or broiler until very hot. Place the swordfish in a nonreactive pan large enough to hold it in one layer. Pour the oil and lemon juice over the fish, and sprinkle with the chopped herbs and capers. Set the fish aside for 5 to 10 minutes to absorb the flavors.

Place the fish on the grill or under the broiler and cook, turning once, until done, approximately 10 minutes per inch of thickness.

GRILLED TUNA SICILIAN STYLE

TONNO ALLA SICILIANA

Serves 4 to 6

SWORDFISH   SHARK   MAHIMAHI

The melted butter finish combines with the flavor of rosemary in another unique Sicilian marriage of flavors. Thanks to Anna Gossetti della Salda's *Le Recette Regionali* for the inspiration.

½ **cup white wine**

1 tablespoon finely chopped fresh rosemary, plus additional whole sprigs for garnish

2 garlic cloves, peeled and finely chopped

Salt and freshly ground black pepper to taste

4 to 6 6-ounce tuna steaks

Olive oil for grilling

2 tablespoons unsalted butter

6 anchovy fillets, rinsed and finely chopped

1 lemon, cut into wedges

Make a marinade by mixing together the wine, rosemary, garlic, and salt and pepper in a small bowl. Place the fish in one layer in a glass or enamel baking dish. Pour the marinade over the fish and set aside for at least 1 hour, turning occasionally. The fish can be refrigerated in the marinade for up to 24 hours.

Heat a charcoal or gas grill, ridged stovetop griddle, or broiler until very hot. Lightly rub the grill with an oil-soaked towel to prevent the fish from sticking. Transfer the fish steaks to the grill or broiler, reserving the marinade. Cook, basting with the reserved marinade, for approximately 3 minutes per side, or until the fish feels firm when pressed with your finger. Transfer the fish to individual plates or to a large serving platter. Melt the butter with the chopped anchovies and pour the mixture over the fish. Garnish with lemon wedges and sprigs of rosemary. Serve hot.

Tuna with Rosemary and White Wine

TONNO IN VINO BIANCO AL ROSMARINO

Serves 4 to 6

The tuna is prepared with a rosemary-garlic stuffing that is enhanced by the protection of a crunchy breading.

3 sprigs fresh rosemary, leaves only, finely minced, plus additional sprigs for garnish

3 garlic cloves, peeled and minced

1½ to 2 pounds tuna, cut into 1½-inch-thick steaks

1½ cups white wine

Olive oil for grilling

Salt and freshly ground black pepper to taste

2 to 3 large eggs, beaten

½ cup dried bread crumbs

Mix together the chopped rosemary and garlic. Cut several ¼-inch-wide incisions, about ½ inch deep, in the tuna steaks. Press the rosemary and garlic mixture into the slits. Arrange the tuna in a baking dish just large enough to hold the steaks in one layer. Pour the white wine over the steaks and marinate in the refrigerator for at least 2 hours, turning the fish once.

Heat a charcoal or gas grill, ridged stovetop griddle, or broiler until very hot. Lightly rub the grill with an oil-soaked towel to prevent the tuna from sticking. Remove the tuna from the marinade and let the excess marinade run off. Season with salt and pepper. Dip the tuna steaks first in the beaten eggs, then in the bread crumbs. Grill or broil the fish, turning once, until a golden crust has formed and the fish is cooked through, about 6 minutes. Transfer to a serving platter or individual plates. Garnish with rosemary sprigs, and serve immediately.

SWORDFISH WITH AN OREGANO CRUST

PESCE SPADA COPERTO CON ORIGANO

Serves 4 to 6

In a stone farmhouse with no electricity or refrigeration, a young Sicilian housewife treated me to this dish cooked on a stone grill. The scent of the charred dried oregano perfumed the air throughout the area, and we soon found ourselves hosting an impromptu party for the neighbors. In this dish, as with all Italian food, it is important to use Mediterranean or Greek oregano.

1½ to 2 pounds swordfish, cut into ½-inch-thick steaks
Salt and freshly ground black pepper to taste
Olive oil for grilling
½ cup dried oregano
Lemon wedges

Season the swordfish steaks with salt and pepper. Cover the bottom of a pie plate with olive oil. Spread the oregano in another pie plate. Dip each swordfish steak in the oil and then dredge in the oregano to coat.

Heat a charcoal or gas grill or a ridged stovetop griddle until very hot. Lightly rub the grill with an oil-soaked towel to prevent the swordfish from sticking. Grill the fish on both sides until just cooked, about 4 minutes in all. Transfer to a serving platter or individual plates and garnish with lemon wedges. Serve immediately.

PEPPER-CRUSTED TUNA STEAKS

TONNO AL PEPATO

Serves 4 to 6

SWORDFISH

One of my favorites: A Tuscan way with beef is borrowed for meaty tuna. A thin steak is dredged in coarse black pepper, grilled quickly so the fish remains rare, and served with flavored butter and lemon wedges.

> 1½ to 2 pounds tuna, cut into ½-inch-thick steaks
> Salt to taste
> Olive oil for grilling
> ½ cup coarsely ground black pepper
> 4 to 6 tablespoons Chive Butter (page 308)
> Lemon wedges

Season the tuna steaks with salt. Cover the bottom of a pie plate with olive oil. Spread the ground pepper in another pie plate. Dip each tuna steak in the oil and then dredge in the pepper to coat.

Heat a charcoal or gas grill or a ridged stovetop griddle until very hot. Lightly rub the grill with an oil-soaked towel to prevent the tuna from sticking. Grill the fish, turning once, until it is cooked, about 4 minutes in all. Transfer to a serving platter or to individual plates and top each tuna steak with a tablespoon of the butter. Serve immediately, accompanied with lemon wedges.

SAFFRON-TINTED TUNA WITH RAISINS

TONNO ALLO ZAFFERANO

Serves 4 to 6

SHARK   SWORDFISH

An extraordinary dish with the complexity of saffron, the sharpness of rosemary, the acidity of vinegar, and the sweetness of raisins. The ingredients combine to create an explosion of rustic elegance. The intense flavor of grilled raisins and the splashes of orange color as the saffron tints the fish entice everyone at the table.

1½ pounds tuna, cut into ½-inch-thick steaks
1 recipe Saffron-Raisin-Rosemary Marinade (page 292)
Salt and freshly ground black pepper to taste

Arrange the tuna in one layer in a nonreactive dish. Cover with the marinade. Marinate for at least 30 minutes, preferably longer, turning the fish once in the marinade. Heat a charcoal or gas grill, ridged stovetop griddle, or broiler until very hot. Lightly rub the grill with an oil-soaked towel to prevent the tuna from sticking. Remove the fish from the marinade, and pour the marinade into a small saucepan. Set the saucepan on the grill and heat the marinade while you grill the tuna. Season the tuna steaks with salt and pepper, and grill for about 2 minutes on each side, until done. Transfer to a serving platter and pour the heated marinade over the fish. Serve immediately.

TROUT RUBBED WITH RED PEPPER PASTE

TROTE AI PEPERONI

Serves 4 to 6

CATFISH   COHO SALMON

Small whole fish can be grilled either in the normal fashion or "open-face" as I do here. To enable you to open out the fish like a bear rug, you will have to make a slit in the belly the whole length of the fish and remove the backbone. It's a bit of extra work for you (or your fishmonger) but well worth it. The fish covers the whole plate and makes an impressive presentation.

4 to 6 whole small trout, scaled and cleaned (see page 5)
1 recipe Roasted Red Pepper Paste (page 303)
Olive oil for grilling
Lemon wedges
Sprigs of fresh basil

Open each trout so it lies flat. Rub the flesh and skin side of each fish with the red pepper paste. Refrigerate for at least 1 hour.

Heat a charcoal or gas grill, ridged stovetop griddle, or broiler until very hot. Lightly rub the grill with an oil-soaked towel to prevent the trout from sticking. Cook the trout flesh side down for 2 minutes. Turn the fish carefully with a spatula and cook for another 2 minutes, or until the fish are golden brown. Transfer to individual plates and garnish with lemon wedges and basil sprigs.

Tuna and Grilled Radicchio with Black Olive Paste

TONNO ALLA NUOVA CUCINA

Serves 4 to 6

SWORDFISH   BONITO

At Alberto Ciarla in Trastevere, the food is uncharacteristically *nuova cucina*. The interior is stark and glossy, and our fish was served on shiny black plates. The balsamic-oil marinade tames the bitterness of the radicchio. The fresh clean flavor of the rare tuna is sweetened by the grilled vegetable, and the olive paste adds a reinforcing salty sharpness.

3 large heads radicchio
Olive oil for grilling
¼ cup balsamic vinegar
¼ cup extra-virgin olive oil
Salt and freshly ground black pepper to taste
1½ to 2 pounds tuna, cut into ½-inch-thick steaks
¼ cup Pesto di Olive (page 298)
Lemon wedges

Cut out the core of each head of radicchio, and carefully remove the leaves. Heat a charcoal or gas grill, ridged stovetop griddle, or broiler until hot. Lightly brush the radicchio leaves with olive oil and place on the grill. Cook just until wilted. Transfer to a small bowl and toss with the vinegar and extra-virgin olive oil. Season with salt and pepper and let marinate for 30 minutes.

Make sure the grill is very hot, and lightly rub the grill with an oil-soaked towel to prevent the tuna from sticking. Season the fish steaks lightly with salt and pepper. Grill the fish on both sides until grill marks are clearly visible and the steaks are cooked, about 4 minutes in all. Arrange the marinated radicchio leaves on a serving platter or on individual plates. Place the tuna on top of the radicchio, drizzle with the Pesto di Olive, and garnish with lemon wedges. Serve immediately.

GRILLED STUFFED TUNA ROLLS

INVOLTINI DI TONNO

Serves 4 to 6

SWORDFISH   MAHIMAHI

A traditional specialty of Messina in Sicily, this is one of the most popular dishes presented in our regional Italian dinner series at Trattoria Angeli.

1½ to 2 pounds tuna in one piece
½ medium onion, peeled and finely chopped
2 celery stalks, finely chopped
1 garlic clove, peeled and minced
¼ cup olive oil
1 zucchini, chopped
Handful of chopped fresh Italian parsley
2 tablespoons capers
8 green olives, pitted and chopped
2 Roma tomatoes, peeled, seeded, and chopped
Juice of ½ lemon
Salt and freshly ground black pepper to taste
Oil for grilling
Lemon wedges

Slice the tuna into ¼-inch slices. Finely chop enough tuna to measure 1 cup. Set the remaining tuna slices aside.

In a large skillet, sauté the onion, celery, and garlic in the oil until wilted. Add the zucchini and sauté until the vegetables are soft. Add the 1 cup of chopped tuna and the parsley, and cook, stirring, over moderate heat until the tuna is completely cooked. Transfer to a small bowl. Add the capers, olives, tomatoes, lemon juice, and salt and pepper, and mix well.

Place a heaping tablespoon of the stuffing on the narrow edge of a slice of tuna. Roll up the fish and secure with toothpicks. Continue until all the pieces of tuna are stuffed and rolled. Brush the rolls with oil and season with salt and pepper to taste. Heat a charcoal or gas grill, ridged stovetop griddle, or broiler until moderately hot. Cook the tuna rolls, turning 2 or 3 times, until just cooked, no more than 3 or 4 minutes. Serve accompanied by lemon wedges.

WHOLE FISH INFUSED WITH CAPER, ONION, AND OREGANO PASTE

PESCE AL PESTO DI CAPPERI E ORIGANO

Serves 4 to 6

STRIPED BASS   GROUPER   YELLOWTAIL

The bite of capers and onions mixes with the earthy saltiness of anchovies to imbue the fish with an explosion of flavor. A friend recently gave me a case of capers unlike any I had ever seen. Packed in coarse salt from the volcanic island of Pantelleria, they are large and taste nearly like perfume. They give another dimension to this dish. For a refreshing alternative, try rubbing the fish with Mint Pesto (page 301).

1 large whole fish (approximately 4 pounds), scaled and cleaned (see page 5)
½ recipe Caper, Onion, and Oregano Paste (page 302)
Olive oil for grilling
Sprigs of fresh oregano
Lemon wedges

Cut a few ½-inch-deep incisions in the fish. Fill the incisions with some of the caper-onion-oregano paste. Rub the inside cavity of the fish with the remaining paste.

Heat a charcoal or gas grill, ridged stovetop griddle, or broiler until very hot. Lightly rub the grill with an oil-soaked towel to prevent the fish from sticking. Cook the fish for approximately 10 minutes per inch of thickness, turning the fish once halfway through the cooking process. Place on a serving dish. Garnish with oregano sprigs and lemon wedges, and serve immediately.

SKEWERS

I SPIEDINI

*I*mpaling food on the tip of a stick and holding it over a fire is one of the oldest cooking methods known to man. In Italy, this peasant cookery is elevated to an art form. Fresh herbs are threaded on the skewers along with tidbits of fish, shellfish, vegetables, cheese, or cured meats. The best spiedini combine lean and fat foods for the most tender result.

A skewer made of metal is the best tool because the food also cooks from the inside out as the metal conducts the heat. The result is food that cooks more quickly and is less likely to be dry. The alternative is the bamboo skewer, which comes in many sizes from short enough to hold just one biteful to nearly a foot in length. It's advisable to soak bamboo skewers in water overnight or for an hour or two at the very least so they don't burn on the grill. As you thread the food onto skewers, make sure the pieces are well secured so they don't rotate on the skewers when you turn them or fall into the flames below. Shrimp is best threaded with its tail tucked in so that the skewer pierces it in three places. Make sure that vegetables are tightly secured between two pieces of sturdy food that will hold them stable when they soften during cooking.

SHRIMP SKEWERS

SPIEDINI DI GAMBERONI

Serves 4 to 6

As the pancetta cooks, it bastes the shrimp with its fat, leaving them tender and subtly flavored with peppery meatiness. The garlicky bread crumb mixture adds the additional richness of butter and the extra bonus of the texture of crunchy bread crumbs.

    2 to 3 slices pancetta, cut ½ inch thick

    30 large shrimp, shelled and deveined (see page 9)

    1 bunch fresh sage

    2 sprigs fresh rosemary, leaves only, finely chopped, plus additional
        sprigs for garnish

    ½ cup extra-virgin olive oil

    4 garlic cloves, peeled and minced

    Olive oil for grilling

    ¼ pound unsalted butter

    ¼ cup dried bread crumbs

    Lemon wedges

If using bamboo skewers, soak them in water for at least 2 hours to prevent them from burning on the grill.

Cut the pancetta into 24 chunks just big enough to fit onto a skewer. Thread the shrimp, pancetta, and fresh sage leaves onto 6 skewers in that order, continuing until there are 5 shrimp per skewer. Reserve any remaining sage for garnish. Mix the rosemary, olive oil, and half the garlic together in a small bowl. Lay the skewers in a shallow baking dish or a pie plate, pour the herbed oil over, and let marinate for at least 1 hour.

Heat a charcoal or gas grill, ridged stovetop griddle, or broiler until very hot. Lightly rub the grill with an oil-soaked towel to prevent the shrimp from sticking. Melt the butter in a small pan. Remove from the heat and stir in the remaining garlic and the bread crumbs. Place the shrimp skewers on the grill. As they cook, drizzle with the melted butter and bread crumb mixture. Cook for approximately 2 minutes per side, or until the shrimp feels barely firm when pressed with your finger. Transfer the shrimp skewers to individual plates or a large serving platter. Garnish with lemon wedges and sprigs of sage and rosemary.

SKEWERED MUSSELS WITH POTATOES AND BREAD CRUMBS

SPIEDINI DI COZZE

Serves 4 to 6

These spiedini are a modern take on the traditional Pugliese pairing of mussels and potatoes. Here tender mussel meat and sturdy potato cubes are threaded onto skewers and then dredged in bread crumbs flavored with lemon zest and thyme. These also make great hors d'oeuvres to pass around at parties.

> 36 black mussels, cleaned (see page 8)
> ½ cup white wine
> 1 pound boiling potatoes, peeled
> ¼ cup olive oil
> 3 garlic cloves, peeled and minced
> 1 teaspoon finely chopped lemon zest
> 4 sprigs fresh thyme, leaves only, chopped very fine, plus additional sprigs for garnish
> ½ cup dried bread crumbs
> Olive oil for grilling
> 3 large eggs, beaten
> Lemon wedges

If using bamboo skewers, soak them in water for at least 2 hours to prevent them from burning on the grill.

In a large covered skillet over moderately high heat, steam the mussels with the white wine just until they open. Let cool slightly, then remove the meat from the shells and set aside. Cut the potatoes into approximately 1-inch dice, or the same size as the cooked mussels. Cook the potatoes in boiling salted water until they are barely tender; they should still be fairly firm. Drain and transfer to a bowl of ice water to stop the cooking process. When the potatoes are cool, drain again and pat dry with a towel. Thread the mussels and the potatoes alternately onto 12 skewers, with 3 mussels and 3 potato chunks on each skewer.

Heat the oil in a small pan over low heat until it is warm. Add the garlic, lemon zest, and chopped thyme and cook for 1 minute. Remove from the heat and cool for 5 minutes. Stir in the bread crumbs. Transfer to a pie plate.

Heat a charcoal or gas grill, ridged stovetop griddle, or broiler until very hot. Lightly rub the grill with an oil-soaked towel to prevent the skewers from sticking. Dredge the skewers first in the beaten eggs, then in the bread crumb mixture. Grill for about 2 minutes on each side. Transfer to a serving platter and garnish with thyme sprigs and lemon wedges.

Shrimp Skewers with Mozzarella on Polenta

SPIEDINI DI GAMBERI CON MOZZARELLA E POLENTA

Serves 4 to 6

Few dishes are as pretty as this one. The pink shrimp, melting creamy mozzarella, and charred herbs and mushrooms sit atop deep golden broiled polenta. Italians often oven-broil skewers. Simply find a pie plate or bread pan that allows the skewers to rest on the edges and place it in the middle of a very hot oven until browned and crisp.

1 pound fresh mozzarella

24 large shrimp, shelled and deveined (see page 9)

12 bay leaves

18 small mushrooms

1 recipe Polenta (page 147), poured into an oiled loaf pan, cooled, and cut into ½-inch-thick slices

Olive oil for broiling

¼ pound unsalted butter

¾ cup extra-virgin olive oil

4 sprigs fresh thyme, leaves only, chopped, plus additional sprigs for garnish

4 garlic cloves, peeled and minced

Lemon wedges

If using bamboo skewers, soak them in water for at least 2 hours to prevent them from burning.

Cut the mozzarella into 18 chunks just big enough to fit onto a skewer. Thread the shrimp, bay leaves, mushrooms, and mozzarella onto 6 skewers in the following order: shrimp, mozzarella, mushroom, shrimp, and so on; interweave 2 bay leaves per skewer, between the shrimp and mushrooms.

Preheat the broiler. Brush the polenta slices with olive oil and broil on both sides until slightly toasty. Transfer to a serving platter. Meanwhile, in a small sauté pan, melt the butter with the extra-virgin olive oil, chopped thyme, and garlic. Place the shrimp skewers under the broiler, and broil, basting them with the melted butter mixture, for approximately 2 minutes per side, or until the shrimp feels barely firm when pressed with your finger. Arrange the shrimp skewers on top of the polenta. Garnish with lemon wedges and sprigs of thyme.

Fennel-Marinated Fish Skewers
SPIEDINI DI PESCE AL FINOCCHIO

Serves 4 to 6

SOLE   ORANGE ROUGHY   PERCH

Americans rarely thread boneless fillets on skewers, but Italians often do. You can get away with skewering varieties of fish that might normally be too tender to lay directly on the grill because once threaded, the fillet will only touch the grill in a couple of places. So experiment with thin tender fillets. The licorice bite of fennel is one of my favorite Italian flavors. For this dish I first dust the fillets with a mixture of ground and whole fennel seeds and a pinch of hot pepper to add some kick.

1½ pounds cod fillet, cut into portions
1 tablespoons fennel seeds
2 teaspoons ground fennel
½ teaspoon red chile pepper flakes
½ cup extra-virgin olive oil
Salt to taste
Olive oil for grilling
Lemon wedges

If using bamboo skewers, soak them in water for at least 2 hours to prevent them from burning on the grill.

Place the fillets in a baking dish large enough to hold them without overlapping. Scatter the fennel seeds, ground fennel, and red chile pepper flakes over the fillets. Then drizzle the olive oil over them. Marinate in the refrigerator at least 2 hours. When ready to cook, thread each cod fillet onto a skewer. Season with salt.

Heat a charcoal or gas grill, ridged stovetop griddle, or broiler until very hot. Lightly rub the grill with an oil-soaked towel to prevent the skewers from sticking. Grill the skewers until the fish is cooked, about 3 minutes, depending on the thickness of the fillets. Transfer to a serving platter or individual plates and garnish with lemon wedges. Serve immediately.

SEA SCALLOPS DOUSED IN BLACK PEPPER VINAIGRETTE

CAPE SANTE PEPATO

Serves 4 to 6

The scallop is a Venetian specialty featured at the Rialto, still snug in its gorgeous pink shell. The famous Venetian fish market is a treat, with a selection of fish quite different from what you may find in other large Italian cities. Razor clams, crabs of varying kinds, edible barnacles create an indelible still life.

> 1½ pounds large sea scallops, tough side muscles removed
> Olive oil for grilling
> Juice of 2 lemons
> ½ recipe Black Pepper Dressing (page 297)
> Lemon wedges

Heat a charcoal or gas grill, ridged stovetop griddle, or broiler until very hot. If you wish, thread the scallops onto skewers for easier grilling. Lightly rub the grill with an oil-soaked towel to prevent the scallops from sticking. Grill the scallops for about 1 minute on each side, drizzling the lemon juice over them, until grill marks are clearly visible and the scallops are opaque. Transfer the scallops to a serving platter or individual plates and drizzle generously with the dressing. Garnish with lemon wedges. Serve immediately.

SEA SCALLOPS WITH BROWN BUTTER BREAD CRUMBS ON SOFT POLENTA

CAPE SANTE SULLA GRATICOLA CON POLENTA

Serves 4 to 6

The union of tender scallops and soft polenta results in a dish of incredible succulence. If you don't have the time to make the polenta from scratch, use one of the imported instant products now on the market. Instant polenta cooks in about five minutes and has an exceedingly tender texture.

> 8 tablespoons (1 stick) unsalted butter
> 4 garlic cloves, peeled and minced
> Handful of chopped fresh Italian parsley, plus additional whole sprigs for garnish
> ¼ cup dry bread crumbs
> Salt and freshly ground black pepper to taste
> 1 recipe soft Polenta (page 147)
> Olive oil for grilling
> 1½ pounds sea scallops, tough side muscles removed
> Lemon wedges

In a sauté pan, heat the butter over medium heat until it just begins to brown. Add the garlic and chopped parsley and cook until the mixture becomes golden brown. Remove from the heat and add the bread crumbs and salt and pepper. Stir until well mixed.

Prepare the polenta according to the recipe directions; begin cooking the scallops about 5 minutes before the polenta is done. (If using instant polenta, prepare it while the scallops are cooking.)

Heat a charcoal or gas grill, ridged stovetop griddle, or broiler until very hot. Lightly rub the grill with an oil-soaked towel to prevent the scallops from sticking. Grill or broil the scallops until they are opaque, basting frequently with the buttered bread crumb mixture. Pour the soft polenta into individual serving dishes. Top the polenta with the scallops. Garnish with lemon wedges and parsley sprigs.

Baked Fish

Few dishes are as easy to prepare as a baked casserole layered with herbs, tomatoes, potatoes, and boneless fish fillets or a simple baked whole fish or steak topped with herbs and other piquant ingredients moistened with wine, oil, or butter. The aroma wafting from the oven fills your home while you get your kitchen in order, set the table, and prepare for your family and friends to partake of the meal. Baking often makes for impressive yet simple dining. Most of the recipes I've included here are extremely easy and call for everyday ingredients. The few recipes that are more complex can easily be made in stages, often a day ahead, thus simplifying your life even more.

The word *casserole* fills many of us with dread as we recall 50s-era concoctions full of canned creamed soups, canned fish, potato chips, and canned fried onions. I was lucky enough to be subjected to these dishes only when visiting friends, and in fact thus thought they were quite exotic. Upon my return home, my mother, queen of the simple, fresh, and abundant table, would shake her head in amusement but would never give in to what she called ''ersatz,'' or artificial, food. Later on in life, when I was introduced to the simple, homey combinations of the Italian kitchen, I came to fully appreciate her drive for direct flavors. In my cooking classes, I often spend much of the lesson reminding my students that simplicity can be more elegant and satisfying than gratuitous complexity.

Small Fish Baked in an Herbal Marinade

PESCE IN MARINATURA

Serves 4 to 6

TILAPIA   TROUT   COHO SALMON   POMPANO

 classically simple dish in which fresh herbs add flavorful and visual dimensions.

4 to 6 small whole fish, scaled and cleaned (see page 5)

½ cup extra-virgin olive oil, plus extra for drizzling

Salt and freshly ground black pepper to taste

Juice of 1 lemon

1 cup white wine

2 handfuls of chopped fresh Italian parsley

1 bunch fresh thyme or oregano

4 to 6 garlic cloves, peeled and thinly sliced

2 lemons, cut in thin slices, plus lemon wedges for garnish

Lightly oil the fish inside and out with some of the olive oil. Rub with salt and pepper both inside and out. Make 2 small diagonal slashes on each side of the fish to absorb the marinade. To marinate the fish, place them side by side in a nonreactive baking pan just large enough to hold them in one layer. Pour the remaining oil, the lemon juice, and wine over the fish. Sprinkle half the chopped parsley over the fish, then arrange the sprigs of thyme or oregano over them. Cover with plastic wrap and refrigerate for about 1 hour.

Preheat the oven to 400°. Lift the fish out of the marinade and stuff them with the garlic and lemon slices. Return them to the baking pan with the marinade, laying the fish on top of the herbs. Drizzle with olive oil. Bake for about 10 minutes per inch of thickness. To serve, carefully remove the fish from the baking pan to a large serving platter. Discard the whole herbs. Spoon any accumulated cooking juices over the fish. Garnish with lemon wedges and the remaining chopped parsley.

BAKED WHOLE FISH WITH WINE AND BUTTER

PESCE IN BIANCO

Serves 4 to 6

STRIPED BASS   RED SNAPPER   SALMON   WHITEFISH

Few dishes express drama as effectively as a large whole fish garnished with herbs and lemon. This is an impressive dish with the woodsy richness of a rosemary-flavored butter.

1 large whole fish (approximately 4 pounds), scaled and cleaned (see page 5)

Salt and freshly ground black pepper to taste

2 garlic cloves, peeled and minced

½ recipe Garlic-Rosemary Butter (page 307)

2 handfuls of chopped fresh Italian parsley, plus a few sprigs for garnish

1 cup white wine

¼ cup White Fish Broth (page 79) (optional)

Lemon wedges

Preheat the oven to 400°. Season the inside cavity and outside of the fish with salt and pepper. If you wish, make 2 small diagonal slashes on each side of the fish. Rub the minced garlic all over the fish and place it in a flameproof baking pan just large enough to hold it. Generously dot the fish with the flavored butter and sprinkle half the parsley over it. Pour the wine, and the broth if desired, over the fish. Bake, uncovered, basting occasionally with the accumulated juices, until done, about 10 minutes per inch of thickness. The fish should be firm yet give a little to the touch. Transfer to a serving platter. Put the baking pan on the stove over high heat and simmer until the cooking juices reduce and thicken slightly. Pour the reduced sauce over the fish and scatter the remaining chopped parsley over. Serve immediately, garnished with lemon wedges and sprigs of parsley.

EMERALD SNAPPER

PESCE SMERALDA

Serves 4 to 6

STRIPED BASS   SALMON   WHITEFISH

In this recipe the dramatic presentation of a whole fish is made even more beautiful by drenching the snapper with a salsa verde, or traditional green sauce, when it comes out of the oven. The piquant sauce bathes the steaming fish with the biting flavors of garlic, anchovy, and capers, while the parsley acts as an emerald blanket.

1 large red snapper (approximately 4 pounds), scaled and cleaned (see page 5)

Salt and freshly ground black pepper to taste

4 garlic cloves, peeled and minced

1 cup white wine

¼ cup White Fish Broth (page 79) (optional)

2 handfuls of chopped fresh Italian parsley

2 tablespoons capers, coarsely chopped

2 to 4 anchovy fillets, minced

¼ cup fresh lemon juice

¾ cup extra-virgin olive oil

Lemon wedges

Preheat the oven to 400°. Season the inside cavity and outside of the fish with salt and pepper. Make 3 small diagonal slashes on each side of the fish. Rub half the minced garlic all over the fish. Place it in a baking pan just large enough to hold it. Pour the wine, and the broth if desired, over fish. Sprinkle half the parsley over the fish. Bake uncovered until done, about 10 minutes per inch of thickness. The fish should be firm yet give a little to the touch. Meanwhile, make a salsa verde by mixing together the remaining garlic and parsley, the capers, anchovies, lemon juice, oil, and salt and pepper to taste in a small bowl. When the fish is done, transfer it to a serving platter. Immediately pour the salsa verde over the fish and serve garnished with lemon wedges.

CRUNCHY BAKED TROUT WITH CAPER-ANCHOVY SAUCE

TROTE AI CAPPERI

Serves 4 to 6

COHO SALMON   TILAPIA   POMPANO

A dish that incorporates the best of two techniques—marinating and breading. Marinating enhances the natural briny trout flavor, and the breading seals in the flavors of the marinade and adds crunch to the final dish.

4 to 6 small whole trout, scaled and cleaned (see page 5)
1 recipe Caper-Anchovy Sauce (page 296)
1 cup dried coarse bread crumbs
Lemon wedges

To marinate the fish, place them side by side in a nonreactive pan just large enough to hold them in one layer and pour the sauce over them. Rub some of the sauce into the fish cavities. Cover with plastic wrap and marinate in the refrigerator for at least 1 hour.

Preheat the oven to 400°. Lift the fish out of the marinade, reserving the marinade. Roll each fish in the bread crumbs, and place side by side in a lightly oiled baking pan. Drizzle a bit of the reserved marinade over the fish. Bake until the bread crumbs are golden brown and the fish is cooked through, about 10 minutes per inch of thickness. Garnish with lemon wedges and serve.

Herbal Trout Wrapped in Prosciutto

TROTE AL PROSCIUTTO

Serves 4 to 6

COHO SALMON   TILAPIA   POMPANO

Although we often serve fish as an alternative to meat, the Italians have a long tradition of enriching simple fish dishes with cured meats, especially prosciutto. I take the idea of enrichment one step further by adding a chive-based compound butter to self-baste the fish.

4 to 6 small whole trout, scaled and cleaned (see page 5)
2 teaspoons dried thyme leaves
Salt and freshly ground black pepper to taste
½ recipe Chive Butter (page 308)
4 to 6 thin slices prosciutto
Lemon wedges
Sprigs of fresh thyme

Preheat the oven to 400°. Rub the trout inside and out with the thyme and salt and pepper. Put a nut of the butter inside each fish. Lay a slice of prosciutto vertically on a work surface and dot it with butter. Lay a fish across the prosciutto and wrap the prosciutto around the trout. Repeat with the remaining fish. Place the prosciutto-wrapped trout side by side in a lightly oiled baking pan. Dot with the remaining butter. Bake until done, about 10 minutes per inch of thickness. Arrange the baked fish on a large platter and garnish with lemon wedges and thyme sprigs. Serve immediately.

BAKED SMELTS WITH PANCETTA AND HERBS

PESCE SEMPLICE AL FORNO

Serves 4 to 6

In Italy *pesce azzurro,* or "blue fish," is a beloved fish category that encompasses anchovies and sardines. I often use smelts in traditional dishes that call for fresh sardines or anchovies when they are unavailable.

½ pound pancetta, diced

1 medium onion, peeled and diced

3 garlic cloves, peeled and minced

2 sprigs fresh rosemary, leaves only, minced

2 tablespoons extra-virgin olive oil

1½ pounds smelts, cleaned

1 cup white wine

Handful of chopped fresh Italian parsley

Salt and freshly ground black pepper to taste

Preheat the oven to 400°. Sauté the pancetta, onion, garlic, and rosemary in the olive oil until the pancetta renders its fat and the onion is soft. Place the smelts side by side in a lightly oiled baking dish. Top with the pancetta-onion mixture. Pour the wine over all and finish by sprinkling with the parsley and salt and pepper to taste. Cover with aluminum foil and bake for 10 minutes. Remove the foil, baste the fish with the accumulated juices, and bake uncovered for another 10 minutes. Serve hot or at room temperature.

WHOLE FISH IN THE STYLE OF LIVORNO
PESCE ALLA LIVORNESE
Serves 4 to 6

RED SNAPPER   PORGY   PERCH

A traditional dish that originated in the Jewish community of Livorno in Tuscany, this couldn't be simpler. Small whole fish are sautéed until golden, then baked in a simple tomato sauce. (Or braise the fish on top of the stove if you prefer.) This recipe is the stripped-down version still served in small seaside trattorie. You can easily enrich the sauce with wine and fish broth if you wish.

> **4 to 6 small whole fish, scaled and cleaned (see page 5)**
> **Flour for dredging**
> **½ cup extra-virgin olive oil, plus extra for drizzling**
> **2 celery stalks, thinly sliced**
> **4 to 6 garlic cloves, peeled and minced**
> **4 large ripe tomatoes or 8 Roma tomatoes, peeled, seeded, and chopped**
> **Generous handful of chopped fresh Italian parsley**
> **Salt and freshly ground black pepper or red chile pepper flakes to taste**

Preheat the oven to 400°. Dredge the fish in flour and shake off the excess. Heat the oil in a large skillet and sauté the fish until crusty and golden on both sides. Remove the fish to a platter, reserving the oil remaining in the skillet. To prepare the sauce, cook the celery in the same skillet over moderate heat until it wilts. Add the garlic and sauté for about 1 minute. Add the chopped tomatoes and parsley, and cook over moderate heat until the tomatoes break down and form a sauce. Add salt and black or red chile pepper to taste. Arrange the fish in a baking pan and pour the sauce over them. Drizzle with extra-virgin olive oil. Bake, covered, for about 15 to 20 minutes, or until the fish flakes off the bone. Serve immediately.

SWORDFISH BAKED WITH PINE NUTS AND CURRANTS

PESCE SPADA ALLA SICILIANA

Serves 4 to 6

TUNA   CORVINA   BONITO   MAHIMAHI

Combining swordfish with currants and pine nuts is a Sicilian signature. Green olives add an extra bit of sharpness to balance the raisins. This dish is easily adapted for other varieties of rich, oily fish.

2 onions, peeled and thinly sliced

3 tender inner celery stalks with leaves

¼ cup extra-virgin olive oil, plus extra for drizzling

3 garlic cloves, peeled and minced

¼ cup currants, plumped in hot water for 20 minutes and drained

2 tablespoons pine nuts

10 green olives, pitted and torn in half

Salt and freshly ground black pepper to taste

1½ to 2 pounds swordfish steaks

2 ripe tomatoes, sliced

Preheat the oven to 400°. In a sauté pan, cook the onion and celery in the olive oil over moderate heat until very soft and beginning to take on a bit of color. Add the garlic and sauté for 1 minute. Transfer to a bowl and let cool. Add the drained currants, pine nuts, and olives to the cooled onions, and season with salt and pepper.

Lay the swordfish steaks side by side in an oiled oven-to-table baking dish. Arrange the sliced tomatoes in an overlapping pattern over the swordfish. Season with salt and pepper. Spread the onion mixture over the tomato-topped swordfish. Drizzle extra olive oil on top. Cover with aluminum foil and bake for 15 minutes. Remove the foil and bake for an additional 10 minutes, or until the top layer of onions is a deep golden brown. Serve immediately.

Mackerel Layered with Fried Sweet Peppers and Potatoes

TEGAME DI PESCE E PEPERONI

Serves 4 to 6

A wonderfully hearty "bake," perfect for a one-dish summer supper, accompanied by a simple green salad.

3 large russet potatoes, peeled

4 red and/or yellow bell peppers, cored, seeds and ribs removed, and cut into strips

½ cup extra-virgin olive oil

1 bunch fresh basil, leaves only

2 tablespoons capers, rinsed

1½ to 2 pounds mackerel fillets

Salt and coarsely ground black pepper to taste

Parboil the potatoes in salted water until half cooked, about 12 minutes; drain. Peel the potatoes, cut them into 1-inch dice, and let cool to room temperature. While the potatoes are boiling, gently sauté the peppers in the olive oil until soft and sweet. Stir in the basil and capers, remove from the heat, and let cool to room temperature.

Preheat the oven to 400°. Oil an oven-to-table baking dish. Layer the potatoes in the bottom of the dish. Top with the fish fillets, then top with the peppers and their accumulated cooking juices. Season with salt and pepper. Bake, covered, for approximately 15 minutes. Uncover and bake for an additional 5 minutes, or until the fish is cooked and the potatoes and peppers are heated through.

Monkfish with Green Olives, Orange Zest, and Oregano

CODA DI ROSPO ALL'ARANCIA

Serves 4 to 6

STURGEON

The monkfish sold in fish shops is in fact just the tail of an unbelievably ugly animal, but few fish have as satisfying a taste and texture. I love to cook with monkfish. It has no bones and is unique in that it combines a meaty texture, sweet flavor, and pure white color. These similarities to the clawed crustacean are why it is often called the poor man's lobster. It's forgiving and versatile, as at home in baked dishes as in soups. In this recipe, the Sicilian flavors of oranges, oregano, and green olives are combined in a marinade. The delicate fish is briefly sautéed in a polenta crust before it is baked in the marinade.

1½ to 2 pounds monkfish fillet in one piece
Grated zest of 2 oranges
1¼ teaspoons dried oregano
½ cup dry white wine
2 tablespoons plus ¼ cup extra-virgin olive oil
⅓ cup all-purpose flour
¼ cup polenta or coarse cornmeal
Salt and freshly ground black pepper to taste
⅓ cup pitted green olives, cut in half lengthwise
½ cup White Fish Broth (page 79) or water
Orange wedges

Place the monkfish fillet in a nonreactive bowl or glass pie plate. Rub with the orange zest and oregano. Pour the wine and 2 tablespoons of the oil over the fish. Cover with plastic wrap, refrigerate, and let marinate for at least 1 hour.

Preheat the oven to 375°. Lift the fish out of the marinade, reserving the marinade, and blot dry. Mix the flour and polenta or cornmeal together. Season the monkfish with salt and pepper, roll in the flour mixture, and shake off excess.

In an ovenproof skillet or shallow flameproof casserole, heat the remaining ¼ cup olive oil over medium heat. When the oil is hot, carefully place the fish in the pan, and sear until crusty and golden on all sides. Remove the skillet or casserole from heat and add the reserved marinade, the olives, and fish broth or water. Bake until done, approximately 10 minutes per inch of thickness. Remove the fish from the oven and let rest for 5 minutes. Slice the monkfish at an angle starting at the tail end. Drizzle the olives and pan juices over the fish. Garnish with orange wedges and serve immediately.

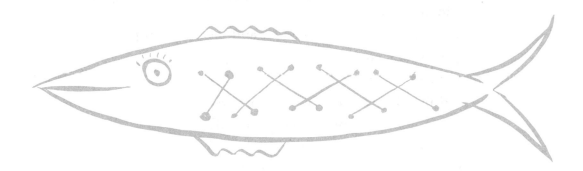

ROASTED MONKFISH WITH PIQUANT SWEET PEPPERS

CODA DI ROSPO AL FORNO CON PEPERONATA

Serves 4 to 6

The sweet-sour bite of the peperonata sets off the sweet flesh of the monkfish. The color contrast of the red peppers against the pure white of the fish is stunning.

1 large red onion, peeled and coarsely chopped

¼ cup olive oil, plus extra for drizzling

7 garlic cloves, peeled and cut into slivers

4 red bell peppers, cored, halved, seeded, and cut lengthwise into ½-inch strips

6 Roma tomatoes, peeled, seeded, and coarsely chopped

¼ cup balsamic vinegar

1 to 3 teaspoons sugar

Salt and freshly ground black pepper to taste

1½ to 2 pounds monkfish fillet in one piece

To make the peperonata, sauté the onion in the olive oil in a large skillet until it begins to soften. Add two thirds of the garlic and the peppers and cook slowly over low heat until the peppers are soft and very sweet. Add the tomatoes and cook over moderately high heat until they break down and form a sauce. Add the vinegar and just enough sugar to produce a subtle sweet-and-sour taste, and cook until the sugar dissolves. Taste for salt. Let cool to room temperature.

Preheat the oven to 400°. To prepare the fish, make a number of small incisions on both sides of the fillet and insert the remaining garlic slivers into them. Rub a drizzle of olive oil and salt and pepper to taste over the fish. Place in an oiled baking dish and roast until done, about 15 minutes. To serve, cut the monkfish into thick diagonal slices and present with the peperonata on the side.

Parchment-Baked Sea Bass Fillets with Black Olives
Branzino in Cartoccio
Serves 4 to 6

RED SNAPPER   HALIBUT   SALMON

To cook *in cartoccio,* meaning wrapped in paper or foil, is simple yet has the potential for endless variations. To vary the dish simply add any herb, or tomato, or lemon slices to the fish and carefully wrap your inspiration in foil. To keep the fillets moist, always include a liquid such as broth, wine, or lemon juice—or even a couple tablespoons of water.

2 pounds Chilean sea bass fillets, cut into serving portions
¼ cup Black Olive Paste (page 298)
1 small onion, peeled, halved, and thinly sliced
2 to 3 garlic cloves, peeled and thinly sliced
Salt and freshly ground black pepper or red chile pepper flakes to taste
Handful of chopped fresh Italian parsley
½ cup Moroccan olives, pitted
Extra-virgin olive oil for drizzling
½ to 1 cup White Fish Broth (page 79) (optional)
Lemon wedges

Preheat the oven to 450°. Rub the fillets with the olive paste. For each portion, cut aluminum foil or parchment paper into a rectangle twice as wide as the piece of fish.

Make a small bed of the onion slices on each piece of foil. Lay an olive-rubbed fillet on top of each mound of onions and top with the garlic slices, salt and black or red pepper, and parsley. Tuck a few olives around each fillet. Drizzle a bit of olive oil, and the fish broth if desired, over each fillet. Enclose the fish fillets by folding over and crimping the aluminum foil or parchment. Place the packets on a baking sheet and bake for 10 minutes per inch of thickness. Remove the foil packets from the oven and carefully open them. Lift the fillets to individual plates and top with the onions, olives, and accumulated cooking juices. Garnish with lemon wedges.

"Parchment"-Baked Whole Stuffed Fish
PESCE NEL ALUMINIO
Serves 4 to 6
TROUT   PERCH   GRAY MULLET

I saw this technique for the first time many years ago, during the first summer of my Italian studies in Perugia. A group of us went camping at Lake Trasimeno, one of the largest of all freshwater lakes in Italy. It is a tranquil place, and the lake still yields sweet-fleshed fish. There, around a campfire with almost no "batterie de cuisine," one of the students threw together a stuffing of leeks, aromatic vegetables, and bread crumbs along with a few ingredients she had brought along. She stuffed the freshwater fish we caught, wrapped it in foil, and tucked it into the dying embers of the fire. The succulent, aromatic treat that awaited us when we unwrapped the foil was memorable. This is the recipe.

1 large whole fish (approximately 4 pounds), scaled and cleaned (see page 5)

Salt and freshly ground black pepper to taste

1 bunch fresh thyme, plus additional sprigs for garnish

1 leek, washed and finely chopped

1 celery stalk, trimmed and minced

1 carrot, peeled and minced

2 garlic cloves, peeled and minced

¼ cup extra-virgin olive oil, plus extra for drizzling

1 cup homemade dried bread crumbs (see page 12)

1 lemon, cut into thin slices

1 cup dry white wine

¼ cup White Fish Broth (page 79) (optional)

2 handfuls of chopped fresh Italian parsley

Lemon wedges

Season the inside cavity and the outside of the fish with salt and pepper. Rub the fish inside and out with a few of the thyme sprigs. Make 3 small diagonal slashes on each side of the fish. To make the stuffing, sauté the leek, celery, carrot, and garlic in the oil until soft and tender. Add the bread crumbs and mix well. Taste for salt and pepper. Let the stuffing mixture cool to room temperature.

Preheat the oven to 400°. Carefully fill the fish cavity with the cooled stuffing. Close the cavity with toothpicks. Place the fish on a piece of heavy-duty aluminum foil twice its size, tucking half the remaining bunch of thyme under the fish, near the slashes. Lay the remaining thyme over the slashes on the top. Arrange the lemon slices in an overlapping pattern on top of the fish. Pour the wine, and the broth if desired, over the fish. Sprinkle half the parsley over all. Enclose the fish by folding over and crimping the aluminum foil. Place the package in a shallow baking pan just large enough to hold it and place in the oven. Bake for 10 minutes per inch of thickness. Remove the fish from the oven and carefully open the package. Lift the fish to a large serving platter, and remove the toothpicks. Spoon out the stuffing and transfer it to a small serving bowl. Pour the accumulated cooking juices over the fish and sprinkle on the remaining parsley. Serve garnished with lemon wedges and thyme sprigs.

ROASTED SCALLOPS AND GARLIC
CAPE SANTE AL FORNO
Serves 2

I first sampled these delicious, mouth-numbing scallops several years ago in Chioggia, near Venice. The brilliance of the stark presentation remained with me until finally I had to experiment myself. To do this dish justice you need plump sea scallops, an uncompromisingly good olive oil, a young head of garlic, and a *very* hot oven.

½ pound sea scallops, tough side muscles removed
10 to 20 garlic cloves, peeled
20 cherry tomatoes, stems removed, cut in half
1 tablespoon fresh thyme or oregano leaves
Salt and freshly ground black pepper to taste
Extra-virgin olive oil for drizzling
Lemon wedges
Olio Santo (page 15) for drizzling

Preheat the oven to 450°. Divide the scallops, garlic cloves, cherry tomatoes, and thyme or oregano between two individual-sized oven-to-table casseroles. Season with salt and pepper and liberally drizzle olive oil over all. Place on a rack in the upper third of the hot oven and roast just until the scallops are cooked through, about 10 minutes. Place the hot casseroles on plates to serve, and accompany with lemon wedges to spritz on the hot scallops and Olio Santo or additional extra-virgin olive oil for drizzling.

BAKED TILAPIA WITH MUSHROOMS AND BESCIAMELLA

TEGAME DE PESCE AL FORNO

Serves 4 to 6

SOLE   PLAICE   ORANGE ROUGHY

 creamy, buttery dish bubbling with the golden touch of Parmesan and the earthy taste of mushrooms.

4 tablespoons unsalted butter

2 tablespoons extra-virgin olive oil

¼ pound shiitake or portobello mushrooms, stems removed, thinly sliced

1 garlic clove, peeled and minced

10 fresh sage leaves

Salt and freshly ground black pepper to taste

1½ to 2 pounds tilapia fillets

Salt and freshly ground black pepper

2 cups Besciamella Sauce (page 289), cold or at room temperature

¼ cup freshly grated imported Parmesan cheese

Preheat the oven to 400°. Heat the butter and oil in a small skillet. Add the mushrooms, garlic, and sage and sauté over high heat just until the mushrooms are tender. Season with salt and pepper to taste. Remove from the pan and let cool to room temperature.

Season the fish fillets with salt and pepper and place them side by side in a buttered baking dish. Top the fish with the cooled mushrooms. Spoon the besciamella over the fillets and smooth with a spatula or the back of a spoon. Sprinkle with the Parmesan cheese. Bake for 20 to 25 minutes, until the fish flakes at the touch of a fork and the besciamella is lightly golden and bubbly.

HALIBUT TOPPED WITH RICH GARLIC MASHED POTATOES

PESCE AL PURÈ AGLIATA

Serves 4 to 6

SEA BASS COD

This dish is a take on *baccalà mantecato,* in which fresh cod is served with an intensely rich purée of salt cod and oil. When these already addictive mashed potatoes are combined with the besciamella, they become downright decadent.

1½ to 2 pounds halibut fillets, cut into serving portions
Salt and freshly ground black pepper to taste
2 teaspoons minced fresh rosemary or 10 fresh sage leaves, minced
1 recipe Garlicky Mashed Potatoes (page 279)
1 cup Besciamella Sauce (page 289)

Preheat the oven to 350°. Rub the fillets with salt and pepper and the rosemary or sage. Arrange the fillets side by side without crowding in a buttered baking dish or casserole. Mix the Garlicky Mashed Potatoes and the besciamella together. Adjust the seasoning if necessary. Spoon the potato mixture around and over the fish. Bake until the potatoes are golden brown, about 25 to 30 minutes. If the potato mixture begins to brown too quickly, cover the pan with aluminum foil. Serve immediately.

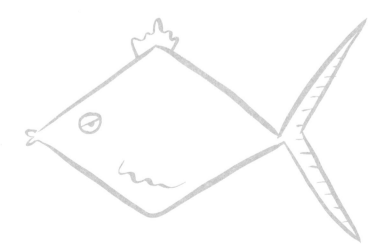

Sea Bass with Tomato and Red Wine Marinade

BRANZINO AL VINO ROSSO

Serves 4 to 6

HALIBUT   MONKFISH   MACKEREL

I like the unexpected touch of red wine combined with fish and find it works particularly well in dishes that include tomatoes. The shallot both deepens and sweetens the flavor of the dish.

2 pounds Chilean sea bass fillets

Salt and red chile pepper flakes to taste

2 garlic cloves, peeled and minced

Handful of chopped fresh Italian parsley

2 sprigs fresh oregano, leaves only, or 1 healthy pinch dried oregano

1 shallot, peeled and minced (optional)

2 tablespoons extra-virgin olive oil

½ cup red wine

1 ripe tomato, finely diced

Season the fillets with salt and red chile pepper to taste and place them side by side in an oiled baking dish. In a small bowl, mix together the garlic, parsley, oregano, shallot if using, olive oil, red wine, and diced tomato. Spoon over the fish. Cover the baking dish with plastic wrap and marinate for at least 1 hour in the refrigerator.

Preheat the oven to 400°. Bake the fillets for about 15 minutes, or until the fish is firm to the touch. Serve immediately.

TEGAME

The Italian words *tegame, tiella,* and *tortiera* all sound more country-simple and earthy than *casserole,* our lone English equivalent. The American casserole, so often made with canned ingredients, has been given such a bad rap that it is hard to overcome the negative connotations of the word, but what else do we call ingredients that are combined or layered in an ovenproof dish, and then baked? From time immemorial these simple combinations have saved the day for many a working woman (or man) by providing a savory, simple dinner of readily available ingredients.

LAYERED "BAKE" OF TUNA AND TOMATO
TONNO E POMODORO AL FORNO
Serves 4 to 6

SWORDFISH   MAHIMAHI

In this dish, sliced tomatoes are simply layered with herbs and tuna and baked, but the resultant juices alone are reason enough to try it. Serve with plenty of crusty bread and a *vino da tavola.*

2 cups fresh bread crumbs
2 tablespoons plus ½ cup extra-virgin olive oil
5 large ripe tomatoes, cored and cut into ½-inch slices
2 to 4 garlic cloves, peeled and thinly sliced
1½ to 2 pounds tuna steaks
6 anchovy fillets
Red chile pepper flakes to taste
1 bunch fresh oregano or 2 pinches of dried oregano

Preheat the oven to 400°. Combine the bread crumbs with 2 tablespoons of the oil in a small bowl. Set aside. Place a layer of half the tomatoes in an oiled ovenproof baking dish large enough to hold the tuna steaks in one layer. Top the tomatoes with the sliced garlic. Lay the tuna steaks over the tomatoes and top with the anchovy fillets, red chile pepper flakes to taste, and oregano. Layer the remaining slices of tomato over the fish and pour the remaining ½ cup oil over all. Bake for 10 minutes. Then sprinkle the bread crumbs over the casserole and continue baking until the fish is done and the bread crumbs are crunchy and golden brown. Serve immediately.

The "bakes" that follow are traditional *tegame* from Apulia, where humble ingredients, such as potatoes, rice, and bread crumbs, are characteristically combined in an artful way.

"BAKE" OF MUSSELS AND RICE
TIELLA DI COZZE E RISO
Serves 6 to 8

2 onions, peeled and thinly sliced
4 garlic cloves, peeled and minced
2 handfuls of chopped fresh Italian parsley
5 ripe tomatoes, thickly sliced
Extra-virgin olive oil for drizzling
1 cup grated Pecorino Romano cheese
Salt and freshly ground black pepper to taste
1½ cups rice, rinsed in cold water
1 pound mussels, steamed open and meat removed from shells
3 cups water and/or fish broth

Preheat the oven to 350°. Spread the onions in the bottom of an oiled casserole. Sprinkle half the garlic and parsley over them. Make a layer of half the tomatoes, drizzle with olive oil, and sprinkle with ½ cup of the Pecorino and salt and pepper to taste. Spread the rice over the cheese. Lay the mussels over the rice, then finish off with the remaining garlic, parsley, and tomatoes. Drizzle more oil over the casserole, and add the water and/or fish broth. Bake until the rice is tender, about 40 minutes. About 10 minutes before the casserole is done, sprinkle the remaining ½ cup Pecorino over the top and let cook until golden and crusty. Serve hot or at room temperature.

"Bake" of Mussels, Tomato, Potato, and Zucchini
TEGAME DI COZZE
Serves 6 to 8

 traditional "bake" from Puglia, where mussels and potatoes share a place on many serving platters.

2 large russet potatoes, peeled and thinly sliced

3 large onions, peeled and thinly sliced

48 mussels, steamed open and meat removed from shells

4 garlic cloves, peeled and minced

Handful of chopped fresh Italian parsley

1 bunch fresh basil, leaves only, chopped

4 ripe tomatoes, sliced

Extra-virgin olive oil for drizzling plus 2 tablespoons

1 cup grated Pecorino Romano cheese

Salt and freshly ground black pepper to taste

3 zucchini, cut into thin rounds

½ cup White Fish Broth (page 79) (optional)

1 cup fresh bread crumbs

Preheat the oven to 350°. Arrange the potatoes in an overlapping fashion on the bottom of an oiled casserole. Top the potatoes with half the onions, then distribute half the mussels over the onions. Sprinkle half the garlic, parsley, and basil over the mussels. Layer half the tomatoes over the herbs. Drizzle with olive oil and sprinkle with ½ cup of the Pecorino and salt and pepper to taste. Arrange the zucchini over the tomatoes, and top with the remaining onions and mussels. Finish with the remaining garlic, parsley, basil, tomatoes, and ½ cup Pecorino. Pour the fish broth over the top if desired, and drizzle more oil over the casserole. Bake until the vegetables are soft and the flavors marry—depending on your taste, anywhere from 40 minutes to more than an hour. Meanwhile, mix the bread crumbs with the 2 tablespoons olive oil. Ten minutes before you remove the dish from the oven, sprinkle the bread crumbs over the top. Serve hot or at room temperature.

Baked baccalà dishes are another traditional category of *tegame*. Baccalà, an inexpensive year-round staple, is soaked, cooked, boned, and flaked, then incorporated into casseroles with milk, potatoes, and greens.

"BAKE" OF BACCALÀ, POTATOES, AND MILK
TEGAME DI BACCALÀ
Serves 4 to 6

2 tablespoons extra-virgin olive oil plus ¼ cup

2 large onions, peeled, cut in half, and thinly sliced

6 garlic cloves, peeled and minced

20 fresh sage leaves, cut into julienne

Handful of chopped fresh Italian parsley

Salt and freshly ground black pepper to taste

5 russet potatoes, peeled and thinly sliced

1 large sprig fresh rosemary, leaves only, minced

2 pounds boned cooked baccalà (see page 6), fresh cod, or halibut fillets, flaked

1 cup water or fish broth

3 cups milk, plus more if necessary

1 cup fresh bread crumbs

2 tablespoons melted unsalted butter

Preheat the oven to 375°. Oil an ovenproof casserole with 2 tablespoons of the oil. Heat the remaining ¼ cup olive oil in a large skillet. Sauté the onions over moderate heat until soft, adding the garlic, sage, and parsley halfway through the cooking time. Spread half the onion mixture on the bottom of the oiled casserole. As you arrange the ingredients in layers, add salt and pepper to taste. Arrange half the potatoes over the onions, overlapping them slightly. Sprinkle the rosemary over the potatoes. Top with the cooked fish, and spread the remaining onion mixture over the fish. Arrange the remaining potatoes over the onions in an overlapping pattern. Add the water or broth and milk. Cover the casserole and bake for 50 minutes, adding additional milk if the casserole looks dry during cooking. Meanwhile, mix together the bread crumbs and melted butter. Sprinkle the bread crumbs on top of the casserole, and bake for an additional 10 minutes, or until the bread crumbs and potatoes are golden brown.

Baccalà Baked with Greens
BACCALÀ IN ZIMINIO
Serves 4 to 6

**2 pounds baccalà, center cut, soaked and cut into serving portions
(see page 6)**

Flour for dredging

¼ cup extra-virgin olive oil, plus extra for drizzling

1 onion, peeled and diced

4 celery stalks, diced

1 large carrot, peeled and diced

1 fennel bulb, trimmed, cored, and diced

6 garlic cloves, peeled and minced

1 pound spinach or chard, stems trimmed, washed, and chopped

½ pound mustard greens or arugula, washed and chopped

Generous handful of chopped fresh Italian parsley

4 bay leaves

½ cup white wine

1 cup water or fish broth

Preheat the oven to 375°. Pat the fish fillets dry with kitchen towels, then lightly dredge in flour and shake off the excess. Heat the ¼ cup oil in a skillet. Fry the floured fish fillets over high heat until they are barely golden, about 1 minute per side. Using a spatula, remove the fillets to a platter. Cook the onion, celery, carrot, and fennel in the oil remaining in the skillet until they are soft. Add the garlic and sauté for about 1 minute. Add all the greens, the herbs, wine, and water or broth, cover, and cook until the greens are wilted. Remove from the heat. Layer half the greens in the bottom of an oiled baking dish. Lay the sautéed fish fillets over the greens. Top with the remaining greens. Drizzle with a bit of oil. Bake until the fish is done, about 25 to 30 minutes.

BAKED LOBSTER IN SPICY TOMATO SAUCE
ARAGOSTA AL DIAVOLO
Serves 4

A quick and easy way to prepare lobster. I sometimes intentionally cook more lobster than I know I will need just for the leftovers, which are great on pasta. (Messy! Serve with plenty of napkins and bibs!)

2 live Maine lobsters, split in half lengthwise (see page 8)
4 cups cold Salsa all'Arrabiata (page 287)
1½ cups Garlicky Bread Crumbs (page 12)

Preheat the oven to 400°. Place the lobsters in an ovenproof baking dish, side by side, meat side up. Cover the lobsters with the arrabiata sauce. Cover the dish and bake for approximately 15 minutes, basting the lobsters once or twice. Sprinkle the bread crumbs over the lobsters and continue baking, uncovered, for 5 to 10 minutes, or until done. Remove the lobsters from the baking dish and place on a serving platter. Pour the sauce into a bowl for dipping.

STUFFED CALAMARI IN ROSEMARY SAUCE
CALAMARI RIPIENE ALLA SALSA DI ROSMARINO
Serves 4 to 6

My favorite way to cook squid is a dish that crosses all regional boundaries. The flavors of the squid itself and of the stuffing melt into the fresh tomato sauce. The addition of rosemary is my obsessive touch, which I borrowed from the rolling hills of the Tuscan countryside. On one of my early trips to Italy, I was treated to a weekend at the country home of an acquaintance. The gravel entrance was lined on both sides with the blue-green of traditional upright Tuscan rosemary. My addiction to the herb began with the *cucina* of that household, and there is no end in sight!

3 slices day-old country bread, crusts removed

Milk or water for soaking

1 small onion, peeled and finely chopped

1 celery stalk, peeled and minced

½ cup extra-virgin olive oil

3 garlic cloves, peeled and minced

1½ pounds cleaned squid, tentacles finely chopped (see page 10)

5 ripe tomatoes, peeled, seeded, and chopped

Small handful of chopped fresh Italian parsley

Salt and freshly ground black pepper to taste

½ cup dry white wine

10 fresh basil leaves, chopped

1 small sprig fresh rosemary

Preheat the oven to 325°. Soak the bread in milk or water until soft. Squeeze it dry, then chop it. Cook the onion and celery in ¼ cup of the olive oil until soft. Add one third of the garlic and the chopped squid tentacles, and sauté until the tentacles firm up. Transfer to a bowl and add the chopped bread, 1 tablespoon of the chopped tomatoes, half the parsley, and salt and pepper to taste. Mix thoroughly.

Stuff the squid sacs half full with the bread filling, leaving room for the stuffing to swell. Fasten the open ends with toothpicks. Heat the remaining ¼ cup olive oil in a medium skillet. Add the remaining garlic and sauté briefly. Add the remaining tomatoes, the white wine, basil, and rosemary, and cook over moderately high heat until the tomatoes begin to break down and form a sauce. Arrange the stuffed squid in a lightly oiled oven-to-table baking dish, and pour the tomato sauce over the squid. Bake until tender, approximately 1 hour. Serve hot.

Salmon Wrapped in Greens with Scented Butter

FILETTO ALLE FOGLIE

Serves 4 to 6

RED SNAPPER   WHITEFISH   HALIBUT

You can use any large lettuce or chard leaves in place of the romaine. The greens add their delicate flavor while allowing the basil butter to baste the fillets. The finished presentation is a striking plate of glossy light green bundles of pink salmon. This elegant dish is easy to prepare and serve for a large group.

1 large head romaine lettuce

8 to 12 tablespoons Basil Butter (page 309), at room temperature

1½ pounds salmon fillets, cut into serving portions

¾ cup white wine

Sprigs of fresh basil

Remove the outer, darker leaves from the romaine, and reserve the heart for another use. You will need 1 leaf for each fillet. Remove most of the stem from the lettuce leaves by cutting a narrow triangle out of the base of each one. Bring a medium saucepan of salted water to a boil. Add the lettuce leaves and blanch for 30 seconds. Drain the lettuce and immediately submerge in a bowl of ice water to stop the cooking process. When the leaves are cool, lay them on a towel and carefully pat dry.

Preheat the oven to 375°. Lay 1 lettuce leaf on a work surface. Spread approximately 1 tablespoon of the Basil Butter on one side of a salmon fillet and place it buttered side down in the center of the lettuce leaf. Spread 1 more tablespoon of the butter on the top of the fillet. Fold the leaf over so that the fish is wrapped in a neat packet, with the pink edges peeking out slightly. Repeat with the remaining fillets. Lay the fish packets side by side in an ovenproof baking dish large enough to hold all of them in one layer. Pour the wine over the packets. Bake until done, about 10 minutes per inch of thickness. Serve immediately on a serving platter or on individual dishes, spooning a little of the cooking juices over the top of each packet. Garnish with the basil sprigs.

Sautéed and Fried Fish

The recipes in this chapter fit into two categories: pan-sautéing (in oil or butter) and deep-frying. Few dishes are as delicious as a delicate fish fillet lightly dredged in bread crumbs and sautéed or deep-fried to a satisfying crunch.

When faced with a menu full of fish choices, I will nearly always order the simplest sautéed fillet. The aim of a sauté is to achieve a thin, crispy, yet yielding crust while retaining a moist, tender interior. To accomplish this, you need to cook with high heat and move quickly. Use a large nonstick pan, if necessary, that doesn't crowd the fillets. It is important to give the fillets enough room. Use clarified butter, the essential ingredient for achieving perfectly sautéed fish. When you clarify butter, you remove the solids and water, which are what cause butter to burn at high heat. When sautéing, I add enough fat to the pan so that there is a very thin coating that completely covers the bottom of the pan. Resist the temptation to turn fish more than once as you sauté it. The more you handle delicate fillets, the more likely they are to break apart. If you have access to a good restaurant supply or gourmet cookware shop, look for a flexible metal spatula. They have long slotted blades and the flexible metal allows you to negotiate easily between the edge of the pan and the fillet itself. A well-prepared fish sauté needs only a lemon wedge and a sprinkle of chopped parsley as enhancement.

To deep-fry properly you need a deep heavy saucepan. The heaviness of the pan helps it to maintain a consistent temperature as you add food to the pan. High sides accommodate the oil, which increases in volume when heated. A slotted spoon and paper towels are indispensable for draining. I recommend using olive oil for frying because of the flavor it imparts to the food, but by no means feel that you need to use extra-virgin. Pure olive oil is of sufficient quality for deep-frying. As with sautéing, it is important not to crowd the pan. Unlike sautéing, though, it is important to move the food frequently in the pan. Food should be well dried before it is dredged in flour, bread crumbs, or batter to ensure that the coating adheres. Adjust the heat according to what you are deep-frying: high and fast for small fish, shellfish, and thin-cut vegetables, more moderate for larger fish and dense vegetables like cauliflower to allow slower, even cooking. Use plenty of oil so the ingredients have enough room to circulate. As the ingredients cook, remove each piece separately as it is done.

SOLE IN BUTTERY BREAD CRUMBS

SOGLIOLA NELLA MOLLICA

Serves 4 to 6

SAND DABS   ORANGE ROUGHY   JOHN DORY

This classic preparation is still one of my very favorites and stands as edible proof that simplest is often best. Whisking the butter in at the end results in a delicate, creamy sauce that blends harmoniously with the fresh flavors of lemon and parsley. Quick, easy, and always satisfying.

1½ pounds sole fillets
Salt and freshly ground black pepper to taste
¾ cup milk
1 cup fresh bread crumbs
Clarified butter for sautéing (see page 14)
2 tablespoons unsalted butter or Chive Butter (page 308)
Handful of coarsely chopped fresh Italian parsley
Juice of 1 lemon
Lemon wedges

Season the fish fillets with salt and pepper. Dip in the milk and lift to let excess run off. Then dredge the fillets in the bread crumbs. Heat a thin layer of clarified butter in a nonstick sauté pan large enough to hold the fillets in one layer without crowding. When the butter is very hot but not smoking, add the fish fillets. Gently nudge the fish a bit with a flat metal spatula to prevent sticking, and cook for about 1 minute on each side. With the spatula, carefully transfer the fillets to serving plates or a platter. Lower the heat and add the 2 tablespoons butter and the parsley to the pan. Whisk the butter until it is smooth and creamy; do not overheat or the butter will break down and the sauce will separate. Add the lemon juice and adjust the seasoning. Immediately pour the sauce over the fish fillets. Garnish the fish with lemon wedges and serve immediately.

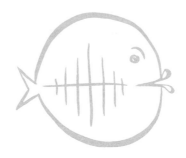

GOLDEN POLENTA-SAUTÉED TROUT
TROTE DORATO
Serves 2

An easy dish of trout dredged in polenta. The corn meal lends a beautiful color and crunchy texture to the fish.

2 small whole trout, cleaned and cut open with backbone removed (see page 5)
Salt and freshly ground black pepper to taste
4 sprigs fresh thyme, leaves only, finely chopped, plus additional sprigs for garnish
Polenta (page 147) or corn meal for dredging
Extra-virgin olive oil or clarified butter (see page 14) for sautéing
Lemon wedges

Season the trout with salt and pepper. Sprinkle with the chopped thyme. Dredge each fish in the corn meal to coat.

In a large cast-iron or nonstick pan, heat a thin layer of olive oil or clarified butter over medium-high heat until hot but not smoking. Place 1 trout in the pan flesh side down. Cook until a golden-brown crust forms, then turn the fish over. Continue cooking until the fish is done, about 3 minutes longer. Transfer the fish to a large platter and loosely cover with aluminum foil. Cook the second trout, adding more oil or butter to the pan, if necessary. Transfer to the platter and garnish the fish with lemon wedges and fresh thyme sprigs. Serve immediately.

Sautéed Salmon with Garlicky Wilted Greens

SALMONE ALLA VERDURA

Serves 4 to 6

Few foods are as beautiful as a peachy pink fillet of salmon. Although salmon is rarely served in Italy, I have found that pairing it with a traditional Italian sauté of garlic and greens makes for a delicious meal. Use any combination of greens you like. Arugula or mustard greens will be peppery, Swiss chard will be rich and earthy, and spinach will be light and clean.

> 1½ pounds salmon fillet, cut into portions
> Salt and freshly ground black pepper to taste
> ¼ cup extra-virgin olive oil, plus extra for sautéing
> ¼ cup white wine
> Juice of ½ lemon
> 2 garlic cloves, peeled and minced
> 1 pound greens

Season the salmon with salt and pepper. In a large nonstick pan, heat a thin layer of olive oil over medium heat until hot but not smoking. Add the salmon and sauté for about 2 to 3 minutes per side. Add the wine and lemon juice, and remove from heat. Transfer the salmon to a serving platter or individual serving dishes, and pour the pan juices over the fish. Heat the ¼ cup olive oil in another sauté pan. Add the garlic and greens, and cook, tossing constantly, just until wilted, about 1 minute. Serve the salmon accompanied with the sautéed greens.

SAUTÉED JOHN DORY WITH FENNEL

PESCE SAN PIETRO AL FINOCCHIO

Serves 4

SOLE   TILAPIA

Complex-tasting yet simple to make, this dish combines the light anise flavor of fennel with the freshness of mint and the bite of red chile pepper and vinegar.

¼ cup extra-virgin olive oil

1 large fennel bulb, trimmed, cored, and sliced

Clarified butter for sautéing (see page 14)

1½ pounds John Dory fillets

Salt and freshly ground black pepper to taste

Flour for dredging

10 fresh mint leaves, chopped

Small handful of chopped fresh Italian parsley

Pinch of red chile pepper flakes

¼ cup red wine vinegar

4 tablespoons unsalted butter or Fennel Butter (page 310)

Heat the olive oil in a sauté pan over medium heat. Add the fennel and cook until soft. Remove the fennel from the pan and keep warm. Heat a thin layer of clarified butter in a large nonstick sauté pan until very hot but not smoking. Sprinkle the fish fillets with salt and pepper to taste. Dredge the fillets in flour and shake off the excess. Gently lay the fillets in the pan, being careful not to splash the hot fat. Cook for approximately 2 minutes per side, turning the fish once. Carefully remove the fish to serving plates or a platter. Add the mint, parsley, red chile pepper flakes, and red wine vinegar to the pan and bring to a simmer. Lower the heat and whisk in the butter until smooth and creamy. Adjust the seasoning. Immediately pour the buttery pan juices over the fish fillets. Garnish the fish with the sautéed fennel.

GOLDEN HALIBUT AND GARLIC PURÉE
PESCE DORATO ALIATO

Serves 4 to 6

SEA BASS

An unusual element of this recipe is that the fish is cooked without any spices or herbs. This allows the pure, mild flavor of the fish to meld with the mellow, nutty flavor of the garlic purée. For a real treat, accompany this dish with mashed potatoes.

1½ pounds halibut fillet, cut into portions
Milk for soaking
About 40 cloves of Caramelized Garlic in its oil (see page 13)
Salt and freshly ground black pepper to taste
Flour for dredging
Olive oil for pan-frying
Lemon wedges

Soak the halibut fillets in milk for 30 minutes. Meanwhile, remove the garlic from its cooking oil using a slotted spoon and purée it in a food processor with a steel blade or in a blender, using as much of the oil as necessary to create a spreadable consistency. Add salt and pepper to taste.

Lift the fish out of the milk, dredge well in flour, shaking off the excess, and set aside on a plate. Pour enough oil in a large sauté pan to come about ¼ inch up the sides. Heat the oil until it is hot enough to sizzle a tiny piece of fish when you drop it in. Lay the floured fillets in the hot oil, being careful not to crowd the pan, and cook without disturbing the fish until a good crust forms. Carefully turn the fillets, using a spatula, and cook until golden on the second side. Transfer the fish to a serving platter. Mound the garlic purée in the center of the platter. Garnish with lemon wedges. Serve some of the purée with each fillet.

MONKFISH FROM PALERMO
CODA DI ROSPO AL PALERMITANO
Serves 4 to 6

The use of anchovies and rosemary is a characteristic of the cooking of the Sicilian city of Palermo. Monkfish is usually baked or braised because of its dense, meaty texture, but cutting it into thin medallions before sautéing allows it to become tender in no time.

2 eggs

3 tablespoons milk

½ cup fresh bread crumbs

5 anchovies, minced

2 sprigs fresh rosemary, leaves only, minced

1½ to 2 pounds monkfish fillet, cleaned and sliced into ½-inch-thick medallions

Salt and freshly ground black pepper to taste

Clarified butter for sautéing (see page 14)

Juice of 2 lemons

Handful of chopped fresh Italian parsley

Mix the eggs and milk in a shallow bowl. Combine the bread crumbs, anchovies, and rosemary in another shallow bowl. Season the fish with salt and pepper. Dip the monkfish medallions first in the eggs, and then in the bread crumbs, coating them completely. Set aside on a plate. In a large nonstick sauté pan, heat a thin layer of clarified butter over medium heat. When it is hot but not smoking, carefully place the monkfish in the pan. Cook until golden brown on both sides, turning the fish once with a spatula. Transfer to a serving platter. Drizzle with the lemon juice and sprinkle with the chopped parsley.

GARLICKY SHRIMP WITH BUTTER
SCAMPI ALL'AGLIO

Serves 4 to 6

This classic preparation is redolent with garlic and butter. Serve with a salad of arugula, radicchio, and Belgian endive dressed with balsamic vinegar and extra-virgin olive oil, and accompany with mountains of crusty bread to soak up the juices.

½ pound (2 sticks) unsalted butter

8 to 10 garlic cloves, peeled and minced

Red chile pepper flakes to taste

30 to 36 large tiger prawns, with heads if possible, deveined but shells left on (see page 9)

Generous handful of chopped fresh Italian parsley

Juice of 2 lemons

Salt to taste

Melt the butter in a large skillet. Add the garlic and red pepper flakes, and cook for just a few seconds. Add the prawns and cook, stirring frequently, until done, approximately 8 to 10 minutes. Add the parsley and lemon juice, and season with salt to taste. Serve immediately.

SHRIMP SAUTÉ WITH TOMATOES, ALMONDS, AND PINE NUTS

GAMBERI ALLA MANDORLE E PIGNOLI

Serves 4 to 6

A luxurious dish of Sicilian origin. The crunchiness of the nuts accentuates the firm bite of the sautéed shrimp.

2 tablespoons olive oil
¼ cup blanched slivered almonds
2 pounds medium shrimp, peeled and deveined (see page 9)
2 to 3 garlic cloves, peeled and minced
4 round tomatoes or 12 Roma tomatoes, coarsely chopped
5 fresh basil leaves, chopped
¼ cup white wine
Small handful of coarsely chopped fresh Italian parsley
¼ cup toasted pine nuts

Heat the olive oil in a medium sauté pan. Add the almonds and toast until slightly browned. Add the shrimp and sauté until slightly colored. Remove the shrimp from the pan and set aside. Add the garlic to the pan and cook until it releases its characteristic aroma. Add the tomatoes and basil, and cook until the tomatoes begin to break down and form a sauce. Add the white wine and cook until the mixture thickens. Return the shrimp to the sauce to reheat, and add the chopped parsley. Transfer to a serving platter or individual serving dishes. Garnish with the pine nuts. Serve immediately.

ORANGE-SCENTED SHRIMP WITH VERMOUTH AND FENNEL

GAMBERI ALL'ARANCIA E FINOCCHIO

Serves 4 to 6

Another Sicilian-inspired dish fragrant with the characteristic flavors of orange and fennel.

1 fennel bulb with feathery top

6 tablespoons extra-virgin olive oil

4 garlic cloves, peeled and minced

1 to 1½ pounds shrimp, peeled and deveined (see page 9)

10 fresh basil leaves, finely chopped

¼ cup finely chopped orange zest

½ cup dry vermouth

Juice of 1 lemon

Salt and freshly ground black pepper to taste

Remove the feathery fronds from the fennel bulb, reserving a large handful. Cut the fennel bulb in half lengthwise and remove the core. Cut into thin slices. Finely chops the reserved tops.

Heat the olive oil in a large sauté pan over medium heat. Add the sliced fennel and cook until softened, about 10 minutes. Add the garlic and cook for 1 minute. Add the shrimp, basil, chopped fennel tops, and orange zest and cook until the shrimp turn pink. Add the vermouth and lemon juice and cook for 1 minute over high heat. Season with salt and pepper to taste. Serve immediately.

SOUTHERN-STYLE CALAMARI SAUTÉ

CALAMARI DEL SUD

Serves 4 to 6

"Southern-style" here refers to Italy from Rome south to the tip of the boot, where pine nuts, raisins, and olives are often combined with tomatoes to create sweet and savory dishes. Squid can become very rubbery if sautéed for too long. The key to this dish is time. It requires only four minutes at most in the pan.

¼ cup extra-virgin olive oil

2 garlic cloves, peeled and minced

1½ to 2 pounds cleaned squid, body sacs cut into rings, and tentacles trimmed (see page 10)

Juice of ½ lemon

2 large tomatoes, chopped

Handful of Kalamata olives, pitted and cut lengthwise in quarters

¼ cup dark raisins, soaked in warm water to plump and drained

¼ cup toasted pine nuts

Salt and freshly ground black pepper to taste

Heat the olive oil in a large sauté pan over medium heat. Add the garlic and sauté until it releases its characteristic aroma. Add the squid, and sauté for 30 seconds. Add the lemon juice, tomatoes, olives, raisins, and pine nuts and cook just until heated through. Season with salt and pepper and serve immediately.

Soft-Shell Crabs with Herb Butter

MOLECHE CON BURRO ALL'ERBE

Serves 4 as an entrée or 8 as an appetizer

There are few foods that can compete with the unique flavor and texture of soft-shell crabs. A seasonal treat, they can easily become addictive. Your fishmonger can prepare the crabs for cooking, but remember that they are extremely perishable and must be used within four hours once cleaned. In this recipe, they are sautéed and served with an herbal butter and lemon.

> 8 large soft-shell crabs, prepared for cooking (see page 8)
> 6 eggs, beaten
> ¼ cup extra-virgin olive oil
> Salt and freshly ground black pepper to taste
> Flour for dredging
> Juice of 2 lemons
> 6 tablespoons Garlic-Rosemary Butter (page 307) or Basil Butter (page 309)
> Handful of chopped fresh Italian parsley
> Lemon wedges

Place the crabs in a baking dish and pour the beaten eggs over them. Refrigerate for 1 hour.

In a sauté pan, heat the olive oil over medium-high heat. Season the crabs with salt and pepper, dredge in flour, and gently pat to shake off excess flour. Sauté the crabs quickly on both sides just until a light golden crust forms. Transfer the crabs to a serving platter and reduce the heat under the pan to low. Add the lemon juice to the pan and scrape up any browned bits clinging to the bottom of the pan with a wooden spoon. Whisk in the herb butter until smooth and creamy. Adjust the seasoning. Immediately pour the buttery pan juices over the crabs. Garnish with chopped parsley and lemon wedges. Serve immediately.

MIXED SEAFOOD FRY

FRITTO MISTO

Serves 4 to 6

A dish to serve when you have a house full of friends or relatives to help. It is well worth the work involved. Huge platters of golden deep-fried nuggets accompanied by bowls of lemon wedges and any of the nontraditional dips I have suggested make for a beautiful, impressive, and decadent dinner. A classic fritto misto also often includes deep-fried mashed potato croquettes and fried stuffed rice croquettes; I would rather reserve my appetite for the gargantuan feast, but accompany with a simple green salad if you must. Serve with bottles of chilled light white wine, such as Pinot Grigio or Tocai Friulano.

Choose some or all of the following:

> **Firm-fleshed white fish fillets, such as cod, halibut, or baccalà, cut into small portions**
>
> **Whitebait or other very small whole fish**
>
> **Shrimp, preferably with heads, deveined but in the shell (see page 9)**
>
> **Sea scallops, tough side muscles removed**
>
> **Black mussels, steamed open and meat removed**
>
> **Squid, cleaned and cut into rings (see page 10)**
>
> **Soft-shell crabs, prepared for cooking (see page 8)**

Some vegetables that can be used are:

> **Zucchini, sliced into rounds or cut lengthwise into strips**
>
> **Zucchini flowers or Anchovy-Filled Zucchini Flowers (page 45)**
>
> **Artichoke hearts or bottoms, parboiled until just slightly underdone**
>
> **Cauliflower florets, parboiled until just slightly underdone**
>
> **Radicchio leaves**
>
> **Any fresh herb, particularly parsley, basil, and sage**

These can be used for coating the ingredients (see below):

Flour

Milk or half-and-half

Club Soda Batter (page 243)

Beer Batter (page 243)

Wine Herb Batter (page 242)

Beaten eggs

Dried bread crumbs

For Fish:

Dip in Club Soda Batter, Beer Batter, or Wine Herb Batter and fry.

For Shrimp and Scallops:

Flour and fry.

For Mussels:

Dip in flour, egg, then bread crumbs, and fry.

For Squid:

Soak in milk or half-and-half for at least 1 hour. Drain, dredge in flour, and fry.

For Vegetables:

Dip in Club Soda Batter or Wine Herb Batter and fry.

Fry the seafood in at least 4 inches of vegetable oil heated to 375°. Carefully drop the battered, floured, or crumbed seafood into the oil. The seafood should bubble immediately when immersed in oil. Do not overcrowd; fry only so much at one time that seafood can float freely in the oil without touching. Use a metal spoon to move the seafood around in the oil, turning it so that all surfaces become golden brown. When done, transfer with a slotted spoon to paper towels to drain.

Vegetables should be fried using the same method in clean oil at a slightly lower temperature, about 350°.

Serve with lemon wedges and any of the following:
Salsa all'Arrabiata (page 287)
Garlic-Herb Mayonnaise (page 305)
Red Pepper Mayonnaise (page 305)
Tomato-Herb Mayonnaise (page 304)

WINE HERB BATTER

Makes about 3 cups

The combination of wine and herbs gives this batter a more complex flavor. Very light.

1 extra-large egg
2 cups all-purpose flour
¾ cup white wine
1¼ cups water
Handful of finely chopped fresh Italian parsley
Handful of finely chopped fresh basil
Salt and freshly ground black pepper to taste

In a mixing bowl, beat the egg with a whisk. Whisk in the flour. Slowly pour in the wine and water, and beat until smooth. The batter should just coat the surface of a wooden spoon; if necessary, add additional water or flour to adjust the consistency. Fold in the herbs and season with salt and pepper to taste. Refrigerate for at least 30 minutes. Just before using, adjust the consistency if necessary with more water or flour.

CLUB SODA BATTER

Makes about 3 cups

This batter forms a crisp coating.

1 extra-large egg
2 cups all-purpose flour
2 cups club soda
Salt and freshly ground black pepper to taste

In a mixing bowl, beat the egg with a whisk. Whisk in the flour. Slowly pour in the club soda and beat until smooth. The batter should just coat the surface of a wooden spoon; if necessary, add additional club soda or flour to adjust the consistency. Season with salt and pepper to taste. Refrigerate for at least 30 minutes. Just before using, adjust the consistency if necessary with more club soda or flour.

BEER BATTER

Makes about 3 cups

This batter cooks quickly and results in a deep golden-colored coating.

2 extra-large eggs
2 cups all-purpose flour
¼ teaspoon cayenne pepper
1 cup beer
Salt to taste

In a mixing bowl, beat the eggs with a whisk. Whisk in the dry ingredients. Slowly pour in the beer and beat until smooth. The batter should just coat the surface of a wooden spoon; if necessary, add additional beer or flour to adjust the consistency. Season with salt to taste. Refrigerate for at least 30 minutes. Just before using, adjust the consistency if necessary with more beer or water or more flour.

Salads

The salads in this chapter encompass a complete repertoire, from the simplest assortment of raw seasonal vegetables accompanied by a hot "bath" of butter, garlic, and anchovies to the most elaborate of all Italian seafood salads, the Ligurian specialty known as *cappon magro,* a baroque pyramid of fish, seafood, and vegetables drowned in a green sauce. The term *salad* is used loosely, as many of these, such as the classic Insalata Frutti di Mare or the Salmon Salad with Parsley Dressing, are nearly pure seafood or fish and have absolutely no greens. Some are combinations of sautéed or grilled vegetables with fish and seafood used as lean garnishes, while others are primarily leafy green salads with the embellishment of shrimp, scallops, or fish.

BAGNA CAUDA

Makes 1 cup dipping sauce

The traditional Piemontese hot bath of oil, butter, garlic, and anchovy is a perfect wintry dip for any raw vegetables you choose. While cardoons and celery are the most traditional, I use everything dippable in season.

Clean, peel, and/or slice any or all of the following assortment of vegetables:

> Carrots
>
> Inner ribs of celery
>
> Fennel
>
> Asparagus
>
> Radicchio leaves
>
> Sweet bell peppers of any color
>
> Green onions
>
> Radishes

For the sauce

> ½ cup extra-virgin olive oil
>
> 4 large anchovy fillets, rinsed
>
> 3 garlic cloves, peeled and minced
>
> 8 tablespoons (1 stick) unsalted butter, softened
>
> Salt and freshly ground black pepper to taste

In a small saucepan, heat ¼ cup of the oil over low heat and sauté the anchovies until they fall apart. Add the remaining ¼ cup oil and the garlic and heat slowly for 5 minutes. Whisk in the softened butter bit by bit. Season with salt and pepper. Keep warm. Serve with the raw vegetables.

Classic Seafood Salad

INSALATA FRUTTI DI MARE

Serves 4 to 6

How could anyone experience Italy and not encounter this salad? This is the benchmark of all Italian seafood salads. Composed only of shellfish, it is luxuriously rich. I prefer to present it as is, with no adornments except for lemon wedges.

1 lemon, cut in half

4 bay leaves

1 teaspoon cracked black peppercorns

1 pound shrimp, peeled and deveined (see page 9)

1 pound squid, cleaned (see page 10)

½ pound bay or sea scallops, tough side muscles removed if necessary

2 cups white wine or water

½ cup pure olive oil

2 pounds mussels, cleaned (see page 8)

2 pounds soft-shell clams, cleaned (see page 7)

6 to 8 garlic cloves, peeled and cut in half

About 1 cup extra-virgin olive oil

½ cup fresh lemon juice, or more to taste

2 handfuls of chopped fresh Italian parsley

Salt and freshly ground black pepper to taste

Lemon wedges

In a large pot of boiling salted water seasoned with the cut lemon, bay leaves, and cracked peppercorns, blanch the shrimp, squid, and scallops separately just until done. As you remove each type of seafood from the cooking water, plunge it immediately into a bowl of iced water to stop the cooking process. Drain the cooled seafood, and combine the shrimp, squid, and scallops in a large bowl.

Combine 1 cup of the wine or water and ¼ cup of the pure olive oil in a large shallow pan. Add the mussels, cover, and steam open over high heat. Remove the mussels from the pan, and pick the meat out of the shells. Using the same method, steam the clams in the remaining 1 cup wine or water and ¼ cup pure olive oil. Pick the clam meat out of the shells. Combine the mussels and clams with the other shellfish. Add the remaining ingredients except lemon wedges and mix well. Cover with plastic wrap and marinate for at least 2 hours in the refrigerator. Remove the garlic before serving if desired. Adjust the seasonings, adding more lemon juice and olive oil if needed. Garnish with lemon wedges.

SAUTÉED SEAFOOD SALAD
INSALATA DI PESCE FRITTA
Serves 4 to 6

An unusual but authentic technique of first dredging and sautéing fish and then marinating it adds another layer of flavor and richness. Sage and rosemary are herbs not commonly used in salads, but because they are combined with the deeper flavors of fried seafood, their assertive flavors work well in this salad. This recipe is adapted from Anna Gosetti della Salda's *La Ricetta Regionali Italiane,* the bible of regional Italian cooking.

Olive oil for pan-frying

Flour for dredging

Salt and freshly ground black pepper to taste

1 pound shrimp, peeled and deveined (see page 9)

1 pound squid, cleaned and cut into rings (see page 10)

**½ pound bay or sea scallops, tough side muscles removed
if necessary**

½ pound swordfish, cut into cubes

2 pounds mussels, cleaned (see page 8)

1½ cups extra-virgin olive oil or more to taste

1 cup white wine or water

2 pounds soft-shell clams, cleaned (see page 7)

⅓ cup white wine vinegar

1 red onion, cut in half and very thinly sliced

4 to 6 garlic cloves, peeled and minced

2 handfuls of chopped fresh Italian parsley

1 tablespoon minced fresh rosemary leaves

1 bunch fresh sage, leaves only, chopped

Juice of 1 lemon, or more to taste

In a sauté pan, heat enough oil to come about ½ inch up the sides. Season the flour with salt and pepper. Dredge the shrimp in the flour and shake off the excess. Sauté until cooked through. Use a slotted spoon to transfer the shrimp to a nonreactive bowl. Repeat the dredging and sautéing with the squid, scallops, and then the swordfish. As they cook, add them to the shrimp.

Place the mussels, ¼ cup of the extra-virgin olive oil, and ½ cup of the wine or water in a shallow covered pan and steam over high heat. Remove the mussels from the pan and pick the meat out of the shells. Using the same method, cook the clams in another ¼ cup olive oil and the remaining ½ cup wine or water. Pick the clam meat out of the shells. Add the mussels and clams to the sautéed shellfish.

Add the remaining 1 cup olive oil and all the remaining ingredients to the seafood. Season with salt and pepper to taste, and mix well. Cover with plastic wrap and marinate for at least 2 hours in the refrigerator. Before serving, adjust the seasonings, adding more lemon juice and olive oil if needed.

Niçoise Salad
INSALATA NIZZA
Serves 4 to 6
CRABMEAT   SHRIMP   LOBSTER

ice, or Nizza in Italian, enjoys a culinary tradition based on regional ingredients similar to those of Liguria. My version of this famous dish uses the French idea of an arranged salad atop a small bed of greens. The showpieces are rare grilled tuna and blanched scallops, although I have made this salad using crab or lobster. Drizzled with the bracing green flavorful parsley dressing, the vegetables become a colorful mosaic, as striking to the eye as to the palate.

1 pound small red boiling potatoes

24 baby beets, greens removed with just a bit of stem left intact, or 2 large beets, greens removed

½ pound thin to medium asparagus

2 to 3 ears fresh corn, husked

1 lemon, cut in half

¾ pound bay scallops

1¼ pounds fresh Ahi tuna, cut into thick fillets

Olive oil for grilling

Salad greens for serving

4 to 6 hard-boiled eggs, peeled and cut in half lengthwise

1 cup Parsley Pesto Dressing (page 295)

24 fresh basil leaves

⅔ cup Niçoise or other small imported black olives

Paper-thin lemon slices

Cook the potatoes in boiling salted water until tender yet firm. Drain, cool, then cut in half and set aside. Cook the beets in boiling unsalted water until tender but still firm. Cool, then peel. If using baby beets, leave the beets whole; if using large beets, cut into 1-inch cubes. Set aside. Cut the asparagus in half and reserve the bottoms for another use (such as soup or stock). Cook in boiling salted water just until tender, about 2 minutes. Transfer immediately to a bowl of ice water to cool, then remove from the water and set aside. Cook the corn in boiling salted water until done. Cool, then shave the kernels off the cob, being careful to remove the kernels whole as much as possible; set aside.

Bring a medium saucepan of water to a boil. Add the juice from the lemon, and the lemon halves to the water. Add the scallops and cook until they become opaque, 30 seconds to 1 minute. Transfer to ice water to cool, then drain and set aside.

Prepare a fire in a charcoal grill. Brush the tuna lightly with olive oil and grill, turning once, until done. Cool slightly, then break into rough, irregular chunks.

Line individual plates with salad greens. Arrange the tuna, scallops, corn, asparagus, potatoes, hard-boiled eggs, and beets in a mosaic pattern on top of the greens. Drizzle with the dressing. Garnish with whole basil leaves, olives, and thin slices of lemon.

CAPPON MAGRO

Serves 4 to 6

WHITE FISH   CORVINA   SEA BASS

It seems to me that cappon magro is the Italian Riviera's answer to the French salade niçoise. The fish, seafood, and vegetables are each blanched and marinated separately, then arranged in a pyramid atop grilled country bread. A bread-thickened green sauce adorns the colorful structure. What I love most about this dish is the color contrast of the white blanched fish against the intense bright colors of the cabbage, carrots, and beans. A perfect dish for entertaining a special group of friends, as all the preparation can be done well in advance and the result is supremely impressive.

1 fennel bulb, trimmed, cored, and cut into julienne

⅓ pound haricots verts or small green beans, cleaned

3 large carrots, peeled and cut into julienne

24 baby beets, greens removed with just a bit of the stem left intact, or 2 large beets, greens removed

¼ head red cabbage, shredded

Red wine vinegar for marinating

Extra-virgin olive oil for marinating

Salt and freshly ground black pepper to taste

3 lemons

1 onion, peeled and cut in quarters

½ pound medium shrimp, peeled and deveined (see page 9)

½ pound sea scallops, tough side muscles removed and cut in halves or quarters

¾ pound red snapper fillet, cut into ¾-inch cubes

2 to 3 slices country bread, cut in half

1 cup Salsa Verde (page 288)

½ cup small imported black olives

1 small jar pickled pearl onions

Cook the fennel in boiling salted water until softened but still firm, about 2 minutes. With a slotted spoon or strainer, transfer the fennel to a bowl of ice water. Cool, drain, and transfer to a small container. In a large saucepan of boiling salted water, cook the haricots verts, carrots, and beets separately in the order specified. Cool each vegetable separately in ice water and transfer each to a separate container. Cook the cabbage in a large pot of boiling unsalted water for 2 minutes, then cool in ice water, drain, and transfer to a small container. Rub the skins off the beets. If using baby beets, leave them whole; if using large beets, cut them into julienne. Toss each vegetable separately with red wine vinegar, olive oil, and salt and pepper to taste. Set aside to marinate for at least 4 hours.

Meanwhile, bring a medium pot of salted water to the boil. Cut 1 of the lemons in half and squeeze the juice into the pot. Toss in the lemon halves and the quartered onion. Add the shrimp and cook just until the shrimp turn pink. With a slotted spoon or strainer, transfer to a bowl of ice water. Cool, drain, and transfer to a small bowl. Repeat with the scallops and then the fish. Toss the shrimp, scallops, and fish separately with olive oil, the juice from the remaining 2 lemons, and salt to taste. Marinate for at least 2 hours in the refrigerator.

To assemble the salad, grill or toast the sliced bread, and place on individual plates. Layer the marinated vegetables on top of the bread. Top with the seafood. Generously drizzle the salsa verde over the top. Garnish the plates with the olives and pickled onions.

"Green" Grilled Tuna Salad

TONNO VERDE ALL'INSALATA

Serves 4

Years ago, when I visited Sicily for the first time, I roamed the streets of Palermo for several days. This was a different Italy for me, at once rougher and more embellished than what I had seen before. When I came to rest in a small family-run trattoria at the edge of a deserted piazza, the *papa* in charge brought me this salad as I cooled my thirst with an icy aranciata. The grilled tuna is broken into chunks, tossed with a piquant green sauce of capers, green olives, and parsley, and served on torn and dressed escarole leaves.

One of the joys of gardening is being able to grow such beauties as the mild yet full-flavored *pieno cuore* escarole. Its blanched tender white center has just the right subtle touch of bitterness. The tough dark green outer leaves of the standard store-bought escarole will need to be removed—reserve them for flavoring a soup or pesto. This salad can be served warm or at room temperature.

For the dressing
> 2 garlic cloves, peeled
> ½ cup imported green olives, pitted
> 1 tablespoon capers
> 1 cup packed fresh Italian parsley leaves
> ⅓ cup white wine vinegar
> Juice of 1 lemon
> ⅔ cup extra-virgin olive oil

> 4 tuna steaks (about 1 to 1½ pounds)
> Salt and freshly ground black pepper to taste
> Extra-virgin olive oil

1 head escarole, trimmed and cut or torn into small pieces
Coarse salt to taste
Juice of ½ lemon
Lemon wedges
Black Moroccan olives

For the dressing, place the garlic, green olives, capers, parsley, vinegar, and lemon juice in a food processor and process for 30 seconds. With the machine running, pour in the olive oil in a slow stream. Set aside.

Prepare a fire in a charcoal grill or heat a ridged cast-iron stovetop griddle or the broiler. Sprinkle the tuna steaks with salt and pepper and brush with olive oil. Grill or broil close to the heat source until done, about 2 minutes on each side. Set aside until just cool enough to handle. Break up the warm tuna into irregular chunks, place in a bowl, and pour half the dressing over it. Toss until well coated.

In another bowl, toss the escarole with a sprinkle of coarse salt, a generous drizzle of olive oil, and the lemon juice. Make a bed of escarole on each plate and place a mound of the tuna salad in the center. Drizzle the remaining dressing onto the escarole, and garnish with lemon wedges and black olives.

Rice Salad with Seafood

INSALATA DI RISO ALLA MARINARA

Serves 6 to 8

CANNED TUNA   LUMP CRABMEAT

*I*talians traditionally toss bits of leftover fish, cheese, or vegetables into cooked rice and drizzle it with olive oil and vinegar. There is an infinite number of appealing rice salads to be made combining ingredients from the sea and land. Try adding finely chopped cucumbers, sweet pepper strips, grilled corn, and, of course, herbs of any kind.

2 cups long-grain white rice

¼ pound very small cooked shrimp

¼ pound cooked squid

¼ pound cooked bay scallops

1 dozen cooked mussels (meat only)

1 dozen cooked soft-shell clams (meat only)

4 garlic cloves, peeled and cut in half

2 celery stalks, peeled and thinly sliced

¼ small red or yellow onion, peeled and minced

1 carrot, peeled and finely chopped

Handful of chopped fresh Italian parsley

10 fresh basil leaves, torn

½ cup extra-virgin olive oil

Juice of 1 lemon

¼ cup white wine vinegar

Salt and freshly ground black pepper to taste

Cook the rice in abundant boiling salted water until al dente. Drain well. Place the rice in a bowl and add all the remaining ingredients. Toss to mix well and adjust the seasoning if necessary.

QUICK SALAD OF WHITE BEANS AND TUNA
INSALATINA DI TONNO E FAGIOLI

Serves 4

The Italian tradition of combining creamy white cannellini beans with tuna seems to transcend regional boundaries. Many home cooks prepare variations as a healthful dish to throw together at a moment's notice. It also shows up on elaborate antipasti displays in grand ristoranti. The home version usually uses canned tuna—the restaurants, of course, use the fresh. I find it the perfect way to turn a bit of leftover grilled tuna into a new dish.

¼ small red onion, peeled and finely diced
Small handful of chopped fresh Italian parsley
Juice of 1 lemon
½ cup extra-virgin olive oil
Salt to taste
Pinch of red chile pepper flakes or coarsely ground black pepper
1 15-ounce can cannellini or other white beans, drained
2 6½-ounce cans albacore tuna in water, drained and flaked

In a mixing bowl, combine all the ingredients. Transfer to a serving bowl. Serve with bread and a simple green salad.

TUNA AND POTATO SALAD
INSALATA DI TONNO E PATATE
Serves 4 to 6

Another popular salad often seen on antipasti buffets. I make two versions of this salad, one bound with extra-virgin olive oil, the other with anchovy mayonnaise. The humble potato adds its bland, comforting texture to temper the strong taste of the canned tuna. The peppers, rosemary, and oregano are nontraditional additions that elevate this easy-to-make classic.

> 2 large red bell peppers
> 2 pounds small white or red new potatoes
> 2 6½-ounce cans tuna in water, drained and flaked
> 2 sprigs fresh rosemary, leaves only, minced
> 1 sprig fresh oregano, chopped fine
> Handful of coarsely chopped fresh Italian parsley
> Extra-virgin olive oil or Anchovy Mayonnaise (page 306)
> Salt and freshly ground black pepper to taste

Roast the red peppers over a gas flame or in a hot oven, turning occasionally until blackened on the outside. Place in a bag, seal the bag, and let the peppers steam for at least 15 minutes. Remove the peppers from the bag and rinse off the skin and seeds under cold running water. Cut the peppers into thin strips.

Cook the potatoes in boiling salted water just until tender when pierced with a knife; do not overcook. Drain and cut into quarters.

Combine the potatoes, peppers, tuna, and herbs in a bowl. Add enough olive oil or anchovy mayonnaise to hold the mixture together, and mix well. Season with salt and pepper to taste. Transfer to a serving bowl and serve.

INSALATA LATTERIA

Serves 4

Sometimes it's a trip to a foreign land that makes one appreciate the obvious. At La Latteria, a Milanese cheese shop *cum* public kitchen with chairs and tiny tables, I tasted the Italian version of chef's salad and couldn't get enough. While my pregnant friend tucked into her *pure ai formaggi fusi,* mashed potatoes topped with a symphony of melted cheeses, I savored my healthful choice.

½ **head iceberg lettuce, washed and torn into bite-sized pieces**

¼ **cup thickly shredded red cabbage**

1 **large carrot, grated**

Coarse salt to taste

½ **cup extra-virgin olive oil**

Juice of 2 lemons

3 **tomatoes, cut into wedges**

1 6½-**ounce can tuna packed in water, drained and flaked**

4 **hard-boiled eggs, peeled and cut in half lengthwise**

¼ **pound Swiss cheese, cut into thick strips**

¼ **pound fresh mozzarella cheese, preferably** *bocconcini* **(tiny balls of cheese)**

Moroccan oil-cured olives

Lemon wedges

Place the lettuce in a large salad bowl. Add the cabbage and carrot. Add coarse salt to taste, dress with the olive oil and lemon juice, and toss. Arrange the tomatoes, tuna, eggs, Swiss cheese, mozzarella, and olives over the salad, keeping each ingredient separate. Garnish with lemon wedges.

SALMON SALAD WITH PARSLEY DRESSING

INSALATA DI SALMONE

Serves 4 to 6

lthough the recipe calls for oven-poaching the salmon, this salad is equally delicious made with broiled or grilled fish.

1 pound salmon fillet, cut on the diagonal into 4 to 6 medallions
Salt to taste
White wine and water for poaching

For the dressing

    2 shallots, peeled

    1 cup firmly packed fresh Italian parsley leaves, plus whole sprigs for garnish

    ⅓ cup champagne vinegar

    1 cup extra-virgin olive oil

    Juice of ½ lemon

    Salt and freshly ground black pepper to taste

    2 medium cucumbers, peeled

    1 fennel bulb, trimmed

    Lemon wedges

Preheat the oven to 450°. Lightly oil a shallow roasting pan. Lightly season the salmon medallions with salt and place them in the pan. Add enough wine and water to come ¼ inch up the sides of the pan. Cover with parchment, wax paper, or oiled aluminum foil cut to fit inside the pan. Place in the oven and poach until done, 7 to 10 minutes per inch of thickness. Remove from the oven and let the fish cool in the pan.

Place the shallots, parsley, and champagne vinegar in a food processor fitted with a steel blade. Process until puréed. With the machine running, slowly add the olive oil. Add the lemon juice and season with salt and pepper to taste.

Cut the cucumbers in half lengthwise, and carefully remove the seeds with a spoon or melon baller. Cut the cucumbers on the diagonal into very thin slices. Cut the fennel bulb in half lengthwise. Place the two halves cut side down on the cutting board for stability and slice crosswise into very thin slices.

To assemble the salad, generously scatter the cucumber and fennel slices across individual salad plates. Top each serving with a salmon medallion, and drizzle the dressing over the top. Garnish with lemon wedges and parsley sprigs.

COD SALAD WITH ROASTED PEPPERS

MERLUZZO COI PEPERONI

Serves 4

The white poached cod is a beautiful contrast to the roasted red peppers. In fact, with the addition of spinach, this salad looks like the Italian flag: red, white, and green.

5 red bell peppers

½ cup extra-virgin olive oil

2 tablespoons capers

12 fresh basil leaves, julienned

Salt and freshly ground black pepper to taste

1 pound cod fillet, cut into 8 medallions

white wine and water for poaching

2 garlic cloves, peeled and thinly sliced

1 bunch spinach, washed and stems trimmed

Roast the red peppers under the broiler or over a gas flame, turning occasionally, until slightly charred on the outside. Place in a bag, seal, and let steam for 15 minutes. Remove from the bag and rinse off the skins and seeds under cold running water. Cut the peppers into thin strips. In a bowl, combine the peppers, ¼ cup of the olive oil, the capers, basil, and salt and pepper to taste and set aside to marinate for at least 2 hours.

Preheat the oven to 450°. Lightly oil a shallow roasting pan. Lightly season the cod medallions with salt and place them in the pan. Add enough wine and water to come ¼ inch up the sides of the pan. Cover with parchment, wax paper, or oiled aluminum foil cut to fit inside the pan. Poach the fish in the oven until done, 7 to 10 minutes per inch of thickness. Transfer to a platter to cool.

In a small skillet, heat the remaining ¼ cup oil over medium heat. Add the garlic and cook until barely golden. Turn the heat to low, add the spinach, and cook until barely wilted. Transfer to a serving platter.

To serve, top the spinach with the fish medallions. Place the roasted peppers on top of the fish, and drizzle their juices over the top.

SALAD OF FISH AND POTATO
INSALATA DI PESCE E PATATE
Serves 4 to 6

COD   HALIBUT   CHILEAN SEA BASS

The contrast of crunchy celery and fennel and yielding poached fish and potatoes gives a comforting quality to this dish, a refreshing light salad for a summer supper or luncheon.

1½ pounds firm-fleshed white fish fillet

Salt

Milk for poaching

3 pounds small red potatoes

1 fennel bulb

¾ cup extra-virgin olive oil

Juice of 1 lemon

1 tablespoon strong prepared mustard

Freshly ground black pepper to taste

1 small red onion, peeled and minced

4 inner celery ribs, minced

3 garlic cloves, peeled and minced

Generous handful of coarsely chopped fresh Italian parsley

1 bunch fresh sage, leaves only, cut into julienne

5 large Roma tomatoes, cored and cut into quarters

Preheat the oven to 450°. Lightly oil a shallow roasting pan. Lightly season the fish with salt and place in the pan. Add enough milk to come ¼ inch up the sides of the pan. Cover with parchment, wax paper, or oiled aluminum foil cut to fit inside the pan. Poach the fish in the oven until done, 7 to 10 minutes per inch of thickness. Remove from the oven and let cool slightly in the pan. When the fish is cool enough to handle, gently lift it out of the milk. Flake the fish, discarding any bones, and set aside in small bowl. Use a bit of the milk to moisten the fish if it seems dry.

Cook the potatoes in boiling salted water until tender but firm, about 15 minutes. Drain, and peel if you wish. Cut the potatoes in half, and set aside to cool. Trim the fennel bulb, reserving the tops. Remove any tough outer layers. Core the fennel bulb and mince. Chop enough of the tops to measure 1 cup.

Make the dressing by whisking together the olive oil, lemon juice, mustard, and salt and pepper to taste in a small bowl.

In a large bowl, combine the red onion, celery, fennel, fennel tops, garlic, cooked fish, potatoes, parsley, sage, and salt and pepper to taste. Drizzle the dressing over and gently toss. Serve garnished with the tomato quarters.

SHRIMP AND FRIED PEPPER SALAD
INSALATA DI GAMBERI E PEPERONE
Serves 4 to 6

Fried peppers are one of the simple miracles of the Italian kitchen—just the sweet peppers of summer, oil, and salt. I learned to add the shrimp to enrich the salad at a friend's summer home on Lago di Garda in Northern Italy. The secret of the dish is not to skimp on the oil for frying. The peppers must truly fry, not steam—and *slowly,* please. The more slowly they fry, the more concentrated the sugar in the peppers will become, and the sweeter they will be. I prefer this dish without the vinegar, but I was voted down by my kitchen *amici.*

1¼ cups extra-virgin olive oil

3 medium red bell peppers, cored, seeded, and cut lengthwise into thin strips

3 medium yellow bell peppers, cored, seeded, and cut lengthwise into thin strips

Pinch of red chile pepper flakes

4 garlic cloves, peeled and minced

30 medium shrimp, peeled and deveined (see page 9)

Juice of 3 lemons

Handful of chopped fresh Italian parsley

12 fresh basil leaves, cut into julienne

¼ cup red wine vinegar (optional)

Salt to taste

1 bunch watercress

In a large sauté pan, heat 1 cup of the olive oil until very hot. Add the peppers, reduce the heat, and fry until very soft and golden. Transfer the peppers and all their juices to a bowl. In another sauté pan, heat the remaining ¼ cup olive oil. Add the red chile pepper flakes and garlic and sauté briefly. Add the shrimp and sauté until pink. Remove from the heat, add the lemon juice, parsley, and basil, and mix well. Add to the bowl with the peppers. Add the red wine vinegar, if desired, and salt to taste. Mix thoroughly and place in the refrigerator to marinate for at least 2 hours.

Serve the salad on individual plates, garnished with the watercress.

GRILLED SHRIMP SALAD ON ROMAINE

GAMBERI ALL'INSALATA ROMANA

Serves 4 to 6

A composed salad inspired by the orange salads of Sicily. Thick orange slices are grilled to a sweet softness to sit atop crunchy romaine. Then grilled shrimp are tossed with fennel, peppers, and marinated artichoke hearts. (It is acceptable to use boiled rather than grilled shrimp.) Save the feathery fennel tops for a beautiful garnish.

½ **cup olive oil**

1½ **pounds small to medium shrimp, peeled and deveined (see page 9)**

1 **large fennel bulb, trimmed and sliced crosswise, tops reserved and coarsely chopped**

1 **large red bell pepper, cored, seeds and white ribs removed, and cut into quarters**

2 **navel oranges, peeled, white pith cut off, and thickly sliced**

1 **8-ounce jar marinated artichoke hearts, drained and roughly chopped**

1 **bunch fresh sage, leaves only, cut into julienne**

1 **bunch fresh basil, leaves only, roughly chopped**

Extra-virgin olive oil for drizzling

Red wine vinegar for drizzling

Salt and freshly ground black pepper to taste

1 **large head romaine lettuce**

3 **tablespoons fresh lemon juice**

Heat a charcoal or gas grill or a ridged stovetop griddle until very hot. Using a towel dipped in oil, rub oil onto the grids. Lightly brush the shrimp, fennel slices, bell pepper, and orange slices with oil. Grill the shrimp for about 1 minute on each side. Use tongs to remove the shrimp to a platter. Then grill the fennel and the pepper just until grill marks appear and the vegetables begin to wilt. Transfer to the platter. Finally, grill the orange slices for about 30 seconds per side. Be careful not to cook the orange slices so long that they lose their shape.

When the vegetables are cool enough to handle, slice the fennel into thin strips and cut the bell pepper lengthwise into thin strips. In a large bowl, mix together the shrimp, sliced fennel, bell pepper, chopped artichokes, and herbs. Moisten the mixture with a drizzle of olive oil and just a bit of vinegar. Season with salt and pepper and set aside. Wash the romaine and discard the tough outer leaves. Cut out the crunchy core, cut it into thin slices, and then stack the slices and cut into thin matchsticks. Add to the shrimp-vegetable mixture.

Line a serving platter with the tender, innermost romaine leaves. Arrange the orange slices in a pleasing pattern on top of the lettuce leaves. Drizzle a bit of olive oil and the lemon juice over the lettuce and orange slices. Sprinkle with the chopped fennel tops. Gently toss the shrimp-vegetable mixture and spoon on top of the orange slices. Serve immediately.

Warm Shrimp Salad with White Beans

INSALATA DI GAMBERI E FAGIOLI

Serves 4 to 6

While dining at Enoteca Pinchioni, a restaurant in Florence more formal and elegant than my usual haunts, I had a savory combination of scampi with diced tomatoes and beans that inspired this recipe.

For the beans

2 15-ounce cans cannellini beans, drained

½ small red onion, peeled and minced

4 inner celery ribs with leaves, thinly sliced

10 to 12 sprigs fresh thyme, leaves only

Juice of 1 lemon

¼ cup extra-virgin olive oil

Salt and freshly ground black pepper to taste

¼ cup extra-virgin olive oil, plus extra for drizzling

4 to 6 garlic cloves, peeled and minced

½ to 1 teaspoon red chile pepper flakes (to taste)

24 to 36 large shrimp, peeled and deveined (see page 9)

2 bunches arugula, washed and dried

2 round tomatoes or 4 large Roma tomatoes, finely diced

Small handful of coarsely chopped fresh Italian parsley

Lemon wedges

To prepare the beans, mix together the beans, onion, celery, thyme, lemon juice, olive oil, and salt and pepper to taste in a small bowl. Set aside to marinate while you cook the shrimp.

Heat the oil in a medium skillet. Add the garlic and cook just until its characteristic aroma is released. Add the hot pepper flakes and shrimp and sauté until the shrimp are cooked, about 7 minutes. While the shrimp are cooking, line individual plates with the arugula and spoon some of the seasoned beans on each plate. Arrange the hot shrimp over the beans, and top with the diced tomatoes and parsley. To finish, drizzle a bit of extra-virgin oil over the tomatoes, and garnish with lemon wedges. Serve immediately.

WATERCRESS AND SHRIMP SALAD
GAMBARETTI CON CRESCIONE
Serves 4 to 6

A simple salad for a light first course.

1 pound medium shrimp, peeled and deveined (see page 9)
2 tablespoons chopped fresh oregano
2 tablespoons chopped fresh thyme
Grated zest of 1 lemon
Juice of 3 lemons
½ cup plus 3 tablespoons extra-virgin olive oil
2 tablespoons dry white wine
2 cups coarsely chopped watercress or arugula leaves
Salt and freshly ground black pepper to taste

Combine the shrimp, herbs, lemon zest and juice, and ½ cup of the olive oil in a bowl. Cover and marinate for at least 15 minutes, or overnight in the refrigerator.

Remove the shrimp from the marinade, and drain off the excess. Heat the remaining 3 tablespoons olive oil in a sauté pan over medium heat. Add the shrimp and sauté until they turn pink. Add the white wine and scrape up any browned bits clinging to the bottom of the pan. Add the watercress or arugula and toss for a few seconds, until slightly wilted. Season with salt and pepper to taste. Serve immediately.

WARM SHRIMP SALAD

GAMBERI ALL'INSALATA CON PESTO DI OLIVE

Serves 4 to 6

The pink delicacy of shrimp and the dramatic shiny black of olive paste seem forever destined to meet on the plate. A beautiful, simply made dish that you can add to your "fancy" repertoire.

¼ cup extra-virgin olive oil

1¼ pounds medium shrimp, peeled and deveined (see page 9)

4 garlic cloves, peeled and minced

3 large ripe tomatoes, chopped

6 fresh basil leaves, chopped

Juice of 2 lemons

½ fennel bulb, trimmed, cored, and finely chopped

¼ cup Pesto di Olive (page 298)

2 bunches arugula, washed and trimmed

Lemon wedges (optional)

Moroccan olives (optional)

Heat the oil in a large skillet. Add the shrimp and garlic and sauté just until the shrimp turn pink. Add the tomatoes and cook for about 2 minutes, or until they soften. Add the basil, lemon juice, and fennel. Toss gently, add the pesto di olive, and stir just until warm. Serve on a bed of arugula, garnished with lemon wedges and Moroccan olives if desired.

RED AND BLACK SALAD

INSALATA ROSSA E NERA

Serves 4 to 6 as a first course

The beauty of this salad lies in the color contrast between the black-rimmed coral mussels and the silvery-red wilted radicchio. An easy way to present guests with an elegant and unusual combination of tastes.

> 2 pounds black mussels, cleaned (see page 8)
> ¼ cup extra-virgin olive oil
> 2 shallots, peeled and minced
> ¼ cup white wine
> 1½ heads radicchio, cored, washed, and leaves separated
> 1 tablespoon balsamic vinegar
> ¼ cup Garlicky Bread Crumbs (page 12)

Combine the mussels, olive oil, shallots, and white wine in a shallow pan, cover, and steam the mussels open over moderate heat. Remove the mussels from the pan, reserving the juices in the pan, and pick the meat out of the shells. Set aside. Add the radicchio to the pan and heat over low heat just until the radicchio wilts. Remove from the heat, and sprinkle the radicchio with the balsamic vinegar. Arrange the wilted radicchio on individual salad plates. Divide the mussels among the plates, arranging them on top of the radicchio. Top with the bread crumbs and serve.

WARM SCALLOP AND MUSHROOM SALAD ON GREENS

INSALATA BOSCO MARE

Serves 4 to 6

The portobello mushroom has recently burst onto the scene in gourmet supermarkets and produce stands. It is a large cultivated mushroom very deep in flavor—the classic grilling mushroom of Italy. It is characterized by a six- to eight-inch-wide cap that can be nearly two inches thick. When sautéed as in this recipe, portobellos turn a very dark brown and exude a rich deep brown juice.

½ pound portobello or shiitake mushrooms
½ pound white button mushrooms, stems trimmed
¼ cup extra-virgin olive oil, plus extra for drizzling
3 to 4 garlic cloves, peeled and minced
2 sprigs fresh rosemary, leaves only, finely chopped
Small handful of coarsely chopped fresh Italian parsley
Juice of 1 lemon
¼ cup water
1 teaspoon grated orange zest
1 pound bay scallops
Salt and freshly ground black pepper to taste
1 head curly endive, trimmed, washed, and torn into small pieces

If you are using shiitake mushrooms, remove the stems and discard them. Clean all the mushrooms by gently wiping them with a damp kitchen towel, and cut them into thin strips. Heat the oil in a large skillet. Add the mushrooms and sear over high heat for about 2 minutes. Add the garlic, rosemary, and half the parsley and stir until the garlic releases its characteristic aroma. Add the lemon juice, water, and orange zest and cook just until the button mushrooms are tender, about 5 minutes longer. Add the scallops, and stir and cook over medium heat until opaque, no longer than 4 minutes. Add salt and pepper to taste, and remove from the heat. Divide the endive among individual plates. Drizzle the lettuce with olive oil, and spoon the scallops and mushrooms, with some of the cooking liquid, over it. Garnish with the remaining parsley. Serve immediately.

GRILLED SQUID SALAD
INSALATA DI CALAMARI
Serves 6 to 8

Squid always seems most tender when grilled. In this salad, grilled squid is marinated with herbs, a splash of vinegar, and orange juice.

2 pounds cleaned squid (see page 10)

Milk for soaking

Freshly ground black pepper to taste

Olive oil for grilling

2 medium red onions, peeled, halved, and cut into thick slices

1 large red bell pepper, cored, cut in half, and seeds and interior ribs removed

15 fresh basil leaves

Small handful of chopped fresh Italian parsley

3 garlic cloves, peeled and minced

¼ cup extra-virgin olive oil

1 tablespoon red wine vinegar

Juice of ½ large orange

Pinch of dried oregano

Salt to taste

Place the squid in a shallow dish, add milk to cover, and season with pepper. Marinate in the refrigerator overnight.

Drain the squid and dry on paper towels. Slit each squid sac down one side so that it opens flat, and score with a sharp knife. Heat a charcoal or gas grill or a ridged stovetop griddle until very hot. Lightly rub the squid with olive oil. Grill the squid sacs and tentacles until grill marks are visible, about 4 to 5 minutes. (The sacs will curl up into little cylinders.) Remove the squid from the grill and place in a small nonreactive bowl. Brush the onions and pepper with oil and grill until cooked yet still firm. Cut the pepper into thin strips, and add the onion and pepper to the squid. Add the remaining ingredients and let marinate, preferably in a cool spot but not the refrigerator, for at least 1 hour.

Octopus Salad
INSALATA DI POLPO
Serves 4 to 6

The first time I saw octopus outside of an aquarium—and on a plate—was in Bari. I sat waiting for the ferry to Yugoslavia and saw a fisherman beating a large octopus against a rock as if it were laundry—the traditional way to tenderize it. I walked over to him and watched as he turned some already cooked octopus into this salad in about five minutes. Most Asian fish markets sell fresh baby octopus. If you are lucky enough to find them, they are the ideal choice for this dish.

> 1½ pounds octopus, preferably tentacles only, cleaned
> Milk for soaking
> 5 bay leaves
> 1 lemon, quartered
> 2 garlic cloves, peeled and chopped
> 12 Moroccan olives, pitted and torn in half
> Generous handful of chopped fresh Italian parsley
> ½ cup extra-virgin olive oil
> Juice of 1 small lemon
> 1 red bell pepper, cored, seeded, and cut into thin strips

Place the octopus in a shallow dish, add milk to cover, and marinate overnight in the refrigerator.

In a large pot, combine enough water to cover the octopus generously with the bay leaves and quartered lemon and bring to a boil. Lift the octopus from the milk, add it to the boiling water, and simmer for 5 minutes. Remove from the heat and let cool in the cooking water for 15 minutes. Drain. If the tentacles are thin and small, leave whole. If thick and large, cut crosswise into ½-inch pieces. In a bowl, toss the octopus with the garlic, olives, parsley, oil, lemon juice, and pepper strips. Cover and marinate in the refrigerator for at least 2 hours, or overnight, before serving.

Indispensable Accompaniments

ish by its very nature has a soft, yielding texture. The trick to finding appropriate accompaniments is to play on this texture by either emphasizing it with dishes that are somewhat bland and soft in character or by contrasting it with foods that are sharp and crunchy. I therefore usually serve fish with potato dishes or simple salads. Potatoes have a comforting neutral flavor and homey soft texture. Salads add a satisfying crunchy dimension, which is sharpened by the acidic lemon juice or vinegar.

SIMPLE PARSLEY POTATOES
PATATE AL PREZZEMOLO
Serves 4 to 6

2 pounds small red potatoes, cut in half
8 tablespoons (1 stick) unsalted butter
Large handful of chopped fresh Italian parsley
Salt and freshly ground black pepper to taste

Put the potatoes in a large pot of salted water and bring to a boil. Cook until they are tender when pierced with a fork. Drain. Add the butter to the pan in which you cooked the potatoes and melt it over low heat. Return the potatoes to the pan, along with the parsley. Season with salt and pepper to taste. Serve immediately.

GARLICKY MASHED POTATOES
PURÈ DI PATATE GELIATO
Serves 4 to 6

These potatoes can be mashed and whipped with a mixer, but not in the food processor, which gives the potatoes a gluey consistency. I prefer to leave these potatoes unpeeled, but if you want a less rustic look, peel them before cooking.

6 medium russet or 12 yellow Finn potatoes
6 garlic cloves, peeled
½ cup extra-virgin olive oil
Salt and freshly ground black pepper to taste

Cut the potatoes into quarters. Put the potatoes and garlic in a pot of salted water and bring to a boil. Cook until the potatoes are very tender. Drain and return the potatoes and garlic to the pot. Use a potato masher to break up the potatoes. Then use a whisk to whip in the olive oil, adding it a little bit at a time. Whip until the potatoes are fluffy. Season with salt if necessary and pepper to taste.

Mashed Potatoes and Turnips
PURÈ DI PATATE E RAPA
Serves 4 to 6

The richest and most luxurious of all mashed potatoes. The more turnips you use, the sweeter the purée. Cooking potatoes with milk usually requires a longer cooking time, so be patient. Serve with the simplest grilled, sautéed, or baked fish.

4 russet potatoes, peeled and cut into quarters
4 turnips, peeled and cut into quarters
½ medium onion, peeled and finely chopped
Milk
8 tablespoons (1 stick) unsalted butter, cut into 8 pieces
Salt and freshly ground black pepper to taste

Place the potatoes, turnips, and onion in a large saucepan. Pour in enough milk to come halfway up the vegetables, then add enough water to completely cover the vegetables. Add salt and bring to a boil. Cook until the vegetables are very tender. Drain, and return to the pot. Mash with a potato masher. Using a whisk, whip in the butter and continue to whip until fluffy. If the purée seems too stiff, thin out with a little milk. Season with salt if necessary and freshly ground black pepper. Serve immediately.

SIMPLE GREEN SALAD
INSALATA VERDE

I often prefer to dress an insalata verde with just extra-virgin olive oil and salt, without lemon juice or vinegar. I find it more refreshing and less demanding on the palate, particularly when paired with rich, complex dishes. During summer, when my garden is loaded with fresh herbs, I will often toss a few whole basil leaves into the green salad.

Fresh green lettuces, such as romaine, butter, bibb, red leaf, curly endive, and/or escarole

Coarse kosher salt to taste

Extra-virgin olive oil to taste

Lemon juice or red or white wine vinegar to taste (optional)

Wash the lettuce, tear into pieces, and gently dry in a salad spinner. Toss with salt, olive oil, and lemon juice or vinegar if desired. Serve immediately.

MIXED GREEN SALAD

INSALATA MISTA

The classic mixed green salad found in every homey trattoria. Balsamic vinegar is the one untraditional touch. If you wish, substitute red wine vinegar or lemon juice.

Iceberg or other green leafy lettuce
Thickly shredded red cabbage
Peeled, seeded, and diced cucumber
Tomato wedges
Shredded carrot
Coarse salt and freshly ground black pepper to taste
Extra-virgin olive oil to taste
Balsamic vinegar to taste

Wash the lettuce, tear into pieces, and gently dry in a salad spinner. In a salad bowl, toss all the ingredients together. Serve immediately.

THREE-COLOR SALAD

INSALATA TRICOLORE

The most beautiful Italian salad combination: The oil gives a glossy finish to the radicchio, making the salad look elegant and brilliant with color. Using balsamic vinegar to dress the leaves tames the natural bitterness in the radicchio and endive.

Radicchio leaves

Arugula, trimmed of tough stems

Belgian endive, cut lengthwise into thick julienne

Coarse salt and coarsely ground black pepper to taste

Extra-virgin olive oil to taste

Balsamic vinegar to taste

Wash the radicchio and arugula, tear into pieces, and gently dry in a salad spinner. Gently rinse the endive and pat dry with a towel. In a salad bowl, toss all the ingredients together. Serve immediately.

ORANGE–RED ONION SALAD WITH OLIVES
INSALATA SICILIANA
Serves 4 to 6

A variation on the popular and refreshing Sicilian orange salad. The mint and red pepper flakes add another dimension to the dish.

3 large navel oranges

½ red onion, peeled and very thinly sliced

Small handful of finely chopped fresh mint leaves

Coarse salt and red chile pepper flakes to taste

¼ cup oil-cured Moroccan olives

Extra-virgin olive oil for drizzling

Peel the oranges with a sharp knife, removing all the white pith. Slice the oranges crosswise into ¼-inch-thick rounds. Remove any seeds. Arrange the orange slices in an overlapping pattern on a serving platter. Scatter the onion slices over the oranges, then sprinkle the mint and salt and red pepper flakes over all. Garnish the platter with olives, and drizzle olive oil over the salad.

FENNEL SALAD

INSALATA AL FINOCCHIO

Serves 4 to 6

simple salad with a white-on-white look that is the epitome of reductive elegance.

4 fennel bulbs
Coarse salt to taste
Extra-virgin olive oil to taste
Fresh lemon juice to taste
Shaved imported Parmesan cheese

Trim the leafy tops from the fennel and reserve for another use. Trim the bulbs of the tough outer layer if necessary, and trim the cores. Cut in ¼-inch-thick slices, then stack the slices and cut into julienne. Toss the fennel with salt, oil, and lemon juice to taste. Arrange on a serving dish and top with Parmesan.

Sauces, Dressings, and Butters

FRESH TOMATO-BASIL SAUCE

SALSA AL POMODORO E BASILICO

Makes 2 cups

This is the simplest and most characteristically elemental sauce in the Italian kitchen. During the spring and summer months, always use fresh tomatoes, preferably the oval Roma variety. Romas are bred for sauce making, having less water and more bulk. Sauces made with Romas thicken more quickly and require much less cooking time, ensuring a sweeter taste. During the fall and winter, when a tomato filled with its acidic, fruity scent is impossible to find, using high-quality canned pear tomatoes in juice is permissible. I find that a food mill is indispensable in the kitchen. If you desire a smooth tomato sauce, you needn't spend the time to peel and seed the tomatoes before cooking because the food mill will keep back the skins and seeds for you. In addition, unwanted air isn't pumped into the sauce as it would be if you puréed it in a food processor.

¼ **cup extra-virgin olive oil**
2 to 3 garlic cloves, peeled and minced
Pinch of red chile pepper flakes
12 Roma tomatoes, cored and cut in quarters
6 large fresh basil leaves
Salt to taste

Heat the oil in a large skillet over medium heat. Add the garlic and red chile pepper flakes and sauté briefly, just until the garlic gives off its characteristic aroma. Add the tomatoes and cook over moderately high heat until the tomatoes begin to break down and form a sauce: Stir frequently to help the tomatoes break down. Add the basil, season with salt to taste, and continue cooking over moderately high heat, stirring occasionally, until the sauce is thick and no longer juicy. Remove from the heat and put the sauce through the medium disk of a food mill.

"ANGRY" SAUCE

SALSA ALL'ARRABIATA

Makes 2 cups

A devilish sauce, spicy with red chile peppers and garlic. Use cold as a dipping sauce for cold seafood, hot as an accompaniment to fried calamari, or pair with any seafood to dress pasta. Nearly any fillets or shellfish—lobster is particularly good—can be simply baked in this sauce and topped with toasty bread crumbs. The essential character of this sauce comes from the raw garlic added directly to the cooking sauce (rather than cooking it first in olive oil). The pure sharp flavor of garlic is most intense when it is used in this way.

> 1 16-ounce can peeled Italian-style plum tomatoes
> ¼ cup extra-virgin olive oil
> ½ to 1 teaspoon red chile pepper flakes
> 1 to 2 garlic cloves, peeled
> Salt to taste

Purée the tomatoes by putting them through a food mill or by processing in a blender or food processor with a steel blade until fairly smooth. In a medium skillet, heat the extra-virgin olive oil over moderate heat. Add the chile pepper flakes. As soon as the flakes begin to add some color to the oil, add the tomato purée. Stir well to mix, and squeeze the garlic cloves through a press directly into the sauce. Add salt to taste. Cook over moderately high heat until the tomatoes thicken to form a sauce.

GREEN SAUCE

SALSA VERDE

Makes 2 cups

Salsa verde comes from the tradition of sauces emulsified with bread by pounding in a mortar. These sauces have the same satisfying thickness associated with egg-based mayonnaise, while being less rich and without the attendant cholesterol. I present here the more modern method, which uses the food processor.

1½ cups day-old country bread, crusts removed
¼ cup white wine vinegar, or to taste
3 anchovy fillets, rinsed
2 tablespoons capers
2 garlic cloves, peeled
Generous handful of chopped fresh Italian parsley
Freshly ground black pepper to taste
1 cup extra-virgin olive oil

Tear the bread into large pieces and place in a small bowl with the vinegar. Soak the bread for 10 minutes, then squeeze it dry and place in the bowl of a food processor fitted with a steel blade. Add the anchovies, capers, garlic, parsley, and pepper. Process until finely chopped. With the processor on, slowly add the oil in a steady stream and process until the sauce thickens. Add a bit of water and additional vinegar to achieve a more runny texture if desired.

BECHAMEL SAUCE

SALSA BESCIAMELLA

Makes 2 cups

In this book I use this classic white sauce mainly in baked recipes to add a touch of creaminess to certain dishes.

4 tablespoons (½ stick) unsalted butter
3 tablespoons all-purpose flour
2 cups hot milk
Coarse salt and freshly ground black pepper to taste

Melt the butter in a small saucepan over low heat. Add the flour and stir to form a smooth paste. Heat the milk in a separate saucepan. When it is hot but not boiling, pour it into the roux (the butter-flour mixture), stirring constantly with a whisk or wooden spoon. Cook over low heat until the sauce thickens and the flour taste is gone. Add salt and pepper to taste.

SPICY PIQUANT SAUCE

SALSA PICCANTE

Makes 2 cups

Red chile flakes add a kick to this traditional nonemulsified green sauce. It is delicious both as a marinade and as a dressing on cooked fish and shellfish.

1½ cups fresh Italian parsley leaves
1½ tablespoons capers
5 anchovies
1 to 3 teaspoons red chile pepper flakes
1¼ cups extra-virgin olive oil
1 tablespoon fresh lemon juice
Salt and freshly ground black pepper to taste

Combine all the ingredients in a food processor fitted with a steel blade and process until smooth.

Salmoriglio comes from the word *salamoia,* meaning ''brine.'' The first of the following three recipes is a typical Sicilian marinade that is used for moistening and flavoring grilled fish before, during, and after cooking. The marinade is traditionally beaten until homogenous and somewhat emulsified. The two variations that follow produce interesting flavor contrasts and work well as simple nonemulsified mixtures. Although I give suggestions for pairing flavors and fish types, experiment by letting your taste be your guide.

Basic Sicilian Fish Marinade
SALMORIGLIO

Makes 1½ cups

1 cup extra-virgin olive oil

Scant ½ cup hot water

Juice of 2 lemons

1 to 2 garlic cloves, peeled and minced

2 tablespoons coarsely chopped fresh Italian parsley

¼ tablespoon dried oregano

Pour the oil into a small mixing bowl. With a whisk, slowly beat in the hot water and lemon juice. Add the garlic, parsley, and oregano, and whisk until smooth and emulsified.

FRESH OREGANO AND WINE MARINADE

BAGNA OREGANATA

Makes 1 cup

Equally good on meaty fish (such as tuna and swordfish) and more subtly flavored white-fleshed fish (such as sea bass). An excellent marinade for fish fillets that are to be grilled.

½ cup olive oil

½ cup dry white wine

2 to 3 tablespoons chopped fresh oregano or ½ teaspoon dried oregano

2 cloves garlic, peeled and minced

Salt and freshly ground black pepper to taste

Combine all the ingredients in a small bowl.

SPICY MARINADE

BAGNA ARRABIATA

Makes 1½ cups

Great on any rich, strong-flavored fish such as tuna, sturgeon, or swordfish.

1 cup extra-virgin olive oil

½ cup red wine vinegar

2 big pinches of freshly ground black pepper

1 tablespoon red chile pepper flakes

1 teaspoon Dijon mustard

Handful of chopped fresh Italian parsley

Combine all the ingredients in a small bowl. Set aside for 15 minutes before using.

Saffron-Raisin-Rosemary Marinade

BAGNA ALLA ZAFFERANO

Makes 2 cups

There is something about the deep orange of saffron that makes me think of celebration and ritual. This marinade is an easy way to transform a simple fish off the grill into something really special. Pair it only with a gutsy fish that can stand up to the combined strong flavors of saffron, rosemary, and red wine vinegar. The raisins add an intense sweetness to round out the marinade.

Pinch of saffron threads
¼ cup hot water
½ cup red wine vinegar
½ cup roughly chopped raisins
1 tablespoon minced fresh rosemary leaves
1 cup extra-virgin olive oil

Soak the saffron in the hot water for 30 minutes. In a small bowl, combine the saffron and its soaking liquid, the vinegar, raisins, and rosemary. Whisk in the oil.

Arugula Dressing
SALSINA DELLA RUCOLA
Makes 1½ cups

In cooking classes I always describe the flavor of arugula as peppery, similar to watercress but more intense. The inherently spicy nature of the green pairs well with the subtle flavors of fish and seafood. I add chile pepper flakes and mustard to it here to reinforce the spiciness, but they can be omitted for a mellower vinaigrette. The longer the dressing sits, the spicier it becomes. And the more you beat the arugula, bringing out its natural oils, the more pungent the dressing. I usually make this with vinegar for fish and with lemon juice for shellfish. Experiment until you find the contrast you prefer.

¾ cup extra-virgin olive oil
¼ cup red wine vinegar or lemon juice
1 teaspoon Dijon mustard
1 bunch arugula, washed, trimmed, and finely chopped
Pinch of red chile pepper flakes

Whisk the ingredients together in a small bowl.

SPICY TOMATO DRESSING
SALSINA DI POMODORO PICCANTE

Makes 2 cups

This dressing becomes spicier as it sits, so if you like a lot of heat but you prefer to make your dressings ahead, be careful not to add too much of the chile pepper, as it definitely will intensify in flavor. To keep the dressing as lively and full of texture as possible, don't add the tomatoes until the last minute if you make this more than a day in advance.

1 shallot, peeled and minced
1 garlic clove, peeled and minced
1 teaspoon red chile pepper flakes
2 sprigs fresh oregano, leaves only, or 1 healthy pinch dried oregano
½ cup balsamic vinegar
1 cup extra-virgin olive oil
1 cup finely diced ripe tomatoes
Salt to taste

With a wire whisk, beat together all the ingredients except the tomatoes and salt in a bowl. Add the tomatoes and stir gently to mix. Add salt to taste. Set aside for at least 15 minutes. Gently stir before using.

Parsley Pesto Dressing

SALSINA DI PESTO DEL PREZZEMOLO

Makes a generous 2 cups

The Italian word *pesto* actually means "paste," not only the traditional mixture of basil, garlic, Parmesan, and olive oil. *Pesto* is the appropriate term for many herb-condiment pastes. This parsley pesto is brilliant green and suffused with the fresh, sharp flavor of Italian parsley. Although you could make the dressing with curly parsley, the flavor would be somewhat less "green."

1½ cups coarsely chopped fresh Italian parsley
1 garlic clove, peeled and minced
1 tablespoon grated imported Parmesan cheese
1½ cups extra-virgin olive oil
⅓ cup fresh lemon juice
Salt and freshly ground black pepper to taste

Place the parsley, garlic, Parmesan, and ¼ cup of the olive oil in the bowl of a food processor fitted with a steel blade. Process until a smooth paste is formed. Use a rubber spatula to transfer the pesto to a small bowl. Using a wire whisk, beat in the lemon juice and remaining 1¼ cups olive oil. Add salt and pepper to taste.

MUSTARD DRESSING
SALSINA DELLA MOSTARDA
Makes 2½ cups

This is an all-purpose dressing with simple flavors that will enliven a number of salads. I particularly enjoy using it on steamed clams on the half-shell; I add the reserved clam juices to the dressing to round out the flavor.

2 shallots, peeled and finely minced
1½ tablespoons Dijon mustard
2 sprigs fresh thyme, leaves only, or ½ teaspoon dried thyme
¾ cup champagne vinegar
1¼ cups extra-virgin olive oil
Salt and freshly ground black pepper to taste

Using a wire whisk, beat all the ingredients together in a small bowl.

CAPER-ANCHOVY SAUCE
SALSINA DI CAPPERI E ACCIUGHE
Makes about 1 cup

This sauce is simple, quick, and very pleasing with any strong-flavored fish, like tuna.

8 anchovy fillets, finely diced
¼ cup capers
¼ cup chopped fresh Italian parsley
½ cup extra-virgin olive oil
1 tablespoon fresh lemon juice
Salt and freshly ground black pepper to taste

Mix all the ingredients together in a bowl. Set aside for at least 1 hour before serving.

BLACK PEPPER DRESSING

SALSINA DI PEPE NERO

Makes 2½ cups

I like to grind black peppercorns in a coffee mill. You'll find it's more convenient than using a pepper mill every time you need fresh pepper, but you'll still have a fragrant, intense spice on hand to use in your recipes. This simple dressing will do wonders for cooked shrimp or scallops. Just toss with salad greens (or reds in the case of radicchio) for a starter.

1 tablespoon coarsely ground black pepper
1 small garlic clove, peeled and minced
½ cup champagne vinegar
Grated zest of ½ lemon
Juice of 1 lemon
1½ cups extra-virgin olive oil

Using a wire whisk, beat all the ingredients together in a small bowl.

BLACK OLIVE PASTE

PESTO DI OLIVE

Makes approximately 1 cup

Moroccan oil-cured olives are a glittering black color, intense with the meaty taste of olives without the oversalted brininess of salt water–cured olives. This paste is a staple in the Angeli kitchens. To heighten flavor and increase visual appeal there is no equal. Pit the olives by simply pushing out the pits with your fingers.

> 1½ cups pitted Moroccan oil-cured olives
> Grated zest of ½ lemon
> 2 tablespoons fresh lemon juice
> ⅓ cup extra-virgin olive oil
> Pinch of freshly ground black pepper

Place all the ingredients in the bowl of a food processor fitted with a steel blade and process to a smooth purée.

GREEN OLIVE PASTE
PESTO DI OLIVE VERDE

Makes approximately 1 cup

A piquant paste redolent with herbal flavor. Green olives have a particular affinity with fish and shellfish, especially clams.

1½ cups pitted green olives

1 sprig fresh rosemary, leaves only, finely chopped

1½ teaspoons finely chopped fresh thyme or ½ teaspoon dried thyme

1½ teaspoons finely chopped fresh sage or ½ teaspoon dried sage

2 teaspoons finely chopped fresh Italian parsley

1 garlic clove, peeled and minced

¼ cup extra-virgin olive oil

2 tablespoons champagne vinegar

Salt and freshly ground black pepper to taste

Place all the ingredients in the bowl of a food processor fitted with a steel blade and process to a smooth purée.

BASIL PESTO
PESTO GENOVESE
Makes approximately 2 cups

The classic Ligurian paste of fresh basil and garlic is so versatile it's a shame to use it only to dress pasta. Use it to add flavor to soups, salads, marinades, dressings, and even sandwiches.

2 cups firmly packed fresh basil leaves
4 to 6 garlic cloves, peeled
¾ cup extra-virgin olive oil
½ cup grated imported Parmesan cheese
Salt and freshly ground black pepper to taste
¼ cup toasted pine nuts or walnuts

Place the basil and garlic in a food processor fitted with the steel blade. Process until finely chopped. With the machine running, add half the oil in a slow, steady stream. Turn off the processor and add the Parmesan. Process until the cheese is absorbed. With the machine running, slowly add the remaining oil and process until creamy. Add salt and pepper and the nuts. Pulse until the nuts are coarsely chopped. Use immediately, or pour into a container, top with a thin layer of olive oil to prevent the basil from turning dark, tightly seal, and refrigerate.

MINT PESTO

PESTO DI MENTA

Makes 2 cups

Mint has a sweet fresh flavor that combines with garlic to produce an unusual and refreshing herbal boost. Use to marinate whole or filleted fish before grilling or broiling.

> **2 cups fresh mint leaves**
> **½ teaspoon chopped garlic**
> **Juice of ½ lemon**
> **½ teaspoon freshly grated imported Parmesan cheese**
> **¼ cup extra-virgin olive oil**
> **¼ cup fresh Italian parsley leaves**
> **Salt and freshly ground black pepper to taste**

Put all the ingredients in the bowl of a food processor fitted with the steel blade and process until smooth.

Sun-Dried Tomato Pesto
PESTO DI PUMATE
Makes about 1 cup

scarlet-colored pesto vivid with sweet tomato flavor.

1 small jar sun-dried tomatoes packed in oil
2 sprigs thyme, leaves only (optional)
Extra-virgin olive oil as needed

Empty the entire jar of sun-dried tomatoes and its oil into the bowl of a food processor fitted with a steel blade. Add the thyme, if desired. Process into a smooth purée, adding additional extra-virgin olive oil 1 tablespoon at a time if needed to achieve the proper texture.

Caper, Onion, and Oregano Paste
PESTO DI CAPPERI E ORIGANO
Makes 2 cups

apers and oregano share strong aromas that are very perfumatic. Grinding the ingredients in the food processor intensifies their flavors and makes this paste even more pungent.

2 cups fresh oregano leaves
¼ small onion, peeled
1½ teaspoons capers
¼ cup extra-virgin olive oil
Juice of ½ lemon
Salt and freshly ground black pepper to taste

Put all the ingredients in the bowl of a food processor fitted with a steel blade and process until smooth.

Roasted Red Pepper Paste
PESTO DI PEPERONI ROSSI
Makes 1½ cups

A sweet red-orange paste made sweeter by the addition of pine nuts. The bread crumbs give the paste more body and add texture. Slather this paste on fish, or toss it with pasta for a colorful, richly flavored dish.

3 red bell peppers
¼ cup pine nuts
½ cup toasted fresh bread crumbs
3 garlic cloves, peeled
⅓ cup extra-virgin olive oil
Salt and freshly ground black pepper to taste

Roast the peppers over a gas flame or under the broiler until the skin is blackened, turning occasionally with a pair of tongs. Place the peppers in a bag, seal, and let steam for 15 to 20 minutes. Remove the skins and seeds under cold running water.

Preheat the oven to 400°. Place the pine nuts on a cookie sheet and toast in the oven. Keep an eye on them because they can burn quickly. Let cool.

Put the peppers, pine nuts, bread crumbs, and garlic in the bowl of a food processor fitted with a steel blade, and purée. With the machine running, slowly add the olive oil. Season with salt and black pepper.

MAYONNAISE

Mayonnaise is a traditional dip, binder, and dressing for many fish and seafood dishes in Italian *alta cucina* (''high or elevated cuisine'') as well as in the home. The rich, satisfying texture of mayonnaise is often just what is needed to show off a salad or a simple cold poached fish. I tested these recipes with fat-free store-bought prepared mayonnaise and they were still delicious. So enjoy yourself without guilt if you must watch your fat intake.

Tomato-Herb Mayonnaise

MAIONESE ALLE ERBE E POMODORO

Makes 1¾ cups

2 Roma tomatoes
1½ cups mayonnaise
8 sun-dried tomato halves, finely chopped
1 garlic clove, peeled and minced
4 large fresh basil leaves, minced
Salt and freshly ground black pepper to taste

Remove the stem ends of the fresh tomatoes with a sharp knife. Cut the tomatoes in half lengthwise and, using your fingers, scoop out and discard the seeds. Cut the tomato shells into very fine dice. Set aside.

In a small bowl, whisk together the mayonnaise, sun-dried tomatoes, garlic, and basil leaves. Add the diced tomatoes and salt and pepper, and stir to mix.

RED PEPPER MAYONNAISE

MAIONESE DI PEPERONE ROSSO

Makes 1¾ cups

2 roasted red peppers (fresh or canned)

1½ cups mayonnaise

1 garlic clove, peeled and minced

2 tablespoons red wine vinegar

Pinch of red chile pepper flakes

Salt and freshly ground black pepper to taste

In the bowl of a food processor fitted with a steel blade, roughly purée the red peppers. Transfer to a small bowl. Add the mayonnaise, garlic, vinegar, red pepper flakes, and salt and pepper and beat until smooth.

GARLIC-HERB MAYONNAISE

MAIONESE ALL'AGLIO ED ERBE

Makes 1¾ cups

15 garlic cloves, peeled

¼ cup olive oil

1½ cups mayonnaise

2 sprigs fresh thyme, leaves only, or ½ teaspoon dried thyme

1 sprig fresh oregano, leaves only, finely chopped, or 1 pinch of dried oregano

2 tablespoons fresh lemon juice

Salt and freshly ground black pepper to taste

In a small sauté pan, combine the garlic and oil and heat slowly over low heat. When the oil is bubbling and the garlic is beginning to be dotted with golden brown spots, remove from the heat, and let the garlic cool in the oil. When the garlic and oil are completely cool, transfer to the bowl of a food processor fitted with the steel blade, and purée. With a rubber spatula, scrape the garlic purée into a small bowl. Add the remaining ingredients and beat vigorously until smooth.

Anchovy Mayonnaise

MAIONESE DI ACCIUGHE

Makes 1½ cups

8 anchovy fillets, rinsed and dried
1½ cups mayonnaise
1 garlic clove, peeled and minced
Large pinch of chopped fresh Italian parsley
Freshly ground black pepper to taste

Chop the anchovies very fine until they form a paste. Place in a small bowl, add the remaining ingredients, and beat until smooth.

FLAVORED BUTTERS

Flavored butters are an easy way to add richness and additional flavor to simple baked dishes, sautéed fish, or seafood pastas. I always advise students to keep a batch or two on hand in the freezer to help them turn out a delicious meal at a moment's notice.

GARLIC-ROSEMARY BUTTER
BURRO AL ROSMARINO E AGLIO
Makes 1½ cups

¾ **pound unsalted butter, slightly softened**
2 **teaspoons fresh lemon juice**
1 **tablespoon finely minced fresh rosemary**
3 **garlic cloves, peeled and minced**
Grated zest of ¼ lemon
Salt and freshly ground black pepper to taste

Place all the ingredients in the bowl of a food processor fitted with a steel blade or in the bowl of an electric mixer fitted with a paddle, and process until smooth and homogenous. With a rubber spatula, scrape the butter into a small bowl. Or form into a log approximately 1½ inches in diameter simply by spooning the softened butter onto a sheet of wax paper and rolling it up. Refrigerate, or freeze for up to 1 month. Slice off the appropriate amount as needed.

CHIVE BUTTER
BURRO VERDE
Makes 1½ cups

¾ **pound unsalted butter, slightly softened**
1½ **tablespoons snipped fresh chives**
1 **tablespoon fresh lemon juice**
Salt and freshly ground black pepper to taste

Place all the ingredients in the bowl of a food processor fitted with a steel blade or in the bowl of an electric mixer fitted with a paddle, and process until smooth and homogenous. With a rubber spatula, scrape into a small bowl. Or form into a log approximately 1½ inches in diameter simply by spooning the softened butter onto a sheet of wax paper and rolling it up. Refrigerate, or freeze for up to 1 month. Slice off the appropriate amount as needed.

ANCHOVY BUTTER
BURRO ALL'ACCIUGHE
Makes 1½ cups

¾ **pound unsalted butter, slightly softened**
12 **anchovy fillets, rinsed, dried, and roughly chopped**
1 **shallot, peeled and roughly chopped**
1 **teaspoon fresh lemon juice**
Salt and freshly ground black pepper to taste

Place all the ingredients in the bowl of a food processor fitted with a steel blade or in the bowl of an electric mixer fitted with a paddle, and process until smooth and homogenous. With a rubber spatula, scrape the butter into a small bowl. Or form into a log approximately 1½ inches in diameter simply by spooning the softened butter onto a sheet of wax paper and rolling it up. Refrigerate, or freeze for up to 1 month. Slice off the appropriate amount as needed.

Olive Butter

BURRO ALL'OLIVE

Makes 1½ cups

¾ pound unsalted butter, slightly softened
6 Moroccan olives, pitted
12 Kalamata olives, pitted
1 tablespoon roughly chopped fresh Italian parsley
Pinch of freshly ground black pepper

Place all the ingredients in the bowl of a food processor fitted with a steel blade or in the bowl of an electric mixer fitted with a paddle, and process until smooth and homogenous. With a rubber spatula, scrape the butter into a small bowl. Or form into a log approximately 1½ inches in diameter simply by spooning the softened butter onto a sheet of wax paper and rolling it up. Refrigerate, or freeze for up to 1 month. Slice off the appropriate amount as needed.

Basil Butter

BURRO BASILICO

Makes 1½ cups

¾ pound unsalted butter, slightly softened
14 large fresh basil leaves
3 garlic cloves, peeled and minced
Juice of ½ lemon
Pinch each of salt and freshly ground pepper
Pinch of red chile pepper flakes

Place all the ingredients in the bowl of a food processor fitted with a steel blade or in the bowl of an electric mixer fitted with a paddle, and process until smooth and homogenous. With a rubber spatula, scrape the butter into a small bowl. Or form into a log approximately 1½ inches in diameter simply by spooning the softened butter onto a sheet of wax paper and rolling it up. Refrigerate, or freeze for up to 1 month. Slice off the appropriate amount as needed.

FENNEL BUTTER

BURRO AL FINOCCHIO

Makes 1½ cups

1 fennel bulb with leafy tops
1 tablespoon fennel seeds
¾ pound unsalted butter, slightly softened
Juice of ½ lemon
Juice of 1 lime

Remove the greens from the fennel, and chop enough of the greens to make 2 tablespoons. Remove the core from the bulb. Quarter the bulb, and reserve 3 quarters for another use; only 1 quarter is needed for this recipe. Coarsely chop the fennel quarter. Blanch the chopped fennel in boiling water for 30 seconds, drain, and place in a bowl of ice water to cool. Drain again and set aside. In a spice or coffee grinder, grind the fennel seeds to a powder.

Place all the ingredients in the bowl of a food processor fitted with a steel blade or in the bowl of an electric mixer fitted with a paddle, and process until smooth and homogenous. With a rubber spatula, scrape the butter into a small bowl. Or form into a log approximately 1½ inches in diameter simply by spooning the softened butter onto a sheet of wax paper and rolling it up. Refrigerate, or freeze for up to 1 month. Slice off the appropriate amount as needed.

Index

Salmone (cont.)
　　alla verdura, 231
Salmoriglio, 290
Salsa:
　　all'arrabiata, 287
　　besciamella, 289
　　piccante, 289
　　al pomodoro e basilico, 286
　　verde, 288
Salsina:
　　di capperi e acciughe, 296
　　della mostarda, 296
　　di pepe nero, 297
　　di pesto del prezzemolo, 295
　　di pomodoro piccante, 294
　　della rucola, 293
Salt cod, see Baccalà
Sandwiches, 72–76
　　anchovy melt, 73
　　grilled tuna and tapenade, 75
　　pan-fried fish, 76
　　salmon, 72
　　seafood club, 74
Sarde con pomodori al diavolo, 41
Sardenaira, 64
Sardines, 12
　　fennel-scented pizza with, 56
　　Sicilian saffron-tinted pasta with, 116–117
　　with tomatoes and hot peppers, 41
Sauces and dressings, 286–306
　　anchovy mayonnaise, 306
　　"angry" sauce, 287
　　arugula dressing, 293
　　basic Sicilian fish marinade, 290
　　basil pesto, 300
　　béchamel sauce, 289
　　black olive paste, 298
　　black pepper dressing, 297
　　caper, onion, and oregano paste, 302
　　caper-anchovy sauce, 296
　　fresh oregano and wine marinade, 291
　　fresh tomato-basil sauce, 286
　　garlic-herb mayonnaise, 305
　　green olive paste, 299
　　green sauce, 288
　　mint pesto, 301
　　mustard dressing, 296
　　parsley pesto dressing, 295
　　red pepper mayonnaise, 305
　　roasted red pepper paste, 303
　　saffron-raisin-rosemary marinade, 292
　　spicy marinade, 291
　　spicy piquant sauce, 289
　　spicy tomato dressing, 294

Sauces and dressings (cont.)
　　sun-dried tomato pesto, 302
　　tomato-herb mayonnaise, 304
　　uncooked tomato sauce for pizza, 54
　　see also Butters, flavored
Sausages:
　　stuffed mussels farmhouse style, 30
　　surf-and-turf ziti, 141
Scallops, bay, 9
　　baked polenta lasagna with shrimp and, 148
　　classic seafood salad, 248–249
　　fish soup Livornese style, 84–85
　　fusilli with, 109–110
　　linguine with "fruits of the sea," 136–137
　　and mushroom salad on greens, warm, 274
　　Niçoise salad, 252–253
　　rice salad with seafood, 258
　　sautéed seafood salad, 250–251
Scallops, sea, 9
　　with brown butter bread crumbs on soft polenta, 196
　　cappon magro, 254–255
　　classic seafood salad, 248–249
　　cold seafood extravaganza on ice, 40
　　doused in black pepper vinaigrette, 195
　　fish soup Livornese style, 84–85
　　fusilli with, 109–110
　　linguine fini with lemon, butter and, 128
　　marinated mixed grill with veggies and orange juice, 46–47
　　mixed seafood fry, 240–242
　　penne with, in a baked tomato sauce, 129
　　risotto with tomato cream and, 164–165
　　roasted garlic and, 214
　　sautéed seafood salad, 250–251
Scampi all'aglio, 235
Shallots, mussels with garlic, parsley and, 89
Shells, pasta:
　　with mussels and white beans, 113–114
　　summer, with shrimp, 112
Shrimp, 9–10
　　angry, linguine with, 125
　　baked polenta lasagna with scallops and, 148
　　broiled polenta canapés with mixed seafood, 22–23
　　cappon magro, 254–255

Shrimp (cont.)
　　classic seafood salad, 248–249
　　cold seafood extravaganza on ice, 40
　　fettuccine with artichokes, leeks and, 126–127
　　-filled ravioli, 144–145
　　fish soup Livornese style, 84–85
　　and fried pepper salad, 266–267
　　fusilli with, 109–110
　　garlicky, with butter, 235
　　linguine with black olive paste, fennel and, 124
　　linguine with "fruits of the sea," 136–137
　　linguine with pesto and, 127
　　marinated mixed grill with veggies and orange juice, 46–47
　　mixed seafood fry, 240–242
　　mixed seafood risotto, 151–152
　　orange-scented, with vermouth and fennel, 237
　　pesto pizza with, 58
　　pizza with goat cheese and, 57
　　rice salad with seafood, 258
　　risotto from the woods and sea, 152–153
　　risotto with sun-dried tomato pesto and, 162–163
　　salad, grilled, on romaine, 268–269
　　salad, warm, 272
　　salad with white beans, warm, 270–271
　　sautéed seafood salad, 250–251
　　sauté with tomatoes, almonds, and pine nuts, 236
　　seafood caponata, 48–49
　　seafood club sandwich, 74
　　skewers, 189–190
　　skewers with mozzarella on polenta, 192–193
　　summer shells with, 112
　　and watercress salad, 271
Sicilian:
　　fish marinade, basic, 290
　　fish soup with fennel and potatoes, 86–87
　　green olive and clam salad with bruschetta, 69
　　grilled tuna, 179
　　saffron-tinted pasta with sardines, 116–117
　　swordfish pie in sweet orange pastry, 66–67
Side dishes, see Accompaniments
Skewers, 188–194
　　fennel-marinated fish, 194